THE TURN OF THE TIDE IN THE PACIFIC WAR

THE TURN OF THE TIDE IN THE PACIFIC WAR

Strategic Initiative, Intelligence, and Command, 1941–1943

Sean M. Judge

Edited by Jonathan M. House

Foreword by Peter R. Mansoor

University Press of Kansas

Published by the University Press of Kansas (Lawrence, Kansas
66045), which was organized by the Kansas Board of Regents and
is operated and funded by Emporia State University, Fort Hays State
University, Kansas State University, Pittsburg State University, the
University of Kansas, and Wichita State University.

Library of Congress Cataloging-in-Publication Data

Names: Judge, Sean M., author. | House, Jonathan M. (Jonathan Mallory),
1950– editor.
Title: The turn of the tide in the Pacific war : strategic initiative, intelligence,
and command, 1941–1943 / Sean M. Judge; edited by Jonathan M. House;
foreword by Peter R. Mansoor.
Description: Lawrence, Kansas : University Press of Kansas, 2018.
| Series: Modern war studies | Includes bibliographical references and index.
Identifiers: LCCN 2017052560 | ISBN 9780700625987 (cloth : alk paper)
| ISBN 9780700625994 (ebook)
Subjects: LCSH: World War, 1939–1945—Campaigns—Oceania. | World War,
1939–1945—Campaigns—Pacific Area. | Military planning—United
States—History—20th century. | Oceania—History, Military—20th century.
| Strategy—History—20th century.
Classification: LCC D767.9 .J84 2018 | DDC 940.54/26—dc23
LC record available at https://lccn.loc.gov/2017052560.

British Library Cataloguing-in-Publication Data is available.

Printed in the United States of America

10 9 8 7 6 5 4 3 2 1

The paper used in this publication is recycled and contains
30 percent postconsumer waste. It is acid free and meets the
minimum requirements of the American National Standard for
Permanence of Paper for Printed Library Materials Z39.48-1992.

CONTENTS

ILLUSTRATIONS

ACRONYMS AND ABBREVIATIONS

AGF   [US] Army Ground Forces
AIB   Allied Intelligence Bureau
ATIS   Allied Translator and Interpreter Section
CCS   [US-British] Combined Chiefs of Staff; see also JCS
CIC   Commander-in-Chief
CINCPAC   Commander-in-Chief, Pacific
CINCUS   Commander-in-Chief, US Fleet
CNO   [US] Chief of Naval Operations
COMAIRSOLS   Commander Aircraft Solomons
COMAIRSOPAC   Commander Air, South Pacific
COMINT   communications intelligence; a subdiscipline
                  of SIGINT
FEAF   [US] Far East Air Force
FRUMEL   Fleet Reporting Unit, Melbourne
FRUPAC   Fleet Radio Pacific
HUMINT   human intelligence
ICPOA   Intelligence Center, Pacific Ocean Area
IGHQ   [Japanese] Imperial General Headquarters
IJA   Imperial Japanese Army
IJN   Imperial Japanese Navy
JAAF   Japanese Army Air Force
JCS   [US] Joint Chiefs of Staff; see also CCS
JIC   [US or British] Joint Intelligence Committee
JICPOA   [US] Joint Intelligence Center, Pacific Ocean Area
JNAF   Japanese Naval Air Force
JSP   [US] Joint Staff Planners
JSSC   [US] Joint Strategic Survey Committee
JUSSC   Joint U.S. Strategic Committee
MID   [US] Military Intelligence Division, part of G-2,
                  War Department
MIS   [US] Military Intelligence Service, field operating
                  arm of intelligence
ONI   [US] Office of Naval Intelligence

OSINT	open-source intelligence
OSS	Office of Strategic Services
POA	[US] Pacific Ocean Areas (Admiral Chester Nimitz)
SAASS	School of Advanced Air and Space Studies
SIGINT	signals intelligence
SIS	[US] Signal Intelligence Service
SWPA	[US] South West Pacific Area (General Douglas MacArthur)
USAAF	US Army Air Forces (nominally coequal with Army Ground Forces and Army Service Forces; at the strategic level it functioned as a quasi-independent air force)
USAF	US Air Force
USSBS	US Strategic Bombing Survey

FOREWORD

Peter R. Mansoor

War has both physical and intangible characteristics. The former—weapons, soldiers, logistical wherewithal, intelligence, command and control, and so forth—are more readily quantified, analyzed, and documented than such facets as morale, discipline, and training. Even harder to come to grips with are more esoteric concepts such as the principles that various military philosophers have posited since the nineteenth century as key to the successful conduct of war. In *The Turn of the Tide in the Pacific War*, Sean Judge introduces a unique concept, strategic initiative, to explain why and how contending powers design campaigns and use military forces to alter the trajectory of war. He identifies five factors that affect the attainment and retention of the initiative in war: resources, intelligence, strategic acumen, combat effectiveness, and chance, all of them affected by political will. How well contending actors capitalize on these elements determines which side will, to use an analogy from the sport of hockey, "have the puck." In Judge's estimation, "Although it does not grant total control, strategic initiative allows the possessor greater latitude to shape the war toward his ends."

By virtue of excellent leadership, superior training, and in some cases better equipment, Japanese forces possessed a qualitative advantage over Allied forces at the beginning of the Pacific War on December 7, 1941. Japanese military leaders skillfully crafted a series of offensive campaigns—the so-called Centrifugal Offensive—that shaped the contours of the war during its first six months. While many armchair historians believe the initiative then passed from the Japanese to American forces after the Battle of Midway in June 1942, Judge establishes rather that the consequence of that battle was strategic equilibrium. The outcome of the subsequent nine-month struggle in the Pacific was hardly foreordained. At one point during the vicious fighting the US Navy had a single damaged but still operational aircraft carrier left on station in the South Pacific. Judge examines the interplay of the various factors, analyzed for their impact on the fighting in Guadalcanal and New Guinea, which turned the strategic initiative definitively in favor of the United States from 1943 onward. American leaders and the forces they commanded took control of the war before they held the preponderance of resources that became available beginning that year.

Perhaps the most critical of the factors Judge explores is strategic acumen, without which other advantages are easily squandered. The US military was blessed to have senior leaders such as General Douglas MacArthur and Admiral Chester Nimitz designing its campaigns and providing the strategic leadership essential to reversing the tide of war. These leaders then accepted calculated risk to launch two major counteroffensives against Japanese forces before the Imperial Japanese command could recover from the shock of the outcome of the Battle of Midway. Whatever their faults, MacArthur and Nimitz got the vast majority of these big strategic issues right, a far cry from the performance of the Japanese high command, which succumbed to "victory disease" and squandered the temporary advantages gained in the early months of the war. As with the Wehrmacht in Europe, the Japanese military routinely downplayed the criticality of intelligence and logistics in the Pacific War, with commensurate results in both global theaters. Once the virtuosity that propelled Japanese forces to a number of tactical and operational successes in the first months of the struggle diminished with combat losses and mistakes, the foundation of the Japanese war-fighting machine significantly deteriorated. The strategic initiative, once passed to American and Allied forces in the Pacific, would never be relinquished. How and why this happened merits examination, both for the historical consequences and for the education of future strategic leaders.

Sean Judge was a US Air Force lieutenant colonel who had trained in the doctoral program in military history at The Ohio State University to become a professor at the School of Advanced Air and Space Studies at Maxwell Field, Alabama. He was a stellar student in a number of my classes, and I was honored to be a part of his dissertation committee. He had just finished the dissertation upon which this book is based when in the summer of 2011 he was diagnosed with cancer, which tragically took his life a year later. His adviser at Ohio State, John "Joe" Guilmartin, along with colleague Hal Winton at the Air University (who advised Judge's master's thesis while Sean was a student there), determined to revise and publish it. Joe's subsequent sudden and untimely death in 2016 left the project adrift for a short period. Those of us who have worked to bring it to fruition are grateful for the opportunity to share its insights with the historical and armed forces communities, a fitting tribute to the scholarship of its primary author and of the learned adviser who guided him along the path to a deeper understanding of the conduct of war in all of its complexity.

—Columbus, Ohio, July 2016

AUTHOR'S PREFACE

This work had its origins in my School of Advanced Air and Space Studies (SAASS) thesis on "'Who Has the Puck?': Strategic Initiative in Modern, Conventional War," completed in 2008 under the advisement of Dr. Harold R. Winton. A primary goal of this study is to apply the concepts developed in the SAASS thesis in a deeper, more focused analysis of the critical phase of the Pacific War from mid-1942 until early 1943. The original work analyzed strategic initiative more broadly but with less depth, using the case studies of the Soviet–German war of 1941–1945 and the Pacific War from 1941 to 1945. The reader of both works will therefore recognize that my analytical/conceptual framework relies on many of the same terms. Much of Chapter 1: Introduction and Chapter 2: Strategic Initiative borrows heavily from and expands on the theoretical discussion in the previously completed thesis. The reader will also recognize foundational elements taken from the thesis embedded in Chapter 3: The National Command Structures, Chapter 4: Japanese Intelligence Organization in World War II, Chapter 5: American Intelligence Organization in the Pacific during World War II, and Chapter 6: "East Wind, Rain." Yet the influence of the original thesis, of course, pervades throughout this book.

Conventional wisdom holds that Japan waged a hopeless war against foes with vastly superior resources and war-making capacity and was destined to be defeated. The present work does not aim to enter that historical debate directly, although I maintain that the course of the war and its final outcome were by no means foreordained. Instead, my purpose is to use these campaigns as a case study in strategic initiative, reconstructing the organizations, decisions, and events that influenced the shift of initiative from one adversary to the other.

—Sean M. Judge
Columbus, Ohio, 2012

EDITOR'S NOTE

I never met Sean Judge, but by all accounts he was passionately interested, from an early age, in both the US Air Force and the Pacific campaigns of World War II. Like other officers privileged to attend the advanced studies schools operated by the various armed services, he blossomed intellectually, learning to place the complexities of modern battle into the larger contexts of campaigns and strategies for the execution of national policy.

To my mind, therefore, a graduate of the School of Advanced Air and Space Studies who is endorsed by two such distinguished soldier-scholars as Peter Mansoor and Hal Winton deserved serious attention. I anticipated a high level of scholarship from this manuscript, and I was not disappointed. Nonetheless, a doctoral dissertation involves a degree of detailed historiography and documentation that often require reformatting and rephrasing before the general public can appreciate the originality of the author's thought. Having worked with me on other book manuscripts, Professor Winton asked me to make the changes that, had he been granted sufficient time, the author would have made himself prior to publication. In undertaking this reformatting, I made every effort to retain Sean Judge's ideas and phraseology, seeking only to recast both for ease of understanding. Although I added a few sentences for clarification and summation, this version scrupulously retains Sean's original conception of a case study in strategic initiative.

I am indebted to Professor John T. Kuehn, who gave me the benefit of his deep understanding of the Pacific campaigns on which this case study is based.

—Jonathan M. House
Leavenworth, Kansas, August 2017

1

Introduction

THE PACIFIC WAR RAGED FROM DECEMBER 7, 1941, until Emperor Hirohito announced Japan's acceptance of the terms of the Potsdam Declaration on August 15, 1945, leading to the surrender ceremony on the battleship USS *Missouri* in Tokyo Bay on September 2. This conflict was a subset of a wider world war that most historians date to Nazi Germany's invasion of Poland on September 1, 1939. To the Western Allies and the Soviet leader Joseph Stalin, the Pacific represented a secondary theater of far less importance than the European continental contest. Geography contributed in part to the different character of the Pacific War, which included two broad theaters: a continental war in China and Southeast Asia, and a maritime conflict throughout the expanse of the great Pacific Ocean and beyond. This analysis focuses on the maritime conflict in the southern and southwestern Pacific.

The ocean war ranged from the Aleutian Islands in the north to Darwin, Australia, in the south, and from the Hawaiian Islands in the eastern Pacific to Ceylon in the Indian Ocean. The conflict unfolded in three phases. In the first phase (December 1941 to mid-1942), Japan seized the strategic initiative and ran rampant, rapidly achieving its initial expansionist aims of conquering the resource-rich area south of Japan and establishing a defensive perimeter to protect those gains by mid-1942. The second phase embraced a period of strategic dispute, in which the Japanese vied to retain the initiative while the Allies, led by the Americans but with important contributions from Australia and New Zealand, aimed to gain the initiative. Finally, by early 1943 the Allies gained the strategic initiative and retained it until the close of the war.

Our focus is on the pivotal second period of the war, during which the Allies seized the initiative and Japan lost it. Surprisingly, the Allies gained the initiative without the preponderance of material resources that characterized the later stages of the war. Using advantages in other means, the Allies redirected the course of the war toward accomplishment of their objectives while Japan's influence over events steadily diminished. The period thus demands close examination.

Pacific War historiography illustrates the common recognition that the course of the war shifted in the period between mid-1942 and early 1943. Yet, historians differ over the catalysts for the shift, the relative importance of the various campaigns during this period, and even in their terminology for the change, using terms such as "turning point," "strategic initiative," and/or "offensive" and "defensive." This book aims to bring rigor to this argument by investigating the concept of strategic initiative in the context of the Pacific War and by clarifying the interrelationship of the dual campaigns in New Guinea and the Solomon Islands. Indeed, the manner in which the combatants conducted those concurrent campaigns enabled the Allies to seize the strategic initiative before achieving a preponderance of resources. In order to do so, the Allies had to exploit other advantages such as military intelligence and strategic judgment. The Allies also had to fight effectively to overcome the experienced forces the Japanese fielded. Additionally, as in every conflict, chance inserted unpredictable variables to which both sides had to adapt.

Historians, strategists, and military professionals use the term "strategic initiative" often and assume a common understanding, but very few have explicitly defined the term or investigated its supporting elements. Chapter 2: Strategic Initiative discusses the concept in some detail and defines it in more specific language, while also investigating several of the important elements that contribute to the initiative at the strategic level. For the moment, it is important to note that possession of the strategic initiative implies potentially greater influence over the course and conduct of the war. Although it does not grant total control, strategic initiative allows the possessor greater latitude to shape the war toward his ends. For this reason, the process by which strategic initiative is gained, transferred, and lost should be of concern to statesmen, soldiers, and historians alike. (See map 1.)

The mid-phase of the Pacific War is particularly suited to a close study of shifting strategic initiative. The Japanese and the Allies were engaged in two simultaneous and grueling campaigns in eastern New Guinea and on Guadalcanal that changed the course of the war. The latter campaign receives the lion's share of historiographical coverage and the majority of credit for the shift in the course of the Pacific War. Yet, it was the interaction of these campaigns that allowed the Allies to seize the initiative. Far from being just a bloody sideshow, the struggle on Papua New Guinea enticed the Japanese to divide their forces at a critical moment and thereby contributed to their defeat in both campaigns and to their loss of the strategic initiative. Following the Allied victories in these campaigns, Japanese expansion ceased and the Allies were able to exercise the strategic initiative through continued offensive action on New Guinea, New Georgia, and up the Solomon Islands chain. Had Japan emerged the victor, the front would likely have moved south and east, threatening Australia directly and endangering the Allied lines of communications between Australia and Hawaii that passed through New Caledonia, Fiji, and Samoa.

Indeed, the Japanese decision to push on to New Guinea and the Solomons in the spring of 1942 ensured that prewar Japanese and Allied conceptions of the course of the war would be proven wrong. Neither side had planned for large-scale, attritional campaigns involving significant land operations in the South Pacific. Rather, both had envisioned that the two sides would meet in a prolonged series of encounters as the United States projected power across the Central Pacific,[1] culminating in a final decisive battle somewhere in the vicinity of Japan, the Philippines, and Formosa (the island known today as Taiwan). Thus, the unforeseen campaigns in New Guinea and the Solomons must be examined together, and the influence of possession of strategic initiative does much to explain why those campaigns began, why they evolved into desperate struggles, and why the outcome of those campaigns changed the course of the Pacific War writ large.

This book seeks to address a number of important questions:

- *Strategic Initiative:* What is strategic initiative? What elements underlie strategic initiative and contribute to its possession or its loss?
- *Strategic Acumen:* What strategic decision-making structures did the Japanese and the Allies employ? How did those structures contribute to or inhibit maintenance of the strategic initiative in the Pacific during the mid-phase of the Pacific War?
- *Intelligence Apparatuses:* What organizations did the combatants employ in the pursuit of intelligence? How effective were these intelligence organizations in the prosecution of the war?
- *Resources:* How did resources contribute to the outcomes of those campaigns and to the side that held the strategic initiative? How effectively were available resources used?
- *Combat Effectiveness:* How important were combat effectiveness and operational/tactical methods? How did battle successes and failures, and the exploitation thereof, contribute to shifts in strategic initiative?

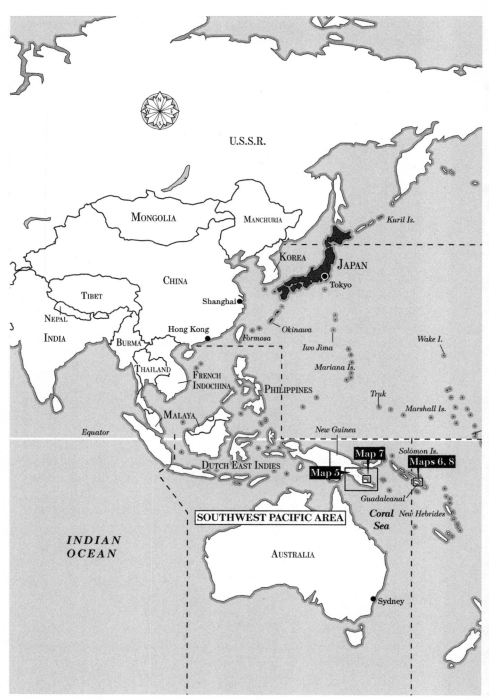

Map 1. Pacific Theater of War

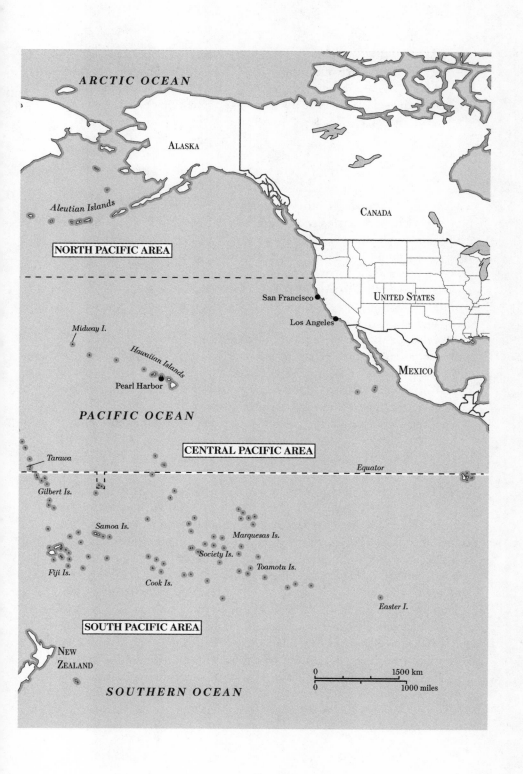

ARCTIC OCEAN

ALASKA

Aleutian Islands

NORTH PACIFIC AREA

CANADA

San Francisco

Los Angeles

UNITED STATES

Midway I.

Hawaiian Islands

Pearl Harbor

MEXICO

PACIFIC OCEAN

CENTRAL PACIFIC AREA

Equator

Tarawa

Gilbert Is.

Samoa Is.

Marquesas Is.

Society Is.

Fiji Is.

Toamotu Is.

Cook Is.

Easter I.

SOUTH PACIFIC AREA

NEW
ZEALAND

0		1500 km
0		1000 miles

SOUTHERN OCEAN

- *Chance:* What was the role of chance? Which side operated more effectively in the face of the unknown? How did this change over time?
- *Political Will:* How did the decisions, desires, and determination of political leaders influence possession and retention of strategic initiative in the Pacific War?

HISTORIOGRAPHY

The dominant campaigns in the Pacific between mid-1942 and early 1943 included General Douglas MacArthur's New Guinea campaign and the simultaneous effort on Guadalcanal under US Navy direction. Historiography has not neglected the period, and strategy is a popular and perennial subject in military history and military science; but there remains room for investigation in both areas. Historians often study these campaigns in isolation, thereby undervaluing the contribution of the Papuan campaign to the outcome of the war.

Moreover, although these accounts frequently refer to possession of the strategic initiative, they rarely define the term. It is possible to exercise initiative at the tactical or operational (campaign) levels while lacking overall strategic initiative. Many of the works do not even mention strategic initiative but refer instead to "turning points."

The best-known official account is Samuel Eliot Morison's fifteen-volume *History of United States Naval Operations in World War II*, covering the naval aspects of the war. Morison also composed a single-volume survey, *The Two Ocean War: A Short History of the United States Navy in the Second World War.* In this latter work, Morison devotes an entire chapter to Guadalcanal but grants only scattered references to New Guinea, which involved far fewer naval combat actions. Morison mentions Allied possession of strategic initiative only after continued fighting in the central Solomons concluded in October 1943, and he offers an implied definition: "They [the Allies] would call the tunes, selecting when and where to fight."[2]

Understandably, the US Marine Corps devoted an entire volume of its official history to the Guadalcanal campaign as a turning point in the war, arguing that the campaign gained the strategic initiative for the Allies while making no mention of any contributions from the concurrent New Guinea operation.[3] Perhaps more surprisingly, however, the exhaustive *United States Army in World War II* series agrees with this assessment. After separate volumes on the New Guinea and Guadalcanal campaigns, the army's historian concludes that it was the latter campaign that wrested the initiative away from the Japanese.[4] In a separate volume, *Strategic Planning for Coalition Warfare, 1941–1942*, the army historians Maurice Matloff and Edwin M. Snell imply that Allied offensive power in New Guinea and the Solomon Islands contributed to the beginning of the shift in strategic initiative to the Allies in December 1942; however, they do not define "initiative."[5] The fourth volume of the US Air Force (USAF) account, *The Pacific: Guadalcanal to Saipan, August 1942 to July 1944*, briefly gives credit to both campaigns for the shift of initiative to the Allies but, again, includes no specific definition or explanation.[6]

Beyond such government works, professional historians and biographers have examined this period and these campaigns from a variety of perspectives. However, many surveys of the Pacific War focus on Midway and/or Guadalcanal as the points where initiative changed hands.[7] Williamson Murray and Allan Millett provide a more nuanced view in *A War to Be Won: Fighting the Second World War*. They conclude that Midway, although it did not give the Allies the strategic initiative in the war, opened the door for them to vie for that initiative.[8]

Other works that analyze the Pacific War typically address the South Pacific campaigns of 1942 and 1943 in greater detail. Dan van der Vat discusses initiative and turning points in his book *The Pacific Campaign: The U.S.-Japanese Naval War, 1941–1945*. In his analysis, three turning points—the Coral Sea, Midway, and Guadalcanal—preceded a slow shift in initiative, which he equates with offensive action, in the Pacific war.[9]

Ronald Spector's influential study *Eagle against the Sun: The American War with Japan* presents yet another perspective on Midway. In Spector's judgment, the Japanese leaders chose to transition to a defensive posture after this battle even though they had sufficient forces to take the initiative if they chose.[10] Spector describes Guadalcanal as a defensive victory, which implies some sort of turning point, but stresses the psychological effects of both jungle campaigns in removing the veneer of the Japanese army's invincibility.[11]

A more recent work examines Japanese calculations in World War II from yet another perspective. *Japanese Military Strategy in the Pacific War: Was Defeat Inevitable?* by James Wood seeks to overturn conventional wisdom that Japan was foreordained to defeat at the hands of the richer Western nations. He argues that Japan had brilliantly executed its initial strategic plans, only to fight three battles—Midway, Guadalcanal, and New Guinea—at the wrong places and times.[12] While he does not clarify his concept of strategic initiative, he clearly feels that the campaigns and battles mentioned above contributed decisively to Japan's loss of that initiative.

One additional work deserves mention: H. P. Willmott's *The War with Japan: The Period of Balance May 1942–October 1943*, originally published in 2002. He rejects the idea of "turning points" in the war but likens the strategic initiative to a "gun lying in the street: it was there for either side to pick [up] and use" following the Battle of Midway.[13]

Turning to primary sources, any such study necessarily requires a look at the "other side" from the Japanese perspective. Unfortunately, primary Japanese sources pertaining to the Pacific War remain limited, particularly for one not versed in the complexities of the Japanese language. The Japanese destroyed much of their documentation when they realized the imminence of their impending defeat in 1945, before Allied forces occupied the island nation. Nonetheless, the postwar interrogations of Japanese officers and leaders conducted under the direction of the United States Strategic Bombing Survey (USSBS) remain a treasure trove of information. Indeed, many historians judge the Japanese participants in these interviews to be more forthcoming and forthright in their responses than were their German counterparts.[14] In addition, in the decades following the war the Japanese produced their own 102-volume history of the conflict, titled *Senshi Sōsho*, portions of which have been translated into English.[15] Finally, the series of postwar "Japanese Monographs" produced by Japanese officers for the US Far East Command provide another source for their perspective.

Studying these campaigns from the Allied perspective is less challenging. The official histories and campaign studies represent solid starting points, but several archival collections located in the United States offer the opportunity to get behind the scenes on the Allied side. Many pertinent US Army, Navy, and Marine Corps records are readily available for examination at the US National Archives II, located in College Park, Maryland. The Naval History and Heritage Command's Operational Archives Branch at the Washington Navy Yard offered additional naval resources, such as Admiral Nimitz's handwritten diary, to supplement the naval records available at the National Archives. Many, if not most, of the supporting US Air Force resources may be found at the Air Force Historical Research Agency at Maxwell Air Force Base in Montgomery, Alabama. Finally, a number of resources are also available through electronic means, including portions of President Franklin Delano Roosevelt's archives in the FDR Library and records of the numerous inter-Allied war conferences.

STRUCTURE

Chapter 2 examines the theoretical concept of strategic initiative and seeks to define the term explicitly in the military context. It then describes several important elements that contribute to the possession of strategic initiative, including resources, intelligence, strategic acumen, and combat effectiveness.

Chapter 3 describes how the Japanese and Allied decision-making structures functioned during the war. It investigates the interaction and working relationships among the political leaders, the army, the navy, and the air force leadership structures down to the units in the field waging the war in the South Pacific.

Chapters 4 and 5 describe and compare the intelligence structures employed by the Japanese and the Allies, in turn. As with the preceding chapter, the examination surveys the structures from national to tactical levels. Although both sides often used common methods of collection and similar sources such as radio intelligence/decryption and aerial photoreconnaissance, their integration of intelligence among the services differed markedly. The Allies developed structures that fostered better cooperation among their land, sea, and air forces than did the Japanese.

The analysis then transitions to the course of the Pacific War between December 1941 and February 1943, evaluating the main theme of shifting strategic initiative. Each chapter recounts a segment of the war, providing a narrative background of events, followed by an analysis of the period utilizing the supporting elements that underlie the possession of strategic initiative.

Chapter 6 is a brief narrative of the first six months of the war, recounting the war of Japanese conquest. It describes Japanese aims and reviews the seemingly irresistible tide of the Imperial advance. It examines the raid at Pearl Harbor as well as the invasions of the Philippine Islands, Malaya, and the Bismarck Archipelago. It also assesses the elements contributing to Japan's possession of strategic initiative during this period.

Chapter 7 recounts the Battle of Midway. It analyzes the significance of this battle and its influence on strategic initiative in the Pacific War, especially the impact of Midway on the strategies of the combatants as well as contemporary assessments of the meaning of the battle.

Chapters 8 and 9 focus on the period of strategic dispute, during which the Allies vied to seize the strategic initiative from the Japanese, from mid-1942 until February 1943. These two chapters analyze the course of the war through the lens of the underlying elements of strategic initiative developed earlier. The resulting analyses attempt to identify where the strategic initiative shifted decidedly to the Allied side and why. The inter-relationships among and interactions of these elements provide a deeper, more nuanced understanding of the course of the Pacific War than has previously been possible. The elements of strategic initiative help explain how and why the combatants engaged in heavy, attritional warfare in the South Pacific when, prior to the war, both anticipated a decisive naval battle in the Central Pacific to determine the war's victor. This interpretation thus provides a fresh look at the interactive effects of the dual, concurrent campaigns, rather than crediting the turn of events in the Pacific solely to the struggle for Guadalcanal and the Solomon Islands.

The first step, then, is to clarify the concept of strategic initiative. What is it, what are the elements that contribute to it, and why is this concept important?

2

Strategic Initiative

A PERUSAL OF MOST WORKS of military history is likely to yield numerous references to "initiative" in many different contexts. Commanders at all levels—whether tactical, operational, or strategic—are expected to exercise initiative. Those who fail to do so often suffer defeat or miss fleeting opportunities and thus endure the recriminations of the public and historians. Accounts of seizing the tactical or operational initiative abound, yet initiative at the strategic level receives only transitory mention. Historians and military professionals often assume a common understanding of strategic initiative, including which combatant possesses it and why. There is, however, neither a clear definition of the concept, nor any significant analysis of the elements that contribute to it. What, then, does the term "strategic initiative" convey?

Crafting useful definitions of abstract terms is always vexing, particularly in the realm of strategy and even more particularly if the concept of strategy is to be a foundational element of that definition. Historians and theorists have proffered a litany of different definitions for strategy, and the conversation continues today. Prudent authors approach the subject with caution and mild trepidation. Indeed, the well-known American military historian and strategist Edward Luttwak crafted his 304-page work titled *Strategy: The Logic of War and Peace* without presenting his own definition of strategy until Appendix A at the end of the book.

Adding to the confusion, many authors, strategists, and current US military doctrine writers recognize different types and/or levels of strategy, although the dividing lines are often murky and obscure. Examples include grand strategy, military strategy, diplomatic strategy, political strategy, economic strategy, and business strategy to name but a few variants.

Certainly, conflicts such as the war in the Pacific involve a number of these levels or types of strategy. The highest level is normally labeled "grand strategy." B. H. Liddell Hart expressed a common theme when he wrote that grand strategy's role is to direct all the resources of one or more nations toward the political object of the war. His discussion of grand strategy also touches upon financial, commercial, and diplomatic influences, but his concept is still dominated by war and military concerns.[1] Paul Kennedy credits Liddell Hart for breaking new ground and builds upon that construct, arguing that a nation's leaders must be able to unite all these elements into a coherent policy.[2] The modern American concept of grand strategy, as encapsulated in the National Security Strategy, expresses much the same concept.[3] Grand strategy, therefore, encompasses war as only one of many options for achieving national objectives.

Elements of grand strategy were at play throughout the war in the Pacific, even among erstwhile allies. The United States was engaged in a global war in which it recognized Nazi Germany in the European theater as the primary threat to American interests. Nonetheless, President Franklin Roosevelt also envisioned a postwar world devoid of the European empires of the past. Great Britain and France, however, fully expected a return to the status quo antebellum and the recovery of their imperial dominions. Similarly, Joseph Stalin and the Soviet Union held opportunistic aims following the defeat of Japan, aims at odds with those of its Western allies. My analysis does not explore this level of international interaction in any detail. Instead, the primary emphasis will be on the military aspects of the maritime struggle between the Japanese and the Allies, although certain elements of grand strategy must inevitably intercede in the conduct of the war.

Conceptualizing military strategy presents similar challenges. Military professionals and historians comfortably discuss the various aspects of war, including the tactical, the operational, and the strategic. What differentiates these presupposed "levels" of war, which in many cases may actually overlap?[4] To define these levels of war clearly, one must leave the level of grand strategy and begin at the lowest form of struggle—tactics—before working upward:

Tactics. Modern US military terminology defines the **tactical level** of war as "the level of war at which battles and engagements are planned and executed to achieve military objectives assigned to tactical units or task forces."[5] Tactics concerns the sharp end of combat, where the bullets fly, the bleeding occurs, and the din of battle dominates.

Operations. Moving up the theoretical ladder we come next to the operational perspective on war. A more recent military concept than either tactics or strategy, the **operational level** involves sequencing and conducting a series of major tactical operations into one or more sustained campaigns with the goal of achieving strategic objectives.[6] By implication, therefore, the operational level usually involves wider geographic areas and longer duration than do tactical actions.

Strategy. As previously noted, there is an ongoing historiographical discussion over the concept of strategy. We have briefly examined grand strategy, but what of the next lower level, military strategy? In general, the **strategic level** involves the interaction of adversaries, seeking to apply the available military resources to achieve the desired end state set by the policy of a nation-state or alliance.[7]

The inherent differences between the levels of strategy and operations require further clarification. Strategy encompasses the factors of time, force, space, and consequences on a higher order than operations, which are generally confined to a shorter period, a smaller force, fewer participants, more limited geographic areas, and less far-reaching stakes. Complexity increases exponentially in the transition from operations to strategy, requiring internal tradeoffs and delicate judgment on the part of the strategist.[8]

A brief examination of the relationship between time and strategy is in order. Time is a useful and often a limited commodity to the military professional. Many a commander has suffered in the judgment of history for moving too slowly or letting opportunities pass. American culture, particularly in the modern age, seems steeped in the mantra of rapid, positive results. Many in the modern US armed forces study the theories of Colonel John R. Boyd, USAF. Boyd, a Korean War fighter pilot, developed a model for enhanced performance in complex situations akin to aerial combat. He based his model for such enhanced performance on the observation–orientation–decision–action time cycle or loop, known in military circles as the OODA loop. The four steps in this loop are to rapidly observe the situation, orient oneself for the evolving environment, decide on a course of action, and then implement that action more quickly than one's enemy. By thus getting inside the enemy's OODA loop, sometimes termed a "decision cycle," one would confuse and disorganize an adversary. The stress is therefore on rapid action and staying ahead of the foe to influence the course of the battle or war to one's own benefit—initiative is implicit. Boyd's OODA loop is often an excellent analytical tool at all levels of war, but it may not be the answer in every situation.[9]

Strategy may not, in fact, always be practiced in a fast-moving situation. Some nations, societies, and cultures may be predisposed to or may consciously select strategic approaches with a longer view of time. For example, in *The Culture of Military Innovation*, Dima Adamsky maintains that the Soviet Union's military culture lacked the fascination with technology prevalent in the United States and that this cultural difference enabled the Soviets to conceive of the broader implications of American advances in military technology before the United States did.[10] Such cultural differences could easily contribute to differences over the concept of time in the formulation of strategy. In addition, depending on the character of the conflict, a less intensive and slower rhythm may supersede and trump a rapidly paced plan of action. The twenty-first century's ongoing war against transnational terrorist organizations such as al-Qaeda could well be one example. The United States and its Western allies must guard against overreaction in an attempt to stay ahead of every move conceivable by their enemies. Such efforts to counter every perceived or possible threat quickly could prove exhaustive and eventually prohibitive. Might not al-Qaeda and its allies benefit from a situation in which the United States and its North Atlantic Treaty Organization allies attempted to wage a high-tempo campaign over the course of two or more decades, with the corresponding expenditure of blood and treasure?

The West and the United States, despite the stereotype of impatience, settled on an enduring strategy during the Cold War to persevere over forty years of confrontation. Rome, in the face of the Hannibalic threat, provides another example. After several disastrous defeats at the hands of the famous Carthaginian, the Roman Senate appointed Q. Fabius Maximus as dictator. He changed the Roman strategy to one of caution, delay, and avoidance of battle and thereby wrested the rhythm away from the previously successful Hannibal. Fabius Maximus's successors soon changed Roman strategy and sought battle once again, resulting in Hannibal's epic victory over the Roman legions at Cannae in 216 B.C. A patient and slow-moving strategy may also impart a sense of ambiguity and confusion to a foe, meeting Boyd's ultimate objectives. Thus one cannot assume, as American military culture often does, that good strategy always requires rapid execution.

In short, strategy is a complex process of competition between thinking opponents in a fluid and uncertain environment. Strategy involves using one's means in effective ways to achieve one's ends. It encapsulates a potentially infinite number of variables. A successful strategy achieves its aims, while more successful strategies do so at lesser cost. Yet, a successful strategy does not require perfection—merely better performance than one's foe or foes.

FRAMING STRATEGIC INITIATIVE

The importance of strategy necessitates a sure grasp of strategic initiative and its underlying precepts. Having the best tactical and operational commanders and methods carries no assurance of ultimate victory in war. In the words of Allan R. Millett and Williamson Murray, "Mistakes in operations and tactics can be corrected, but political and strategic mistakes live forever."[11] The combatants still struggle over where, when, and why certain campaigns and battles are waged or not waged. Operational or tactical success in the wrong fight may or may not be beneficial to victory in the war. It is more advantageous to fight the correct battle adequately than the wrong battle brilliantly. The German army in World War II illustrates the point. The Wehrmacht was among the most potent tactical and operational forces in World War II, yet Germany eventually lost the strategic initiative on all fronts and with it the entire war.[12] *Understanding how to seize, hold, and retain strategic initiative is critical to the effective conduct of war.*

Thus, one must still ask: What is strategic initiative? Sporting analogies may help clarify some of the important aspects of initiative. A potentially helpful indicator of initiative is to ask "Who has the puck?" in hockey or "Who has the ball?" in soccer. The side controlling the puck or ball possesses the general ability to initiate action. The side with possession typically wields greater, though not total, influence over the tempo and style of play, the location of the main effort, and the likelihood of scoring a goal. One important and commonly misunderstood point is that this ability does not necessarily imply constant offensive action. It is possible for a team with the puck to play defensively by simply denying the other team the opportunity to score. Indeed, even possession of the puck or the ball does not necessarily guarantee possession of the initiative. The real crux of the issue is the ability to influence the tempo and style of play. Any sports aficionado may recall contests in which the course of the game favored one side over the other, where one team was forced to play the game in a manner less suited to its strengths and abilities but more favorable to those of its foe. Sports may indeed represent an imperfect analogy to war, but they do illustrate several fundamentals of the concept of initiative.

The introduction's brief historical review mentioned the passing references to strategic initiative by military historians, but a review of current professional military thought reveals a continuing void there as well. There is apparently no generally accepted definition of the term, yet once again there is an underlying assumption of a common understanding. Joint Publication 5-0, *Joint Operation Planning* (2006), refers to potential "forfeiture of strategic or operational initiative" while discussing operational pauses, but that publication provides no definition of strategic initiative.[13] US Air Force doctrine mimics the pattern, using "strategic initiative" in a figure depicting the "Modern View of Conflict" but failing to define the term.[14] Army doctrine defines individual and operational initiative but makes no mention of initiative in the strategic arena.[15] Navy and Marine Corps doctrinal publications likewise seemed to have ignored the concept.

Having examined some of the differences between the operational and strategic levels of war, one can use this knowledge to further our understanding of strategic initiative in the military sense. Clearly, political, economic, and military actions affect strategic initiative; but we may usefully build upon the foundation of operational initiative. Drawing upon the similarities of these various formulations and keeping the focus on the military sphere, strategic initiative in war may be defined as *the ability to influence the course of the conflict by being able to choose to wage those battles, operations, and campaigns most suited to the accomplishment of one's own political ends while avoiding those detrimental to the same.* Here, it is important to note that the side with the strategic initiative may either choose or be compelled to cede operational and/or tactical initiative at times during the conflict. The concepts are not mutually dependent. Referring back to our sporting analogies, the side with possession of the ball or the puck may possess only the operational initiative. For example, they may be playing from behind on the scoreboard, they may be pinned deeply on their own side of the pitch or rink, or time may be expiring. Offensive action and strategic initiative are not synonymous.

One further point of clarification deserves mention. It is possible at times for no combatant to hold a clear advantage or more influence in the course of the conflict. If those situations are also accompanied by comparable resources among the combatants, they may embody situations best described as "strategic equilibrium." H. P. Willmott's aforementioned assessment that strategic initiative was like "a gun lying in the street" following the Battle of Midway would represent such a case.

Strategic initiative as defined here is important on a number of levels. The side with the strategic initiative wields greater influence over the course of the conflict, thereby granting that side more flexibility and more options. This, in turn, implies more potential strategic choices, making the strategists' task more open-ended and complicated while also requiring astute judgment to exercise the initiative effectively. The side with the initiative may not have an easy task, but lacking the strategic initiative implies a more reactive stance with regard to the situation and, therefore, fewer options. Having fewer choices simplifies strategic decision making and clarifies the feasible courses of action. Intuitively, it would seem that the side with possession of the strategic initiative at the close of the war likely would emerge victorious, but this assumption may not be accurate. Analyzing strategic initiative in this one case, and looking at the midpoint of the Pacific War rather than its termination, can neither validate nor disprove this assumption. This potential aspect of strategic initiative requires further investigation.

A better understanding of strategic initiative is imperative for both the historian and the military professional alike. For the latter, understanding when one possesses the strategic initiative in war helps one to recognize opportunities and realize increased freedom of action or inaction. Similarly, understanding some of the underlying elements that contribute to the possession and/or shifting of strategic initiative would enable one to gain that initiative more effectively and thereby help ensure that the war progresses in a fashion beneficial to one's own national interests. For the military historian, an understanding of initiative for past wars allows for a greater appreciation of causation for the twists and turns of those conflicts. It may help to reveal how and why historical actors behaved the way they did as well as how and why campaigns or battles led to their specific outcomes.

The Pacific War combatants on both sides demonstrated awareness of strategic initiative. Allied leaders talked openly of initiative and strategic initiative in correspondence and at Allied conferences. Similarly, Edward Drea's analysis of the Imperial General Headquarters war diary indicates that the Japanese also thought in terms of strategic initiative, at least on some occasions.[16] Yet, like modern historians, their understanding of the concept and their focus on it varied. Interestingly, the Japanese diarist did not note a shift in the strategic initiative just because Japan's forces had stopped advancing by 1943 but did note a shift instead after a critical defeat in the Central Pacific. By early 1943, however, at the Casablanca Conference, the Allies indicated their appreciation of a shift in strategic initiative in the Pacific. Thus, an understanding of strategic initiative helps to analyze the thought processes of actors at the time while also offering a useful method of analysis for historians.

TWO EXAMPLES OF THE INFLUENCE OF
STRATEGIC INITIATIVE

Some historical examples may illustrate the point. The American Civil War progressed from 1861 to 1865 with shifts in strategic initiative. The Union Army attempted to seize the strategic initiative early in the war, hoping to crush the rebellion in its infancy with a march on Richmond, Virginia. Instead, in July 1861, the Battle of First Bull Run, known as First Manassas to the Confederates, stopped the Federal plan and resulted in a period of strategic equilibrium. The overall Union strategy soon evolved into pursuit of two aims: the exhaustion of the South's resources, and the destruction of its armies.[17] Following First Bull Run, the Federals used the strategic mobility afforded them by a superior navy to launch what is known as the Peninsula Campaign in the spring of 1862, a campaign that threatened Richmond from the southeast.

By dint of maneuver, the Union attempted to seize the initiative it had not gained in battle the year before. Nearly simultaneously, the Union won important victories in the western theater at Shiloh, Tennessee, and in New Orleans. The Southerners, under General Robert E. Lee, soon responded with the Seven Days' Battles in June 1862, which relieved Richmond, drove Union forces under General George McClellan back toward Washington, DC, and maintained the strategic equilibrium even though Lee fought on the defensive at the operational level.

Following the victory at Second Bull Run that August, Southern leaders attempted to gain the strategic initiative with an invasion of the North. General Lee marched north in part out of a lack of alternatives, but also with the recognition that the North had been cowed by recent events, and with the hope of turning Maryland to the Confederate cause and forcing Washington to sue for peace.[18] The Federal Army thwarted Lee's invasion at the Battle of Antietam in September 1862. The war remained in a state of strategic equilibrium despite Lee's repulse of the Union attack at Fredericksburg in December.

The Confederates made another attempt to seize the initiative following their victory at Chancellorsville in May 1863, when Lee launched his second invasion of the North. Lee again acted in part out of operational concerns, hoping to feed his troops on Northern crops, but he also saw an opportunity to spread political strife in the North, perhaps achieve foreign recognition for the Confederacy, and thereby force Washington into peace negotiations.[19] Instead, the Confederate defeat at Gettysburg and the simultaneous Federal capture of Vicksburg in Mississippi delivered the strategic initiative into the hands of the Union. The North's strategy of resource strangulation was taking hold, with the victories at New Orleans and Vicksburg giving the United States control over the Mississippi River. Next, the North began to press for its second goal: the destruction of Southern armies. The South still achieved some battlefield successes, such as at the battles at Chickamauga in Georgia and Cold Harbor in Virginia, but the Union maintained the strategic initiative by waging the war predominantly on its terms. In 1864, the Federals exercised that initiative with the campaign in the east under General Ulysses S. Grant and the seizure of Atlanta and the March to the Sea through Georgia by General William Tecumseh Sherman. Grant had decided that the best way to achieve Northern objectives would be to spurn the conventional military wisdom of massing one's forces and, instead, exert pressure on the South through simultaneous advances by different armies.[20] The Union maintained the initiative until the Confederate surrender in April 1865. Thus, the possession of the strategic initiative and the decisions of how to gain and exploit that initiative reveal much, even in a cursory examination, about the course and duration of the Civil War.

The Soviet–German conflict from June 1941 until May 1945 offers another interesting case in strategic initiative.[21] Nazi Germany seized the strategic initiative in that war through its surprise invasion of the Soviet Union in June 1941, which enabled the Germans to wield greater influence in the opening stages of the conflict and wage their war of conquest along a broad front. The Soviets made a crucial stand before Moscow at the end of 1941, but the Germans still retained the strategic initiative.[22] In 1942, the Germans exploited their continued possession of the initiative with a renewed offensive in the south, aiming to strike a death blow at the Soviet economy, seize the Caspian oil fields, and destroy the Soviet forces located in that region. The Soviets countered at the famous Battle of Stalingrad and then seized and held the initiative from mid-1943 until the end of the war.[23]

Following Stalingrad, the Soviets held sway over the course of the war and waged the war by fighting those battles suited to their goals of defeating German military power and overthrowing Nazi Germany. This point is fiercely debated by the participants of the war, many of whom feel the Germans regained the strategic initiative with Field Marshal Erich von Manstein's deft counterstroke that inflicted a serious defeat on the Soviets before Kharkov, in Ukraine, in February 1943. Yet, Manstein's attack was an indicator of operational initiative, not strategic. Manstein reacted to post-Stalingrad Soviet maneuvers and took the opportunity to deal a sound counterstroke that temporarily halted Soviet gains, but the Germans no longer directed the course of the war. Those who hold a different view cite the major German attack on Kursk in July 1943 as an indication of continued German possession of the strategic initiative, but this represents a case in which offensive maneuver is not synonymous with strategic initiative. It is well documented that the Soviet leader Joseph Stalin pressed his leading general, Marshal Georgi Zhukov, to preempt the German attack with a large Soviet offensive. Instead, Zhukov elected to stand on the defensive, with Stalin's grudging approval, and receive the German attack to grind down his foe and then follow it up with a counterstroke of his own. He elected to cede the operational initiative to the Germans temporarily in order to fight the defensive battle of his choosing, thereby exercising strategic initiative in a defensive manner. Following the German defeat at Kursk, the Red Army used the strategic initiative to transition to offensive operations until the surrender of Germany in May 1945. Once again, the understanding of strategic initiative helps clarify the course of the war and the decisions of the players involved.

SUPPORTING ELEMENTS OF STRATEGIC INITIATIVE

Strategic initiative entails the capacity to exert influence. One state's influence derives from a number of different factors depending on the context of the situation. War—our context for strategic initiative—pits two or more thinking opponents against each other in an arena of deadly competition. Effectively analyzing strategic initiative requires determination of those elements that aid or hamper the combatants' ability to seize, retain, dispute, or exploit it. Given the complexities of war, the number of possible factors is potentially infinite, but several stand out as particularly salient: resources, quality of intelligence, strategic acumen, tactical/operational methods (combat effectiveness), chance, and political will.[24] The first four factors correspond to four general determinants of military effectiveness: capacity, knowledge, wisdom, and technique.[25] Although these elements relate to one another in many ways, they can be sufficiently disaggregated to permit discrete analysis. These capabilities will be compared and contrasted for each combatant during the mid-phase of the Pacific War. Questions for this analysis will include: What was the relative significance of each of the factors? How did they operate in concert with one another? How did they combine to result in seizure, retention, loss, and exercise of initiative?

The resources element consists of the "capital" for waging war, or the tools required to fight and to win, including both the quantity and quality of manpower, materiel, and technology. Technological advantage may also be a significant factor in the equation.

Matching one's perception of the total situation with reality is the role of intelligence, which has two components. The first is collection and analysis, including the ability to discern the foe's entire war-making capacity at every level, to divine his intentions and capabilities and to understand the environment in which the two adversaries operate. The second component is counterintelligence and security, which attempts to deny the enemy an accurate understanding of the situation. Both areas contribute to overall intelligence effectiveness, and both play an important role in strategic initiative.

Strategic acumen, the third factor for analyzing possession of strategic initiative, is a broad concept with many ingredients. Fundamentally, it represents the wisdom to shape plans that will work in an environment plagued by uncertainty, friction, and chance. Those endowed with such acumen recognize the correlation between the means they possess, the ends or goals they hope to achieve, and the course of action or way chosen to achieve those ends. They also sense and act upon opportunities. Those gifted in strategic thought weigh the feasibility and payoffs of different courses of action against the risks they incur. Carl von Clausewitz hinted at this when he wrote, "A prince or general can best demonstrate his genius by managing a campaign exactly to suit his objectives and his resources, doing neither too much nor too little."[26]

The first subcomponent of strategic acumen is strategic planning. How effectively does the combatant match its objectives with its capabilities given the context of the existing situation? The Allied landings in North Africa in late 1942 are a good example of matching objectives with capabilities. President Franklin Roosevelt, with the backing of the British prime minister Winston Churchill, forced an invasion that his own military chiefs of staff opposed in order to get American forces into the fight against Germany quickly even if they were capable of achieving only modest military objectives.[27] However, this decision also had important ramifications for force availability in the Pacific theater. The second aspect of strategic acumen is the capacity to achieve surprise. Surprise allows one to accomplish one's mission before the enemy can react; this, in turn, may facilitate transfer of the initiative.[28] Surprise has a close relationship with intelligence but differs slightly in that the focus here is on the ability to conceive and execute deception operations, which are frequently the handmaidens of surprise. Though not always required for strategic acumen, effective deception and surprise may yield extraordinary results. The Japanese torpedo-boat attack on Port Arthur, Manchuria, at the time, in February 1904—before an actual declaration of war—opened the Russo–Japanese War with a surprise move akin to that at Pearl Harbor thirty-seven years later. Operation Fortitude, the Allied effort to mask the Normandy invasion in 1944, stands as an excellent example of deception, as it convinced the Germans that the Allies would strike farther north at the Pas de Calais. Once again, capabilities in these two components may vary widely within one nation or coalition, and each has the potential to play a significant role in determining strategic initiative.

The fourth factor for analyzing possession of strategic initiative is combat effectiveness, measured by a comparison of operational and tactical methods. Superior operational and tactical methods reveal themselves in success on the battlefield, where the bullets fly. According to Peter R. Mansoor, "Combat effectiveness is the ability of a military organization to achieve its assigned missions with the least expenditure of resources (both material and human) in the shortest amount of time."[29] Mansoor also stresses the importance of endurance to sustain operations over time. Although superior performance at the tactical and operational levels is not a guarantee of victory, these factors can contribute noticeably to strategic initiative.

A fifth consideration must be chance. Writing of war, Clausewitz noted that "no other human activity is so continuously or universally bound up with chance."[30] Chance can ruin the most meticulous and sound of plans or, on the contrary, salvage ill-conceived or poorly executed operations. In addition, the human reaction to chance—the ability to operate in uncertain or ambiguous circumstances—looms large.[31] As such, chance may play an important role in possession of the strategic initiative.

Finally, the combatants must demonstrate the political will to want to possess the strategic initiative. President Roosevelt knew he could not force the United States into the war with Japan or Germany but instead had to leave the strategic initiative to the Axis powers until the American people became convinced that war was both inevitable and necessary. Japan's Pearl Harbor attack convinced them, and the tightrope the Allies then walked in balancing the Pacific and European theaters of operations ensued. The Allies had to decide their level of effort in each theater and had to decide whether to seize opportunities or pass them by. Benito Mussolini, as a member of the Axis, had previously attempted to take the strategic initiative with his ill-considered invasion of Greece, an operation that nearly led to Italy's defeat in the Mediterranean and eventually did lead Germany to take over control of the war effort in the Balkans. Leaders may seize the strategic initiative at their peril; sometimes leaders may elect to avoid possession of the initiative or simply may not demonstrate the resolve to act and, therefore, may cede the strategic initiative, also not without risk.

The elements above will not, however, be considered in isolation. Each of these components is related to, and potentially influences, some or all of the others. The examination of the midcourse of the Pacific War must consider how these factors related to one another to influence strategic initiative. Did one factor dominate the others? Did marginal advantages in multiple areas accumulate to deliver strategic initiative into the hands of one side or the other? Was superiority in one or more areas canceled out by disadvantages in the other factors? Examining the war from various perspectives reveals the interplay among elements and between opponents.

The mid-phase of the Pacific War from July 1942 through late 1943 was a period of transition in which the strategic initiative shifted from the Japanese to the Allies. Before examining this critical phase of the war, however, we must understand the strategic decision-making structures of the combatants and gain a greater understanding of their intelligence apparatuses. The Japanese and the Allies entered the war with distinctly different approaches to strategic decision making, and those different approaches shaped the choices they made and the strategies they pursued.

3

The National Command Structures

THE JAPANESE AND THE AMERICANS approached and fought the war with significantly different command organizations. These differences were manifest at nearly every level, from coordination with their respective allies, to their own individual national command structures, on down into the command structures for their fielded forces. Such divergences helped shape the strategies they employed, the decisions and compromises they reached, and their performance in combined and joint operations on the battlefield. Understanding the details of these disparate command organizations is therefore essential to any analysis of the course of the war in the Pacific in the critical phase from mid-1942 into early 1943.

The study of organizations, including their cultures, values, and behaviors, crosses many academic disciplines from history to anthropology, business, and other fields. A full review of such literature is beyond the scope of this book, but brief consideration of some aspects of organizational literature is helpful. Graham Allison and Philip Zelikow examined organizational behavior during the Cuban Missile Crisis in their book *Essence of Decision: Explaining the Cuban Missile Crisis*. The authors examine the inherent foundations of organizations: Governments create organizations to address particular tasks; those organizations often develop their own internal logic for approaching problems and crafting solutions; organizations may also evolve their own particular cultures; and the output generated by the organization typically stems from these factors of logic, culture, and assigned tasks.[1] For example, when presented with the secret buildup of Soviet missiles in Cuba, the US Air Force naturally proposed an air strike to destroy the threat. Such a solution matched the organization's capabilities, logic, and culture.

The implications of this framework are legion for organizations that make strategic decisions. Those that effectively integrate governmental, diplomatic, and military leaders into a coordinated body normally produce decisions and recommendations that qualitatively differ from those of bodies with less effective integration. A modern state requires many organizations to manage the disparate tasks of governing, and coordinating all the associated agencies and bureaucracies to ensure a common direction of effort remains a daunting challenge that grows even more complicated with the introduction of allies. The Japanese and the Allies developed different structures for guiding their efforts during World War II. In general, the Allied decision-making structures integrated the different nationalities, services, and bureaucracies more effectively than did the Japanese.

THE JAPANESE COMMAND ORGANIZATION

At the broadest level, coordination among allies was one of the more glaring differences between the Allied and Axis command structures during World War II. The primary Axis nations—Germany, Italy, and Japan—evinced very little coordination between the European and Pacific theaters of operation. Aside from the maintenance of normal diplomatic contacts and missions between the European Axis nations and Japan, no coordinating structure developed to guide the combatants' actions and harmonize efforts in the east and west for an integrated approach to defeating the Allied powers. Germany and Italy ran the war as they saw fit in Europe and Africa, while Japan operated independently in the Pacific and in Asia.

JAPANESE NATIONAL COMMAND STRUCTURE

By the outbreak of war with the Western Allies in December 1941, the military, and in particular the Imperial Japanese Army (IJA), dominated the Japanese government. Japan's politically restive period during the early 1930s resulted in a de facto veto power of the army over the cabinet. If the army opposed the policies of a cabinet, the war minister could resign and the army would then refuse to appoint a replacement, scuttling the government and preventing the formation of a new one until the appointment of a cabinet more amenable to the army's views.[2]

The IJA enjoyed greater influence within the Japanese structure than did its counterpart, the Imperial Japanese Navy (IJN). After the war, investigators of the United States Strategic Bombing Survey interrogated Prince (and army general) Naruhiko Higashi-Kuni, who was instructed by Emperor Hirohito to form a new cabinet in August 1945 to close out the war. The interrogators queried the prince about the dominance of the army in comparison to the navy concerning control over Japanese industry during the war. Higashi-Kuni matter-of-factly responded through a translator: "He thinks, as a layman again [concerning industry], that the reason was that the army was more powerful than the navy internally."[3] The Japanese reporter Masuo Kato agreed, declaring the decision for war in 1941 an Imperial Army determination: "Japan's decision to attack the United States, Great Britain, and the Netherlands on December 8, 1941, was essentially a now or never decision, and it represented the Army's best judgment as to the precise time at which the greatest opportunity for success might be expected."[4] By contrast, as early as 1937 naval leaders could not alter the actions of the army-dominated government.[5] This does not mean the navy was without influence, but it did play a less significant role than did the army in the formulation of national strategy.

In truth, even the senior levels of the army struggled to control their own subordinates, let alone national policy. The 1937 Marco Polo Bridge incident in China demonstrated serious flaws in the Japanese decision-making apparatus. Local Japanese army commanders in northern China, led by Colonel Renya Mutaguchi, raised tensions with the Chinese to the point of war, with skirmishes soon escalating into multidivisional engagements, all without the blessing of either the War Ministry or the Army General Staff. These incidents, spurred by an aggressive local officer rather than by calculated strategic decisions of the high command, resulted in an undeclared war on mainland Asia and led to the creation of the Imperial General Headquarters (IGHQ) to wage that war.[6] That such a low-level officer could lead his nation into a major conflict demonstrates serious flaws in Japanese command of their forces and in their strategic decision-making.

Emperor Hirohito, the Shōwa Emperor, presided over the Japanese command structure. Despite his divine status in Japanese eyes, his influence over the activities of his government was typically much more nuanced than absolute. In principle, he could wield decisive authority when he so chose, as indicated by his decision to end the war in August 1945. Such occasions, however, were the exception rather than the rule. In theory, all state decisions required Hirohito's sanction, but traditionally the emperor, as the embodiment of the entire nation, remained above party politics and interservice rivalries by simply approving all policies agreed upon by the cabinet and military leaders.[7] In short, he usually rubber-stamped its decisions. According to Japanese postwar arguments, which were perhaps motivated by a desire to shield Hirohito, "The Emperor's non-responsibility clearly defined that the Emperor was not responsible for the entire sovereignty of the nation. This not only applied to domestic and foreign affairs but also to the 'Supreme Command.'"[8] Dan van der Vat characterized the position of Emperor Hirohito as a symbolic head of state and chief executive who did not interfere in daily policy, allowing the actual rulers to conceal their responsibility.[9]

Below the emperor lay a myriad of organizations contributing to the determination of strategy and policy and to the execution of same. These organizations included the Supreme War Council, the Board of Marshals and Admirals, the Imperial Liaison Conference, the cabinet, and the Imperial General Headquarters. Each had its own membership, structure, and expected contribution to the overall war effort.

The Supreme War Council (*Gunji Sangiin*) and the Board of Marshals and Admirals (*Gensuifu*) require only brief mention for the early and middle phases of the war. The US War Department characterized the latter organization as acting only in an advisory capacity to the emperor.[10] The titles of field marshal and fleet admiral carried with them appointment to this board, but that board had no specific military authority.[11]

The Supreme War Council consisted of the Board of Field Marshals and Admirals, the current war and navy ministers, the chiefs of staff of the army and navy, and other senior officers, including former war and navy ministers, appointed by the emperor. Prince Higashi-Kuni, in addition to his aforementioned responsibilities, was also a former member of the Supreme War Council. In his postwar interrogation, the prince stated that the war minister and the army chief of staff placed little faith in that body and did not seek the council's advice or opinions but merely relayed information on programs already enacted by the Imperial Japanese Army.[12] Like the Board of Marshals and Admirals, the Supreme War Council was primarily an honorific body that contributed little to the strategic direction of the Japanese war effort.

The Japanese cabinet constituted a more influential body in the government. It consisted of the prime minister, the war and navy ministers, the foreign minister, and other dignitaries. The cabinet focused on the political and economic administration of the country and the mobilization of resources for the prosecution of the war.[13] On the eve of war, the Japanese army compelled an important change to the cabinet. On October 15, 1941, the army exercised its prerogative and forced the dissolution of the cabinet under Prime Minister Prince Fumimaro Konoye, resulting in the formation of a new cabinet under General Hideki Tojo three days later. Tojo retained his previous office as war minister while simultaneously executing the duties of the prime minister, offering another indication of army dominance in Japanese politics. Even before Tojo had taken over the cabinet, his predecessor felt the strong influence of the military: "I must admit as a prime minister, many of the policies were influenced by the military and it was often necessary to work out certain compromises with respect to policy."[14]

The War and Navy Ministries held specific responsibilities within the Japanese government. Functions of the Ministry of War included administration, supply, and mobilization of the army; it also served as a liaison between the army and the Japanese Diet. The Japanese army Aviation Headquarters was also subordinate to the War Ministry to provide administrative support to Japanese Army Air Force (JAAF) units, which served under the command of the Army General Staff in the field. The minister of war, as noted, was a member of the cabinet and was directly responsible to the emperor and was an active general in the army.[15] Similarly, the Navy Ministry administered the navy, including funding, personnel, training, and logistics. Navy ministers were typically active flag officers in the navy and, as members of the cabinet, were also directly responsible to the emperor.[16] Once again, the military organizations of Japan stood outside of civilian purview.

The Imperial General Headquarters represented the real locus of power for military strategy and operations during the war. IGHQ was not a standing body within the Japanese government but, under the Meiji constitution, was established only during times of war. In November 1937, the Japanese government created the IGHQ that would orchestrate Japan's war effort in response to the ongoing conflict in China. Interservice tensions affected the workings of the body: the army was concerned that any centralized policy mechanism would lead to excessive civilian interference in the conduct of the war, while the navy feared that such centralization would increase the army's influence.[17] Thus, from IGHQ's inception, interservice squabbling and Japanese internal politics limited the ability of the high command to shape the operations and behaviors of the two armed forces into more cooperative and integrated campaigns. That is not to say the Japanese were incapable of effective joint operations, an assertion the opening months of the war certainly debunk. However, the Japanese IGHQ structure certainly did not promote the most effective joint operations or joint strategy.

The historian Edward Drea describes the IGHQ's composition as follows:

> Imperial headquarters was divided into army and navy sections directed by the chiefs of the general staff for both services who were

the emperor's highest advisers on operational matters. The respective staffs came from the directors and selected subordinates of the more important bureaus and departments of the war and navy ministries and the army and navy general staffs. Service leaders agreed beforehand on military policy before seeking the emperor's authorization at special imperial conferences held at IGHQ (*Daihon'ei gozen kaigi*) that included the emperor and his senior military officials and dealt exclusively with military matters. Eight such sessions were held between November 1937 and May 1943.[18]

IGHQ membership included the war and navy ministers, the chiefs of the general and navy staffs, and specially selected staff members from the general staffs of each service. In the rare instances when the army and navy reached accord on a policy or strategic direction, they issued instructions based on so-called Central Agreements. Far more often, however, the Army Section and Navy Section of the IGHQ issued separate directives concerning their own, separate fields of responsibility.[19] As a practical matter, there was no one decision-maker to arbitrate between the two services in the (frequent) event of disagreement.[20] Such a limitation could not help but influence strategic choices and decisions. And, similarly to the war and navy ministers, the chiefs of the army and navy general staffs could appeal directly to the emperor without proceeding through channels with the prime minister or the cabinet.[21]

The Japanese devised the Imperial Liaison Conference (*Dai Hon'ei seifu renraku kaigi*) as the means of creating a semblance of unity of effort at the national level. The liaison conference had no constitutional basis like that of the cabinet, but it represented a structure of mutual agreement, in which all present were responsible for executing the decisions of the conference. The prime minister relayed the agreements from the conference to the cabinet to carry out the government's commitments, while the chiefs of staff followed through on their agreed responsibilities via the IGHQ.[22] The prime minister and foreign minister, together with the two service ministers and chiefs of staff and a few other officials, held liaison conferences with or without the presence of the emperor.[23] When such conferences occurred in the presence of the emperor, their decisions had the force of imperial decrees that were almost irreversible.[24] Yet, once again, final courses of action to interpret and implement these decisions remained dependent on consensus agreements among the liaison conference members, with no arbiter to force a decision if required.

The highest levels of the Japanese command structure therefore demonstrated key shortcomings that adversely influenced the nation's strategic decision-making. Beneath Emperor Hirohito a number of organizations existed, nominally to assist in the strategic direction of the country; but in reality most had only limited influence (see figure 1). The most important organizations for military strategy included IGHQ and the liaison conferences. Additionally, numerous actors enjoyed the privilege of direct access to the throne, placing the military apparatus outside of governmental control. The war and navy ministers, as well as both chiefs of the general staffs, represent such cases. Given Hirohito's traditional reluctance to weigh in on political matters, these structures proved imperfect in achieving conflict resolution among the various competing organizations. The desire for consensus agreements between the services' leaders shaped and limited strategic options and actions.[25]

With the war in full swing in 1942, the command structure of Japan's fielded forces in the South Pacific evolved to meet the requirements of the war. The structure of these forces also influenced the course of the war and the possession of strategic initiative. They require a quick review as well.

JAPANESE FIELD COMMANDS IN THE SOUTH PACIFIC, JULY 1942–NOVEMBER 1943

The Combined Fleet existed as a unique structure within the Imperial Japanese Navy. In practice, it was both an operational seagoing command and another strategic headquarters. The Combined Fleet retained the lion's share of the Imperial Navy's striking power in terms of aircraft carriers and capital ships, which would sortie in support of other fleets or launch independent operations as the war situation required. The well-known and revered Admiral Isoruku Yamamoto assumed the position of Commander-in-Chief (CIC), Combined Fleet, prior to the outbreak of the war, with 10 battleships, 10 aircraft carriers, 18 heavy cruisers, 24 light cruisers, 111 destroyers, and 64 submarines at his disposal.[26]

In theory, Yamamoto's position was subordinate to that of IGHQ and the Navy Department. Reality was rather different than the command flowchart indicated. Yamamoto wielded great influence within the navy and, indeed, the nation, elevating his stature and, therefore, the influence of his office as CIC, Combined Fleet. This led to command difficulties for Japan. His staff included many advocates of naval aviation, which became key to Japan's early successes. However, the Combined Fleet headquarters often perceived itself as struggling against the naval estab-

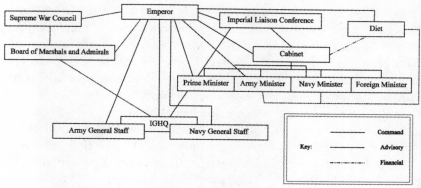

Figure 1. Japanese High Command Structure

lishment. Yamamoto had threatened to resign if the Navy General Staff rejected his proposed raid on Pearl Harbor, resulting in approval for the bold operation. The subsequent success of that attack further enhanced Yamamoto's standing, and with the threat of resignation precedent Yamamoto and the Combined Fleet began usurping the strategic planning function of the Navy General Staff, pitting the Combined Fleet headquarters, based in Hashirajima, against the staff in Tokyo.[27]

This overlap of functions and authority foreshadowed a chronic characteristic of many Japanese organizations throughout World War II. The Japanese did not shy away from complexity; indeed, they embraced it. The dual nature of naval command, the divided IGHQ, plus the numerous bodies and individuals afforded direct access to the emperor all manifested parallel and overlapping bureaucracies. The current US military principles of war regarding "simplicity" and "unity of command" did not permeate Japanese operations or organizations during the war—with sometimes catastrophic effects on the Japanese war effort.

Japan's commitment to the South Pacific grew as the war progressed into its middle phase in the latter half of 1942 and early 1943. During its initial advance in 1942, Japan planned for operations in the South Pacific (known as the Southeast Pacific to the Japanese command) and the conquest of Rabaul in order to protect the southern flank of its naval bastion at Truk. The forces allotted for these operations included the three Imperial Japanese Army infantry battalions that made up the South Seas Force for the invasion of Rabaul in January 1942, plus small naval landing units in conjunction with other infantry companies for occupation of Lae and Salamaua, New Guinea, and other positions in the Solomon Islands

chain. These forces cooperated with the Imperial Japanese Navy's South
Seas Fleet, a regional command that included the 4th Fleet and 11th Air
Fleet.[28] By May, the Japanese forces had successfully completed these initial operations and begun to prepare for the next phase of the war. The
Japanese leaders then planned to expand their perimeter beyond that envisioned prior to the war and soon moved against Papua New Guinea and
the southern portion of the Solomon Islands chain.

As related in the *Senshi Sōsho*, the history of the war compiled by the
War History Office of the Japanese Ministry of Defense after the end of
the war, Imperial General Headquarters reevaluated the situation in the
Southeast Pacific area in May 1942 and laid the foundations for the command organizations that would soon come to the fore in the war:

> At that time, Imperial Headquarters had completed attacks on key
> areas in the southern region. Recognizing that the main base for
> Allied counter-attacks would be the Australian mainland, Imperial
> Headquarters planned a blockade operation to isolate Australia
> from the US. This would involve attacks on the islands of Samoa,
> Fiji, and New Caledonia, the main air and sea relay bases between
> Hawaii and the Australian mainland. The army formed the 17th
> Army (based on 12 infantry battalions), and the navy the 8th Fleet.[29]

Events at the Battle of the Coral Sea in May 1942 and, more significantly,
at the Battle of Midway in June, soon caused the cancellation of the Samoa, Fiji, and New Caledonia operations. These cancellations, however,
forced realignment in the mission of the 17th Army to cooperate with the
navy in the seizure of Port Moresby and eastern New Guinea.[30]

Later in the year, as fighting raged on Guadalcanal and in Papua New
Guinea, the Imperial Army discerned a need for further adjustment in
its command structure. The IJA activated the command of the 8th Area
Army on November 26, 1942, to focus on its southern Pacific operations.[31] Nearly simultaneously, the IJA created the 18th Army under the
8th Area Army to focus on the New Guinea campaign and subordinated
the 17th Army to the 8th Area Army to direct the ongoing battle on Guadalcanal and in the Solomon Islands.[32] Beginning in September 1942 and
thereafter, army aviation units began transferring into the South Pacific
area to assist the IJN air units that had waged the battle to date. The influx of army aircraft began slowly in September 1942 with the arrival of
a reconnaissance squadron and accelerated in late 1942 with the arrival
of the 12th Air Brigade, an elite army fighter unit.[33]

The course of the war also forced the Imperial Japanese Navy to make some command adjustments. As already noted, in mid-1942 the navy created the 8th Fleet to serve in the South Pacific area, thereby reducing the responsibilities of the overstretched 4th Fleet. The 8th Fleet stood up its command on July 14, 1942, and shortly thereafter headed for Rabaul. Thus the South Seas Fleet assumed responsibility for campaigns in the southern Pacific with subordinate units that now included the 8th Fleet and the 11th Air Fleet.[34]

Japan waged the war from late 1941 and into 1943 with these Imperial Army and Navy command structures. It is important to note that, like the necessity for IGHQ to formulate Central Agreements for the conduct of the war, these commands had to negotiate local interservice agreements during the execution of operations in their areas. No overall area commander could force unity of effort based upon his position. The respective army and navy commanders of a given geographic area often received assignments from the high command that delineated separate responsibilities within that area. In the South Pacific, the campaign on New Guinea predominantly fell to the army, while the struggle for Guadalcanal began as a navy operation. Even on the rare occasions when Tokyo ordered them to cooperate, the army and navy headquarters in the field still struggled to coordinate joint operations and to plan effectively for such operations. Without an overall commander to conduct operations in a given area, Japan's two services often fell into the trap of mutual recriminations when operations went awry. The Imperial Japanese Army and the Imperial Japanese Navy each expressed disappointment in the other during the struggle for Guadalcanal.[35] Instead of cultivating effective teamwork, such arrangements did little to mitigate interservice divisions. (See figure 2.)

The organizations in China and Manchukuo are beyond the scope of this analysis but deserve brief mention. Japan's war on the Asian mainland differed substantially from that of the maritime conflict in the Pacific in that it remained primarily an army concern with limited naval participation. Admiral Osami Nagano, former chief of the Navy General Staff, later stated that typically no naval forces were involved; therefore, the navy usually had no part in planning or operations on the continent.[36] This simplified the problem of unity of command because the normal army chain of command had control over its units and the JAAF remained subordinate to the army. No coordination or agreement with the navy was required if naval forces were not participating, which was normally the case.

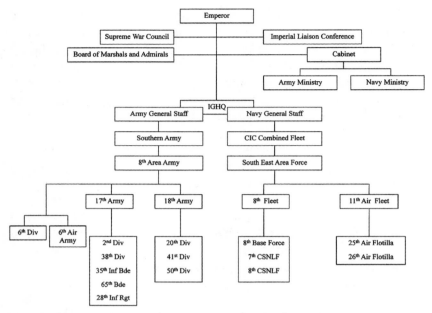

Figure 2. Japanese Command Structure, Late November 1942

Sources: This represents an amalgamation of three separate command charts from three sources: US War Department, *Handbook on Japanese Military Forces* (reproduced Baton Rouge: Louisiana State University Press, 1995), 10. David C. Evans and Mark R. Peattie, *Kaigun: Strategy, Tactics, and Technology in the Imperial Japanese Navy, 1887–1941* (Annapolis, MD: Naval Institute Press, 1997), 459. Gordon L. Rottman, *Japanese Army in World War II: The South Pacific and New Guinea, 1942–43*, ed. Duncan Anderson, vol. 14, *Battle Orders* (New York: Osprey Publishing, 2005), 8.

AMERICAN COMMAND ORGANIZATION

The lack of coordination among the Axis nations meant that Japan ran an independent war effort, free to make strategy as it wished. The Western Allies—the British dominions and their American cousins—represent a stark contrast in this regard. Although agreement often did not come easily, the two powers strove to coordinate their global strategies, one major aim of which was to keep the Soviet Union fighting in the war against Nazi Germany. The different visions of strategy among these Allies often led to serious disagreement over resource allocation and forthcoming operations and could result in unspoken animosity beneath the supposedly placid surface of Allied accord. Nevertheless, they did, in general, succeed in harmonizing their strategies as the war progressed. The key

to that harmonization lay in the Combined Chiefs of Staff (CCS) structure the Western Allies put in place upon America's entry into the war. It
is important to note, however, that this British and American cooperation had important prewar antecedents. The two nations had laid the
foundations for the coalition well before the Japanese attack brought
the United States into the war in December 1941. The soon-to-be allies
sowed the seeds of the now well-known "Germany First" strategy at the
US–British Staff Conference (colloquially known as ABC-1 for America,
Britain, Canada) held in Washington, DC.[37] Talks between the British
and the Americans continued at the Atlantic Conference held in August
1941 off the Newfoundland coast, where the topics included the moral
basis for the war (reflected in the Atlantic Charter) and British ideas on a
peripheral strategy for the defeat of Germany and an invasion of French
North Africa. When the United States entered the war in December, the
British and American Allies established the Combined Chiefs of Staff in
Washington, with the British being represented by a Joint Staff Mission;
the United States created its Joint Chiefs of Staff (JCS) structure to coordinate the global war effort.[38] The Allied ARCADIA Conference, held
in Washington from December 1941 into January 1942, decided on the
charter for the Combined Chiefs of Staff, which was to include a division of combined staff planners.[39] In addition to this ongoing operation
in Washington, the Allies held a series of larger conferences that brought
the president and the prime minister into direct contact. Four such conferences occurred between late 1941 and mid-1943: ARCADIA (Washington, DC) from December 1941 to January 1942; SYMBOL (Casablanca,
Morocco) in January 1943; TRIDENT (Washington, DC) in May 1943;
and QUADRANT (Quebec, Ontario) in August 1943.[40] Such conferences
continued throughout the duration of the war. The British and Americans
also met with the Soviet leader Joseph Stalin and other Allied leaders on
occasion, such as at Cairo and Tehran in 1943 and Potsdam in 1945.

The short-lived American–British–Dutch–Australian Command (known
as ABDACOM) represents the closest example of a combined command
in the Pacific along the lines of those in the European theater. Under the
supreme direction of the British general Sir Archibald Wavell with subordinate commanders and forces from each nation represented in its title,
ABDACOM attempted to stem the Japanese advance in the Far East in
January and February 1942. (See figure 3.)

Suffering a succession of defeats attributable in part to Allied unpre-
paredness, the command evaporated after six weeks, and by the end of
March the Japanese controlled nearly all of the territory ABDACOM

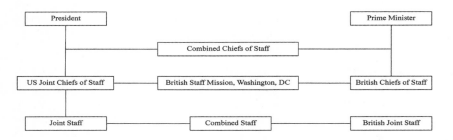

Figure 3. Combined Chiefs of Staff Structure, Late 1942

Sources: Louis Morton, *Strategy and Command: The First Two Years*, United States Army in World War II: The War in the Pacific (Washington, DC: Office of the Chief of Military History, 1962), 232. Taken from a portion of "Chart 3—The Washington High Command and the Pacific Theaters, December 1942."

had been created to defend.[41] The eviction of the major European powers from the maritime geographic areas of the Pacific had important implications for the Allied command structure in that theater as the war progressed. To be sure, Australia and New Zealand wielded influence in the Allied Pacific conflict, but nothing comparable to that of Great Britain in Europe. The United States assumed de facto and de jure leadership in the war against Japan in the Pacific, while China fought its own conflict against Japan on the Asian mainland and Great Britain defended India and had primacy in the war in Southeast Asia.

AMERICAN NATIONAL COMMAND STRUCTURE

Despite this generalization, Combined Chiefs of Staff decisions still directly affected the war in the Pacific following the dissolution of ABD-ACOM in early 1942. However, the main influence of the CCS occurred in resource allocation and the level of effort to be dedicated to the war against Japan. Beyond that, American leaders, not a combined command, directed the military strategy and operations conducted in the maritime environment of the Pacific theater. Allies such as Australia and New Zealand contributed forces, but the chain of command ran from Washington to the unified geographic commands in the various areas of responsibility in the vast Pacific Ocean.

This placed the American president atop the hierarchy of command for the Pacific War. Unlike Emperor Hirohito, however, President Roosevelt

had practical experience as an assistant secretary of the navy and did not
shrink from shaping, or if necessary forcing, strategic modifications on
his military commanders. Eric Larrabee notes this experience had convinced Roosevelt that generals and admirals needed civilian oversight to
maximize their efforts and drive.[42] Further, although the army and navy
were equals in the governmental structure, Roosevelt's close association
with the navy colored his proclivities:

> Perhaps it was an advantage for [General George] Marshall that
> Roosevelt did not take the same proprietary interest in the Army
> that he took in the Navy. It gave Marshall a freer hand, especially
> in the naming of senior commanders, and it did permit him one op-
> portunity—after a discussion in which the Navy was being favored
> unrestrainedly—to answer Roosevelt in kind. "At least, Mr. Presi-
> dent," said Marshall, "stop speaking of the Army as 'they' and the
> Navy as 'us.'" This broke up the meeting. And Roosevelt permitted
> Marshall something he never allowed [Admiral] Ernie King, which
> was to shake apart the cumbersome machinery by which his service
> operated and replace it with a streamlined structure.[43]

Throughout the war, Roosevelt remained a navy man at heart.

Not surprisingly, at the beginning of the war, the American high command required a good deal of modification to manage the requirements
of a global war. The United States began the war with the Joint Army and
Navy Board, or Joint Board, initially established in 1903. In July 1919,
the government had reorganized the Joint Board to include the army chief
of staff, the Chief of Naval Operations (CNO), the chief of the Operations Section of the General Staff, the assistant CNO, and the chiefs of
the War Department and Navy War Plans Divisions. This reorganization
also included the creation of the Joint Planning Committee for strategic
contingency planning.[44] Yet, this organization could not match the British organization of the Imperial General Staff and the numerous divisions
within that structure.

Recognizing the limitations of the Joint Board and faced with superior
cohesion when dealing with the Imperial General Staff during Combined
Chiefs of Staff meetings, the Americans improvised their own version of
the Joint Chiefs of Staff based upon the British model in February 1942.[45]
Nearly simultaneously, the US Army and US Navy implemented several
internal restructuring decisions in March 1942, which enhanced the army
chief of staff's influence, granted greater autonomy to the commander of

the United States Army Air Forces (USAAF) and consolidated the offices
of Commander-in-Chief, United States Fleet, and CNO under Admiral
Ernest J. King. By July 1942, the composition of the JCS included General George Marshall as the army chief of staff, the USAAF commander
General Henry H. "Hap" Arnold (who remained nominally subordinate
to Marshall), Admiral King as CNO and Commander-in-Chief, US Fleet,
and Admiral William D. Leahy (who returned from Vichy France, where
he had served as the US ambassador) as coordinating link to the president
with the ill-defined title Chief of Staff to the Commander-in-Chief. It is
important to note that the JCS enhanced the power of the service chiefs
largely at the expense of the influence of the secretaries of war and the
navy.[46] While still very much subordinate to civilian control, the greatest
form of that civilian control over the military emanated directly from the
president himself rather than through political appointees within his administration. The inclusion of a semiautonomous air force representative,
albeit still subordinate to the army chief of staff, on the JCS represents
a significant difference in comparison to the Japanese high command, in
which the respective air arms remained entirely subordinate to the IJA
and the IJN.

Several important organizations that quickly developed under the JCS
system deserve mention. The Joint Staff Planners (JSP) soon evolved out of
the Joint Board's Joint Planning Committee. The Joint Staff Planners had
army, navy, army air force, and logistical representation, and their work
ranged over all aspects of global operations and logistics. This wide range
of responsibilities soon spurred the development of important subcom-
mittees. The Joint US Strategic Committee (JUSSC), another organization
with a Joint Board legacy, supported the JSP with strategic estimates and
plans to focus on broad strategy. In November 1942, the JCS created the
Joint Strategic Survey Committee (JSSC), with three general officers assigned full-time to consider basic strategy and the long-term implications
of current events and decisions, and to report their findings directly to the
Joint Chiefs, as opposed to the JSP.[47]

These integrated, long-range, joint planning and survey committees
mark another difference from the command structure on the other side
of the Pacific. The Japanese had no such integrated structures. Although
the American system still resulted in interservice differences and competition and the structure did not have a clear superior short of the president,
as a general rule the American forces at least had a system that fostered
closer cooperation among the different services than did Japanese forces.
This structure facilitated operations in the field and bred a familiarity

with interservice capabilities and limitations. Such cooperation and understanding enabled more realistic and effective planning. The JCS made strategic decisions based on the combined expertise of the army and the navy. When they deadlocked, President Roosevelt stepped in to decide, in contrast to Emperor Hirohito, who rarely intervened.

Nevertheless, those interservice differences did manifest themselves in the divided command that marked the Allied forces in the Pacific. The Americans created two major commands to prosecute the war against Japan, one under naval direction, and the other under army direction. Both answered to the JCS. This structure, which was to have serious ramifications throughout the course of the war, demands closer scrutiny.

ALLIED FIELD COMMANDS IN THE SOUTH PACIFIC, JULY 1942–NOVEMBER 1943

A number of factors contributed to the final organization of Allied field commands in the Pacific, including the size of the theater, suggestions from Australia and New Zealand, and the inability of the army and the navy to reconcile their competing claims to theater supremacy. The Allies recognized the need for new command adjustments in the spring of 1942 and considered a number of proposals. Australia and New Zealand attempted to create a command including their nations as well as New Guinea, Timor, and Amboina under the direction of a US commander who would answer to the CCS rather than to the JCS. The CCS, however, recognized that the Pacific theater was likely to come under US purview and simply passed along this request to the Americans. Admiral King rejected this proposal, claiming New Zealand would be a vital link in the line of communication from Hawaii to the southern Allies, while Australia, New Guinea, and the Netherlands East Indies represented an entirely different strategic entity. The army and planners under General Dwight Eisenhower accepted the idea of a divided command in the Pacific but favored a demarcation closer to the Australians' and New Zealanders' proposal. The JCS settled the differences in the proposals between March 9 and 16, 1942, with the general acceptance of the navy's proposal with the modification that the Philippines be included in the Australian area, designated as the South West Pacific Area (SWPA). On March 30, President Roosevelt recognized the political need to give Douglas MacArthur's towering personality a prominent role in the Pacific and approved the proposal, establishing two Pacific commands with MacArthur in charge of the SWPA and Admiral Chester Nimitz in charge of the Pacific Ocean Areas. The JCS retained control over the entire theater and directed the operations in both area commands.[48]

This division of authority and command responsibility also included further geographic areas under the two commands. MacArthur's command consisted of Australia, the Philippine Archipelago, New Guinea, the Solomon Islands, the Bismarck Archipelago, and most of the Netherlands East Indies. Nimitz's area encompassed the remainder of the Pacific and was divided into three subordinate areas for the North, Central, and South Pacific. The South Pacific would be commanded by an officer subordinate to Nimitz, while the first two areas remained under his direct control.[49]

MacArthur's command demanded a multinational organization, but he limited foreign influence within his structure. He assumed command of the SWPA on April 18, 1942, and immediately established the Allied Land, Allied Air, and Allied Naval Force branches, as well as the US Army Services of Supply branch later that July. In an astute diplomatic gesture, MacArthur chose the Australian general Thomas A. Blamey as his ground forces commander. However, MacArthur ignored General Marshall's urging to appoint Australian and Dutch officers to senior staff positions. Instead, his staff was largely American, with Lieutenant General George H. Brett as his air force commander and Vice Admiral Herbert F. Leary (soon replaced by Arthur S. Carpender) in charge of MacArthur's naval forces.[50] MacArthur waged war with this organization throughout 1942 and 1943.

By contrast to MacArthur's coalition forces, the South Pacific Area, subordinate to Admiral Nimitz's Pacific Ocean Areas command, was completely American from its inception. The US Navy tapped Admiral Robert L. Ghormley as Nimitz's subordinate to be Commander, South Pacific Area, although he would not actually take command until mid-1942. Rear Admiral John S. McCain, grandfather of the prominent senator from Arizona, served as Ghormley's air commander. Ghormley's organization retained a distinctly naval flavor, with few army staff officers and initially no separate ground force command. Ghormley did, however, establish subordinate commands for amphibious and service matters. In July 1942, with Admiral King's agreement, the army established a new command under Ghormley (US Army Forces in the South Pacific Area) with Major General Millard F. Harmon at its head. This command exercised no operational control, although General Marshall tasked Harmon with the administration and training of US Army forces, including air elements, in the South Pacific Area.[51] Ghormley's headquarters retained operational control over employment of all the assigned ground forces, including army and Marine Corps units.

A BRIEF COMPARISON OF THE JAPANESE AND AMERICAN COMMAND STRUCTURES

This survey has already identified some salient differences between the Japanese and US command organizations, but the topic deserves a brief recapitulation. The Japanese IGHQ had no clear superior, save the emperor, to break deadlocks or resolve disagreements between the services. The traditional role of the emperor precluded his exercise of such influence, which resulted in the need for consensus among the IJA and the IJN before any joint action could be undertaken. Such a divided command had significant implications for strategic direction because both services could doggedly persist in their parochialisms without fear of being overridden. This often resulted in patchwork planning that protected the individual interests of the services at the expense of the greater good of Japan's war effort. On the US side, the situation was vastly different. The JCS was a much more joint body than was the IGHQ, and it included joint planning and joint strategic-survey bodies, consisting of representatives of both services and the semiautonomous USAAF. Like the Japanese IGHQ, the JCS did not have one supreme officer to break deadlocks and guide joint action should the services disagree, since the president was deliberately vague about Admiral Leahy's authority as the chair. Unlike Hirohito, however, Roosevelt harbored few reservations about guiding policy and settling disagreements among the services. If the army and navy could not come to terms, Roosevelt could and did make decisions that resulted in action. (See figure 4.)

In contrast, the Japanese services tended to resolve their disputes through imperfect compromises that sought to meet the independently developed objectives of both. The Japanese plan for Midway is a good example of this tendency. In that case, the Japanese divided their forces between the Aleutians and Midway, the former to placate the army and the latter to satisfy the navy. This compromise plan resulted in an unmitigated naval disaster. Finally, the inclusion of the semi-independent USAAF chief within the JCS represents a marked difference compared to

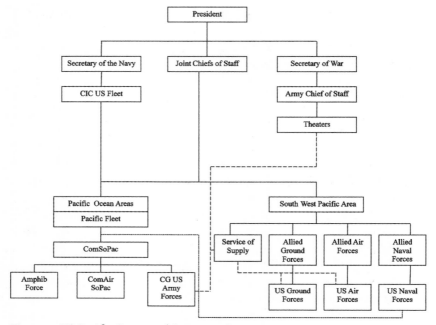

Figure 4. US Pacific Command Structure, Late 1942

Sources: Louis Morton, *Strategy and Command: The First Two Years*, United States Army in World War II: The War in the Pacific (Washington, DC: Office of the Chief of Military History, 1962), 232. Taken from a portion of "Chart 3—The Washington High Command and the Pacific Theaters, December 1942."

the Japanese IGHQ, which excluded the air arms of both services. The American practice allowed for significantly greater consideration of the air perspective in matters of strategy.

The two nations' field commands demonstrate similar differences. Once again, the Japanese forces in the field took direction from their respective service staffs at the IGHQ level and strove to fulfill their service's responsibilities locally. They did not enjoy integrated or unified commands with one supreme commander for a given area. As a consequence, the Japanese army and navy commanders had to broker agreements on a local level, just as their superiors had to do at the national level. By way of contrast, the Allied organizations in the South West Pacific Area and the South Pacific Area had unified commanders with authority to direct all the forces within their purviews. Ghormley and MacArthur both established integrated commands that could direct assets from all the services without requiring the brokered agreements their Japanese counterparts had to arrange. There still existed an imperfect, divided command for American forces in the Pacific between MacArthur's and Nimitz's areas, and many accounts of the war dwell on the disagreements between these two commands. Nonetheless, the JCS and, if necessary, the president were able to resolve operational disputes and competition for resources.

Thus, both sides had to contend with interservice squabbling and disagreements, but they took different approaches to resolving such conflicts. The de facto veto power the Japanese structure afforded the army and navy in strategic decisions required consensus, often resulting in compromise plans with divergent objectives and only limited interservice coordination. The Americans, in the event of a deadlock, could appeal to a president who would decide the issue. The US organizations were certainly not the perfect embodiment of joint action and harmony, but their design—from the international level to the national level and down to the field commands—facilitated and encouraged cooperation in a manner the Japanese structures did not. These command structures gave the United States and the Allies in the Pacific greater strategic agility, especially when confronting rapid changes in the wartime situation, such as that which occurred after the Battle of Midway in June 1942.

4

Japanese Intelligence Organization in World War II

INTELLIGENCE, WITH ITS CORRESPONDING ELEMENTS of collection/analysis and counterintelligence/security, is one of the crucial aspects of military effectiveness. Consequently, intelligence organizations played a role in the gain or loss of strategic initiative during the critical months between Midway and the withdrawal of Japanese forces from Guadalcanal. Just how large a role intelligence played and how it did so will be addressed later. Clearly, however, understanding imperial Japan's approach to and application of intelligence is a necessary precursor to evaluating the events in New Guinea and on the Solomon Islands from mid-1942 to early 1943.

Indeed, familiarity with the general organizations and approach to intelligence and counterintelligence in the IJA and IJN and their associated air arms, from the general staff level down to tactical units, will significantly help in assessing the events of the mid-phase of the Pacific War. Activities such as radio interception and decryption, overseas military/naval attachés' intelligence gathering, use of technical intelligence, reconnaissance, and training of intelligence personnel represent important aspects of Japan's intelligence efforts in World War II. As such, these seemingly arcane functions played a crucial role in the ability of the Japanese armed forces to determine enemy capabilities and intentions, which in turn appreciably influenced Japan's ability to regain the initiative that was placed in dispute after Midway.

ELEMENTS OF INTELLIGENCE

Intelligence collection and analysis are the more intuitively obvious aspects of the concept of intelligence to the layman, but they require more activity, focus, and forethought than meets the eye. What information does one collect? With what means? To what end? Furthermore, information is nothing but meaningless data unless it is analyzed and examined in the context of the strategic, operational, and tactical environment. Collection does not occur in a vacuum but depends on a multitude of sources, all of which intelligence analysts must interpret within their own areas of expertise. Common sources for collection during World War II included, but were not limited to, human intelligence (HUMINT), communications intelligence (COMINT), signals intelligence (SIGINT), open-source intelligence (OSINT), and aerial reconnaissance. Current Department of Defense definitions provide a valuable clarification about the nature of these sources in the modern context. These definitions are a suitable point of departure for discussion of the same types of sources utilized by the combatants in the Pacific War. HUMINT, as the name implies, derives information from human sources, including not just espionage but also military attaché reports, prisoner of war interrogations, and even interviews with tourists who had visited a critical area. COMINT is based on foreign communications.[1] After such information is intercepted over the airwaves, code breakers must decrypt it for application. COMINT is a subset of SIGINT, which incorporates all forms of communications, electronics, and foreign instrumentation signals from foreign sources, however transmitted.[2] Detection of an enemy's radar emissions represents one example of possible SIGINT that is not COMINT, because the emissions themselves do not carry language messages. Open-source intelligence is an anachronistic term to apply to World War II, but the concept certainly existed of using information available in the public domain, such as newspapers, magazines, radio broadcasts, and a multitude of similar sources. Finally, reconnaissance includes any effort to collect information about the activities and resources of an adversary, or about the weather and geographic characteristics of a particular area of operations. Unlike the arcane arts of HUMINT and SIGINT, reconnaissance is an integral part of all military operations.

All of these areas are crucial to a nation's intelligence picture, but collection alone is not enough. Information without context or analysis amounts to little more than raw data. Intelligence, therefore, is "the product resulting from the collection, processing, integration, evaluation, analysis, and interpretation of available information concerning foreign nations, hostile or potentially hostile forces or elements, or areas of actual or potential operations."[3]

The less intuitive, but no less important, defensive elements of intelligence operations include counterintelligence and security, seeking to thwart an opponent's efforts at intelligence collection and reconnaissance.

Taken together, these two aspects are the reverse sides of the intelligence coin whereby one combatant attempts to "blind" the other through a multitude of protective measures, which may include deception.

JAPANESE MILITARY AND NAVAL INTELLIGENCE ORGANIZATIONS

Understanding the Japanese approach to these challenges during World War II is difficult, with a number of factors conspiring to limit the available evidence. Both the IJA and the IJN destroyed the majority of their intelligence documents after the war.[4] The US Strategic Bombing Survey's interrogations of Japanese war leaders confirm the destruction. According to Commander Nobohiko Imai, IJN, the Ministry of Home Defense instituted systematic burning of tabulated naval intelligence in July 1945.[5] Japanese intelligence officers reportedly feared "victor's justice" after the war, especially concerning any aspects of SIGINT; these officers therefore took what they felt were necessary precautions to forestall it.[6] Despite these limitations, one can piece together many of the basic structures and organizations of the Japanese intelligence efforts during World War II. Notwithstanding the reservations mentioned above, it is worth noting that the testimony of Japanese officers interrogated under the USSBS mission seems to display markedly more candor than did the testimony of many of their German counterparts.[7]

Certain aspects of the Japanese approach to intelligence shaped their organizations and processes. There was a distinct divide between military and naval intelligence stemming from the mid-nineteenth century. Japan's experience in World War I was notably different from that of the Western nations, a difference that may have significantly influenced the development of its intelligence structures. Japan did not experience the total war seen in Europe and, therefore, did not develop a comprehensive approach to intelligence.[8]

This analysis, however, is not entirely convincing. Germany experienced the total war of World War I, yet German intelligence in World War II suffered numerous shortcomings. Perhaps the fault lay in the fact that the Japanese army, like its German mentors, retained the tactical intelligence focus of the Prussian nineteenth century–style of limited war. If anything, the IJA and IJN believed that superior tactical intelligence could help compensate for other weaknesses on the battlefield.[9] The USSBS interrogation of Rear Admiral Kaoru Takeuchi, IJN, long-serving intelligence chief of the 5th Section, 3rd Department, Navy General Staff, confirms the limited cooperation between the IJA and the IJN, equating the Japanese concept of intelligence to traditional espionage and spying rather than a comprehensive integration of sources, and indicating that his intelligence section did not analyze its information but simply passed it on to the operational planners on the Navy General Staff.[10] Lieutenant General Seizo Arisue, IJA, Takeuchi's counterpart on the Army General Staff, went even further, suggesting that Japan's recent experiences in China had convinced many army officers that intelligence was unnecessary, an attitude that left them ill prepared to fight the United States.[11] Put simply, Japan's intelligence system had not fully evolved to meet the needs of twentieth-century warfare.

IMPERIAL JAPANESE ARMY INTELLIGENCE ORGANIZATION, JULY 1942–NOVEMBER 1943

Intelligence duties on the Imperial Japanese Army General Staff fell under the auspices of the 2nd Division, whose chief between August 1942 and March 1945 was the aforementioned Lieutenant General Arisue. Elements of the 2nd Division included: the 5th Section covering the Soviet Union and Europe (but excluding Britain); the 6th Section covering America, South America, Britain, and India; the 7th Section covering China and Manchuria; and the 18th Section responsible for SIGINT decryption. Manning was often less than robust. The General Headquarters was reorganized in March 1942 to add the 6th Section, but prior to that reorganization five officers in the 5th Section were responsible for all the areas that both the 5th and 6th Sections covered under the new arrangement. By the end of the war, the 6th Section had grown to twenty-nine officers and five or six noncommissioned officers.[12] In the period leading up to war, the 18th Section boasted a staff of 135 by 1936. The General Headquarters ordered yet another reorganization in July 1943 with important ramifications for SIGINT. The creation of the *Chuo Tokushu Jo-ho Bu*, or Central Special Intelligence Section, signified an increased emphasis on decrypting US cipher traffic. This section consisted of a staff of 301 that grew to more than 1,000 in 1945.[13] By comparison, the British decryption efforts at Bletchley Park in May 1943 employed more than 5,000 people, including a naval section of 1,000 members—and this number does not include the thousands of Americans similarly engaged on the other side of the Atlantic.[14]

Intelligence functions also existed in the subordinate echelons of command, but the emphasis steadily diminished with the level of headquarters. Colonel Kazugi Sugita, IJA, served as a staff officer in the 8th Area Army in the South Pacific in 1942 and later returned to the Imperial General Staff to head the 6th Section of the 2nd Division. Sugita described the intelligence organization of a *Komen Gun* (Area Army), estimated as the equivalent of an American or British army, as being one officer assigned to the G-1 department of the area army staff, which was headed by a colonel. The G-1 department at this level also employed two officers for operations and one for personnel, while the G-2 department assigned three officers to coordinate supply, transportation, and communications.[15] (See figure 5.)

It is important to note that area army commanders had a great deal of command latitude and often exercised independence from IGHQ in many areas, including intelligence. Some area armies established additional intelligence sections within a structure known as *Tokumu Kikan* (Special Service Organization), which also monitored and assisted in governing the local civilian population and procuring local food supplies for the army. The *Tokumu Kikan* of the Kwantung Army tracked Soviet movements, strength, and intentions concerning Manchuria through border observation, interrogation of spies, espionage, communications interception, and analysis of captured materials and news reports. Once again, this organization was independent of headquarters in Tokyo, although IGHQ did monitor its weekly and monthly reports and some IGHQ requests for information were forwarded to the organization from the Kwantung Army.[16] However, there were no *Tokumu Kikan* units assigned to Rabaul under the 8th Area Army, although that army conducted some limited monitoring of Allied transmissions. Not until the late summer of 1943, when the Army General Staff ordered an expansion of interception and decryption efforts against the United States, did the 8th Area Army organize a Special Intelligence Detachment with a staff of 300 and advanced intercept stations at Wewak and Ambon in the New Guinea area.[17]

The next level of command included the individual *Gun*, or numbered army, which was roughly the equivalent to a US army corps with a headquarters and a variable number of divisions and troops. At this level, according to Sugita, all the functions of the G-1 and G-2 departments were typically combined into a solitary section, while the staff at the individual division, or *Shidan*, level below the army consisted of a chief, an operations officer, an intelligence officer, and a supply officer. Sugita elaborated: "This was the [setup] at the beginning of the war. Later, when

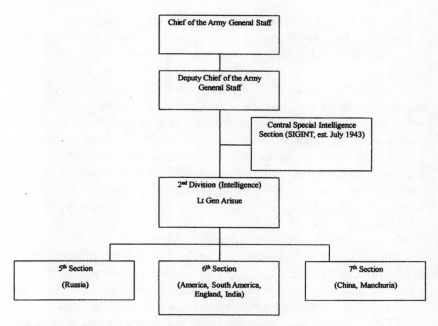

Figure 5. Intelligence Organization of IJA GHQ, 1942–1943

Staff Officers became scarce sections were consolidated. In the 17th Army at Guadalcanal there were 3 junior officers in intelligence. In 8th Army Headquarters at RABAUL there were 5 or 6. This was finally increased to 10 at my request."[18]

At the beginning of the war there were no provisions for intelligence officers below the division level, such as in regimental or battalion structures, and in some division headquarters the intelligence post went unmanned. However, by the end of the war many regiments and some battalions did have intelligence officers or noncommissioned officers assigned. Yet, intelligence functions were not always full-time duties even for these officers.[19]

IJA SIGINT and Codebreaking

The Japanese army did have experience in codebreaking. Beginning in 1921, IJA representatives met regularly with their counterparts in the Signals Traffic Department of the Foreign Ministry as well as the Ministry of Communications but not the IJN. The IJA focused predominantly on the threat from the Soviet Union, and in 1923 it worked closely with

Captain Jan Kowalewski of the Polish army to learn from Polish successes in breaking Soviet codes during their 1919–1920 war with Russia. Following this liaison, the Japanese codebreaking unit was placed in the 7th Section of the 3rd Department (Communications) of the Army General Staff. In July 1930, the IJA assigned the breaking of foreign ciphers to the 5th Section of 2nd Division, which eventually became the 18th Section in 1936.[20] The 1931 publication of *The American Black Chamber*, an exposé on US efforts in cryptanalysis in World War I and the postwar period written by the father of American cryptanalysis, Herbert O. Yardley, revealed US successes against Japanese and others' codes and greatly upset the Japanese.[21] As already noted, the Central Special Intelligence Section was subsequently formed, which increased emphasis on decrypting American codes and ciphers.

These decryption efforts often bore fruit for the Japanese. In 1934, the military police, in a manner worthy of a James Bond thriller, managed to photograph the US codebook for the so-called Brown Code from the consulate in Kobe, enabling the IJA to break that diplomatic code shortly thereafter. The IJA also enjoyed some success breaking the more complicated US diplomatic strip ciphers, which had proven resistant to British and German cryptanalysis; this clearly required much more laborious scientific decoding than simply photographing the codes. The Japanese also scored significant successes, through the efforts of their Kwantung Army, against the Chinese codes of the Kuomintang, or nationalist army, and used their knowledge to indirectly identify British and American intentions in the region.[22] Yet, these achievements did not necessarily parlay into success against the Western Allies' military codes, which used a different system of encryption.

IJA Communications Security

Countering enemy codebreaking requires communications security. Here, too, overall Japanese army performance was mixed but generally effective in the opening stages of the war. Ken Kotani has argued that the IJA focused much of its communications intelligence efforts on decryption, somewhat to the detriment of its own security. Only after Pearl Harbor did the IJA regard the creation of its own codes as a necessity; prior to this, most army officers strongly believed in the security of their infinitely randomized numbered cipher system. Serious reforms in cipher traffic safety measures came only in late 1943 with the establishment of the Cipher Security Committee by the IJA in conjunction with the IJN and the

Ministry of Foreign Affairs. In his influential study *MacArthur's ULTRA: Codebreaking and the War against Japan, 1942–1945,* Edward Drea finds more effective US Army codebreaking of Japanese army communications almost precisely at the time Kotani asserts that the Japanese instituted cipher reforms. According to Drea, the corresponding improvements in US intelligence helped shorten the war through successful operations such as Hollandia in 1944 and contributed to the decision to drop the atomic bombs rather than face the growing Japanese defenses.[23]

Nevertheless, it seems apparent that many of the IJA's assumptions about its cipher system were not wide of the mark, and its security at the beginning of the war—ironically, before the aforementioned reforms— was effective. The IJA used a manual cipher system. Every word had an associated code number, the code was enciphered via a key that changed daily, and the system included false additions to throw off enemy code breakers. Another factor that enhanced Japanese army communications security was the Japanese language itself. According to Drea, "The prevalence of homonyms in Japanese could bedevil the erstwhile translator. For instance, '*kaisen*' might mean 'decisive engagement,' 'sea battle,' 'opening of hostilities,' 'ghost ship,' 'barge,' 'rotation,' 'reelection,' or 'itch.'"[24] For much of the period covered in this study, Japanese army communications were effectively unbreakable.

Open-Source Intelligence

Many of Japan's military attachés stationed abroad placed a premium on using open-source intelligence garnered in the local area of their station. The *Domei* press agency also collaborated with the Japanese government and provided intelligence from the world news services. Although Japan found other such sources difficult to access once war began with the United States, Masao Tsuda, chief of the *Domei*'s branch in neutral Argentina, continued to provide intelligence to his government through analysis of newspapers and journals.[25] Thus, what is today defined as OSINT formed a major part of the Japanese intelligence picture.

IJA Human Intelligence/Prisoner of War Interrogation

Human intelligence played a small role in the IJA's efforts against the United States. Military attachés at embassies and consulates conducted most of the IJA's HUMINT and focused on three main areas: in Manchuria against the Soviet Union, in China against the Kuomintang, and in the

Southern Area against the British and French. The IJA's consistent focus
on continental Asia and Manchuria in particular meant that it regarded
HUMINT against the United States as a task more suited to the Foreign
Ministry and the IJN.[26] General Arisue noted that espionage against the
United States was nonexistent because the IJA's lack of preparation for a
war against the United States meant it did not cultivate the proper contacts and did not place the appropriate personnel in useful locations before hostilities commenced. The Japanese army around Rabaul received
limited information from Allied prisoners of war and got varying levels
of support and information on Allied movements from the natives in the
Solomon Islands and on New Britain. Interestingly, Arisue noted that the
Japanese placed little value on information garnered from prisoners of
war and had almost no instructions concerning how to conduct interrogations.[27]

After-Action Reports and Captured Materials

In stark contrast to his views on the lack of utility of information ob-
tained from prisoners of war, Arisue regarded information garnered from
the battlefront as being more valuable, though with guarded caution regarding air combat:

> Most accurate of all were the reports from the front lines, the direct
> reports of actual conditions. They were considered to be reliable and
> accurate during and after the conflict. As for the air losses, though,
> the one defect was the habit of reporting enemy losses as high and
> own losses as low always. The reason for this was that several re-
> ports would come in from Japanese flyers with regard to one enemy
> plane, and . . . the lack of reports on damage to planes. The major
> losses were given but considerable damages were not reported. We
> could estimate from this side the actual conditions by checking the
> large orders for parts and spares that came in. This was merely an
> estimated figure we had to rely on. It was a very unfortunate way of
> doing things. This was a definite defect.[28]

Those frontline reports were accumulated and assembled at each level
of the chain of command on their way to IGHQ. Lieutenant Colonel
Kokuzo Oya also discussed information gathered from units in the field,
noting that the Japanese identified Allied units and tactics, but during
the latter stages of the war, when the United States was advancing, they
captured only a few pieces of equipment for study.[29] The clear value the

IJA IGHQ placed on these frontline reports may reflect the Japanese tendency to favor tactical information to enhance battlefield success over a more comprehensive approach to intelligence gathering and analysis. Put simply, the Japanese focused more on intelligence of immediate value and related directly to combat at the front than they did on intelligence that provided them with a broader understanding of the Allies' employment of forces and overall capabilities.

Captured documents were another potential source of information. However, during their initial advances in 1941–1942, the Japanese captured few official documents and apparently believed that diaries and other personal items contained little valuable information.[30] Like the neglect of prisoner interrogation, the Japanese attitude toward unofficial documents may have been a form of mirror-imaging, believing that no knowledgeable individual would permit himself to be captured or record sensitive information improperly. Arisue was sufficiently astute, however, to attribute some of the poor results regarding captured materials to the Japanese intelligence organization; in responding to a question about the process for the forwarding of captured materials to IGHQ, Arisue remarked:

> It was left to the decision of theater commanders. Things that they deemed worthwhile to send up here were sent. Because of the general lack of development of the intelligence service—they could have secured many more documents but actually very few got into our hands. When the war was going well, I think that perhaps we secured quite a few, but after the allies began their offensive, we secured nothing that was worthwhile. It was because of the general point of view towards intelligence, the lack of appreciation of it. It resulted in few captured documents. A manual called "Jungle Battle Lessons" from Australian sources was found in the early days of the war in Buna and that helped us greatly in anticipating the lessons you had learned.[31]

It is noteworthy that, once again, Arisue, reflecting the historical Prussian influence on the IJA, chose as his prime example of a valuable captured document one that emphasized the tactical aspects of the battlefield.

Photoreconnaissance

General Arisue stated that IGHQ utilized some aerial photography, although the work was directed in the field with only "certain sets" of

pictures, which he did not specify, being forwarded to Tokyo. Lieutenant
Colonel Oya, when asked about the importance of photo interpretation
at General Headquarters, stated that photo interpretation was done at
Air Headquarters (*Koku Hombu*) and forwarded to *Daihon'ei* (IGHQ).[32]
Colonel Sugita indicated that the IJA had no aircraft in the Rabaul area
until 1943 and thereafter used aerial photography primarily for mapping
purposes. He also asserted that the officers who reviewed the aerial photographs had no special training, so that they did not effectively interpret
infantry positions on the ground.[33] Major Akito Saeki, who commanded
a squadron of Japanese bombers at Wewak, New Guinea, from May to
December 1943, provided some insights on the Japanese use of photoreconnaissance in the Rabaul area: "A reconnaissance squadron attached
to the air division took most of the pictures. On the few daylight missions
flown in NEW GUINEA, the bombers also took photographs." Saeki also
asserted that photo interpretation was done by regular squadron officers,
not specially trained photo interpreters.[34] Colonel Minoru Miyashi, a
Japanese Army Air Force veteran of the Singapore and Palambang operations during the beginning of the war, reported a slightly different experience. According to Miyashi, the *Hikōsentai,* or air regiment, consisting
of three or four *Hikō Chūtai* (air companies) of nine aircraft each, had
two trained photo interpreters assigned, and all aviators were given some
photo interpreter training.[35] Taken together, these differing accounts de-
pict the IJA's use of aerial reconnaissance and photography as somewhat
haphazard.

IJA Intelligence Personnel Selection and Training

Given the lack of emphasis the IJA placed upon intelligence service, Japanese officers did not covet such assignments. General Masakazu Kawabe, the commanding general of Air General Headquarters at the end
of the war, stated that intelligence officers were often second-rate and
untrained men because the army placed much greater emphasis on attack
and operations, much like the German army. When pressed by his American interrogators about the need for better men in intelligence, Kawabe
agreed but asserted that such a change in assignment of officers would
be of little use unless operations officers had much greater confidence in
their own work.[36] One wonders how the intelligence service could ever
change this attitude if it was to be perennially staffed by inferior officers.
Lieutenant General Arisue confirmed Kawabe's assessment in his interrogation with this straightforward evaluation that most personnel assigned

to intelligence were the "dregs" and were often left out of the decision process.[37]

Making matters worse, those supposed dregs had very little in the form of formal intelligence training. In theory, all Japanese army officers received intelligence training at the Japanese War College, but that training left much to be desired. Major Hideo Anno, who served on the General Staff and lectured on occasion at the war college, received very general instruction in communications intelligence concerning radio intercepts and radio security during his war college tour in 1937, and he described some minimal training in preparation of enemy order of battle information. By the end of the war, however, intelligence training at the war college appears to have deteriorated even further. The Japanese army reduced the war college course from three years to six months, with an emphasis on tactics and military history and at most ten hours of intelligence instruction. At this time, the college did not provide any instruction on enemy order of battle deduction and little in the way of prisoner of war handling and use of captured documents; it had also dropped its previous weeklong instruction on reading aerial photographs as map substitutes.[38] Assuming an impending invasion of the home islands, the IJA refocused its abbreviated war college instruction on the basics of ground combat.

Counterintelligence: The War Ministry and the Kempeitai

As the administrative agency of the army, the Japanese War Ministry had its own set of intelligence responsibilities that differed somewhat from those of the IJA proper. The War Ministry conducted covert counterintelligence activities. The ministry also distrusted foreign intelligence provided by field army units and sought to monitor those field units, especially after they began to freelance in Manchuria and China.[39] Furthermore, the Interior Ministry's special higher police, or *Tokko*, monitored foreigners as well as politics in Japan, in addition to foreign diplomatic communications and facilities. With the assistance of the post office, the *Tokko* intercepted foreign mail and even rifled through foreigners' baggage when they traveled via rail.[40]

The most visible aspect of the War Ministry's counterintelligence and intelligence responsibilities was the *Kempeitai*, usually translated as "military police," although that term is too restrictive for its actual functions. Report 97 of the USSBS, titled *Japanese Military and Naval Intelligence*, describes the role of the *Kempeitai*: "Although in the field it worked with the Army, it was under the jurisdiction of the War Ministry and controlled both administrative and judicial police and, as a military organization, was divided into administrative and judicial sections. It had wide powers, vested with the right to exercise Japan's authority over military personnel and the general public alike."[41] The *Kempeitai* used spies, agents, surveillance, documents, mail inspection, interrogation, and COMINT to collect information. Much of this data was passed along to higher officials as raw data.[42] Lieutenant Colonel Yamamura, IJA, the officer in charge of students at the *Kempeitai* school, described the field duties of the *Kempeitai* as including military police duties, discipline, security, and counterintelligence. However, the military police had no connections between the *Kempeitai* and General Arisue's intelligence organization other than some liaison contact.[43] As noted earlier, there were no *Tokumu Kikan* units assigned to the 8th Area Army in the Rabaul area, so those duties fell to *Kempei* units associated with that army.[44] Colonel Sugita confirmed the presence and role of the *Kempeitai* when he stated 100 *Kempeitai* men were at Rabaul, but he indicated that their only intelligence role was to obtain information from natives.[45]

Kempeitai recruits attended the Nakano School located in Tokyo. Lieutenant Colonel Tatsuo Nozaki, IJA, an instructor at that school, stated:

> There was a time when most KEMPEI were volunteers but this turned out to produce men who wanted desk jobs rather than real army service. In recent years, both volunteers and assigned men were taken for a 6–8 month course for officers, and an 8–12 month course for enlisted men. At the end of the war there were about 50 officers and 400–500 enlisted men, organized in three companies at the NAKANO School.[46]

Nozaki described the school's curriculum as including military police, civilian police, law, and thought-control methods.[47]

Intelligence in the Japanese Army Air Force

Like the War Ministry, Japanese army aviation had its own intelligence procedures and characteristics. The Japanese command structure placed the army chief of staff below the emperor in a lateral position vis-à-vis the war minister, with Air Headquarters subordinate to the War Ministry, while the fielded air armies served beneath the respective area armies for their geographic regions. Most of the intelligence work for both ground and air forces was the responsibility of the 2nd Division of the General

Staff, but the air force was responsible for air order of battle and air technical intelligence.[48]

As a practical matter, any military aviator will relate the importance of premission intelligence briefings and postmission debriefings directly to the effectiveness of employment of airpower. Thus, intelligence support in lower-level air units must also be examined.

After the war, interrogators asked Colonel Miyashi what kind of information reached Air Headquarters from lower echelons, to which he replied:

Intelligence from foreign diplomatic sources was sent over from Army General Headquarters; other information came from various units directly. All this was evaluated and reports sent out to lower echelons about every ten days. Most of the information disseminated in this fashion by the Army Air Headquarters (*Koku Hombu*) was pretty much technical—new developments, that sort of thing—but not operational information. That was sent out by the Air General Army [Headquarters] (*Koku Sogun*).[49]

The Japanese established the Air General Headquarters as a tactical air command in 1945, meaning that organization played no role in the New Guinea or Solomon Islands campaigns. Members of the USSBS interrogation team questioned Lieutenant Colonel T. Ashihara, IJA, who worked in the technical intelligence section of the *Koku Hombu* from July 1944 to the end of the war and concurrently acted as chief of the Operational Intelligence Section of the *Koku Sogun* from April 1945 until the end. The summary of Ashihara's interview reveals, once again, manning deficiencies in high-level Japanese intelligence offices, as both of his sections depended on a single group of five to eight officers, three petty officers, one civilian, and ten clerks. Ashihara confirmed the sources of information mentioned by Miyashi and reported the Technical Intelligence Section made reports to its research laboratory at Tachikawa "and occasionally from there to civilian aircraft research laboratories."[50] Major Hiroshi Toga, JAAF, indicated that *Koku Hombu* reports, which at times included information from Germany, assisted with intelligence training and with knowledge of British and American aircraft performance and capabilities.[51] (See figure 6.)

The *Kokugun*, or air armies, which approximated American numbered air forces, were situated immediately below Air Headquarters in the JAAF's hierarchical chain of command. These air armies each had

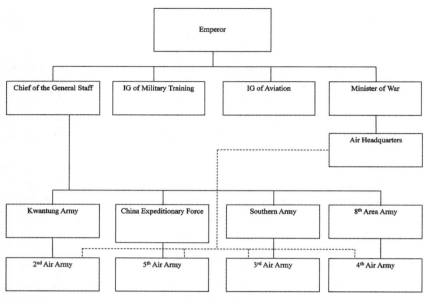

Figure 6. Air Headquarters and Air Army Organization Prior to 1945
Reorganization

clearly defined geographic areas of responsibility, and each functioned
as administrative headquarters for the tactical air units associated with
the corresponding area army. According to the USSBS report on Japanese
military and naval intelligence, the air army was an administrative headquarters with a small staff. For intelligence purposes, it was primarily an
intermediary between the General Staff and field units.[52]

The *Hikoshidan* (air division) constituted the next echelon of command
and represented the largest tactical organization of the JAAF. This unit
exercised operational and administrative control over the subordinate
tactical units in its command. The air division staff consisted of three sections: operations, intelligence, and administration. A lieutenant colonel
or major usually headed the intelligence section, with a staff of three to
six officers and a number of enlisted men. The JAAF assigned any trained
photo interpreters available in the theater to this organization. Among
other duties, the section produced enemy order of battle estimates and
forwarded their estimates of enemy intentions to Tokyo headquarters and
to subordinate commands every ten days.[53] Colonel Miyashi described
his experience as operations officer in the 3rd Air Division from 1940 to
1942, including operations against Singapore and Palambang:

The two things we depended on most were the situation reports and the strength reports. The main thing the situation reports covered were, generally, strength, immediate conditions, changes in the situation, enemy losses. Strength reports were by and large our own strength—how many of our own planes were operational; how many men. This came from the lower units direct to my headquarters by dispatch. It came from the Sentai, jumping one echelon usually, so Shiden got the information as soon as the Dan. Photos were the exceptional thing which came from the Sentai to the Shidan without going to the Dan at all; somebody from the Dan would come up to look at the photos. These photos were developed at the Sentai and sent up by air . . . or by car.[54]

The intelligence roles of the *Hikodan* (air brigade) and *Hikōsentai* mentioned by Colonel Miyashi, as well as the *Hikō Chūtai*, will be discussed below.

The air brigade followed the air division in the chain of command, and typically two or more such brigades served in a division, each containing three or four air regiments.[55] Lieutenant Colonel Shizuma Matsumura, IJA, claimed, based on his experience with the 3rd *Hikodan* in Java in 1943, that the air brigade had no position for an intelligence officer on its table of organization, though usually an officer was assigned such duties, which included relaying information up and down the JAAF chain. He described his duties in the 3rd *Hikodan*: "I was a major at that time. I had a captain below me who was largely used in an intelligence capacity. Both of us doubled in operations and intelligence. There was no provision in the table of organization for an intelligence officer. The commanding officer of the HIKODAN had one staff officer—I was it."[56]

Next in line came the regiment, or *Hikōsentai*, the basic operational unit in the JAAF. According to the USSBS report on military intelligence, the air regiment usually had a staff of five or six officers. The table of organization did not include an intelligence officer for much of the war, although this changed with the April 1945 reorganization for defense of the homeland. Instead, commanders would assign an officer to perform intelligence duties, but given the lack of training of such men, they spent much of the time shuttling information up and down the chain of command while adding little of value.[57]

The *Hikō Chūtai* (air company) represents the final JAAF organization considered. This organization typically consisted of nine to twelve aircraft and closely resembled an American squadron. The USSBS report on Japanese military intelligence summarizes the intelligence operations in these units at the cutting edge of combat:

> Although no special intelligence officer was assigned at squadron level, intelligence duties were performed by an officer, often a flyer, designated by the squadron commander. He kept the files, looked after reproduction, received reports from pilots and air crews who had anything to report and saw to it that studies of enemy tactics, plane recognition and equipment performance were available to pilots. This officer generally did no briefing as this was usually done by the squadron commander. No systematic interrogation of pilots and air crews was attempted following a mission but any man who had something to report was expected to do so, either to the commander or to the officer performing intelligence duties. Mission reports issued by squadrons were usually quite complete. Report forms were prescribed at either air regiment or air division level and called for such data as time of takeoff and landing, gasoline, bombs, and ammunition carried and expended, time of attack, results of attack, unusual sightings, opposition encountered, damage to planes, enemy planes destroyed or damaged, etc. This written report was made for each plane as soon as possible after the mission. Very brief operations reports were made by dispatch immediately after each mission.[58]

Many of these practices remain familiar to the modern US military aviator.

JAAF Aerial Reconnaissance

Aerial reconnaissance also influenced the effectiveness of the JAAF. That air force had very capable Mitsubishi Ki-46 "Dinah" reconnaissance aircraft, and later in the war the IJN fielded the effective Nakajima C6N "Myrt" carrier-based reconnaissance aircraft. However, the USSBS report concluded that both services had very primitive and largely ineffective aerial reconnaissance and photography. The JAAF did have specific squadrons assigned to the reconnaissance mission, though not specifically photoreconnaissance.[59]

Although the IJA apparently gave some limited photo interpretation training to all pilots, fully trained photo interpreters were very rare. The IJA trained a total of eighteen officers in two groups, with the first trained in August–September 1940 and the second group in June 1945. Thirty additional officers were trained as something akin to photographic tech-

nicians. The first class focused its training efforts on studying air instal-
lations and air defenses, but the second class broadened its studies to
include airfield, aircraft, and ship recognition.[60]

Tactical units felt this dearth of trained photo interpreters. Lieutenant
Colonel Matsumura stated there were no trained photo interpreters in
the units beneath the *Hikoshidan* level, which is understandable given the
very limited pool of qualified individuals.[61] As previously noted, Major
Saeki believed that photo interpretation at the reconnaissance squadrons
in New Guinea was accomplished by ordinary pilots who had no special
training in such interpretation.

Lack of emphasis by the JAAF, combined with poor camera quality
that was well below that which was acceptable to the United States, distinctly limited the effectiveness of Japanese photo intelligence during the
war. The USSBS special report on Japanese photographic intelligence
summarized its observations as follows:

> As was the experience of Navy interpreters at Guadalcanal and Java,
> Army photo intelligence officers had their work limited throughout
> most of the war in reporting on airfield progress, AA [antiaircraft]
> defenses, and general development activity at Allied bases for strictly
> air group purposes. Little target work was done, and reports often
> consisted merely of mosaics annotated by the interpreter and sent to
> the appropriate air group section. In the opinion of Major Shimada,
> there was no work done by the Japanese Army prior to the loss of
> Saipan that could really be called photographic intelligence.[62]

This seems an apt summary, but it must be complemented by a detailed
analysis of the IJN's intelligence organization.

IMPERIAL JAPANESE NAVY INTELLIGENCE ORGANIZATION, JULY 1942–NOVEMBER 1943

The most immediate and significant difference between the IJN and the
IJA was the focus of their efforts. Whereas the IJA anticipated hostilities
against the Soviet Union and prepared accordingly, the IJN prepared to
fight the United States. As a result, naval intelligence remained at peacetime levels until Pearl Harbor, with the 5th Section of the 3rd Department
in the Navy General Staff, which specialized in intelligence against the
United States, consisting of fewer than ten people.[63] (See figure 7.)

Intelligence duties on the Navy General Staff resided in the 3rd Depart-

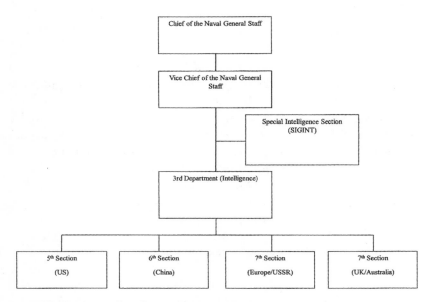

Figure 7. IJN General Staff Intelligence Organization

ment. The 3rd Department, Naval Intelligence, included the 5th Section covering the United States, the 6th Section covering China and Manchuria, the 7th Section responsible for the Soviet Union and continental Europe, and the 8th Section covering the British Empire. Additionally, a Special Intelligence Section for SIGINT existed outside the normal departmental organization, directly under the vice chief of the General Staff, and some cryptanalysis occurred in the 10th Section, which fell under the auspices of the 4th Department (Communications).[64]

The 5th Section included several subsections for analyzing US military capacity and intentions. Rear Admiral Kaoru Takeuchi, IJN, chief of the 5th Section from July 1942 until the end of hostilities, described this organization and the roles of each subsection. His section's assigned duties included: (1) an intelligence and propaganda campaign against the United States and Latin America; (2) estimates of the national affairs of the subject nations; and (3) plans for collecting information on the subject nations. The unit consisted of the admiral and his aide, with a commander or lieutenant commander over each of the four subsections, two clerks, two civilian temporary hires, and thirty-seven new naval officers who arrived in the summer of 1944.[65] Rear Admiral Takeji Ono, IJN, head of the 3rd Department from early 1944 to spring 1945, observed that the staff began the war with a low manning level but greatly increased over time. Within the 3rd Department, subsection responsibilities were as follows: the "A" branch studied the US home country and all aspects of American life; "B" branch covered overseas territories, Alaska, Hawaii, and Guam; "C" branch analyzed Latin America; and "D" branch, headed by a naval engineer, was devoted to the study of US aircraft. The US fleet fell under the auspices of the "A" branch when it was in a home port and the "B" branch when it was at sea or in a Pacific port.[66] (See figure 8.)

As in the IJA, intelligence organizations below the General Staff level steadily diminished in influence and emphasis. The USSBS interrogation summary for Commander Chikataka Nakajima, IJN, states the following concerning intelligence at the Combined Naval Force (more commonly referred to as the Combined Fleet) level, just below the Navy General Staff:

> The concept of intelligence at the Combined Naval Force, of [*sic*] fleet, headquarters level in the Japanese Navy was not a center through which intelligence matters flowed to higher and lower levels, but rather a center for estimating Allied strength and intentions as a basis for policy and operations orders issued by the Commander-in-Chief. Originally a one-man job, this section in the closing phases of the war had been augmented by eight other officers, most of whom had no training other than aviation administration.[67]

In his USSBS interrogation, Captain Y. Arita, IJN, claimed that each naval base and major fleet unit had a radio intelligence and sighting center. Yet, the USSBS report concluded that the only formal intelligence staffs, with specialized personnel, were within the Navy General Staff and the Combined Naval Force (or Fleet).[68] Rear Admiral Ono's statements support this assertion, indicating that ship captains performed their own intelligence tasks, with one intelligence staff officer for each numbered fleet.[69]

These specialized intelligence officers at the Fleet level did not operate as separate staff entities. Commander Tonosuke Otani, IJN, a staff operations officer for 2nd Fleet in 1943 and 1944, explained:

> Each Fleet has an intelligence section attached to the Staff. As a rule, the Communications Officer doubles as Intelligence Officer. Under him there is generally on officer who is a Lt. or Lt. Cmdr. charged directly with intelligence. He has two or three assistants of the rank normally of Lt. (j.g.) or Ensign. Then there will be 16 or 17 petty

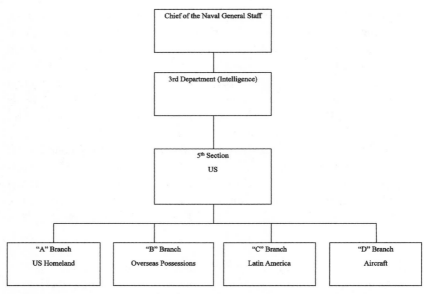

Figure 8. Organization of the 5th Section of the 3rd Department, IJN General Staff

officers included in the section. Squadrons under the Fleet do not ordinarily have their own intelligence section.

Otani characterized duties of Fleet intelligence as tactical in nature.[70] The USSBS report on IJN intelligence succinctly states: "At Fleet level (both surface and air) intelligence was additional duty assigned to the communications officer responsible only to the commanding officer of his fleet and this officer simply correlated available information for the immediate tactical use of his commander."[71]

The intelligence structure below fleet level was virtually nonexistent, and, as with the army, at these lower levels the IJN made intelligence an additional duty for officers with other responsibilities. In addition to asserting that there were no intelligence sections for the squadrons below the fleets, Otani also seconded Ono's contention that individual ships did not generally have their own intelligence officers. Intelligence at these levels was again associated with the communications officer, as confirmed by the testimony of Commander Nikichi Handa, IJN, who served as a communications staff officer in both the 3rd Destroyer Squadron and the 5th Cruiser Squadron. Handa indicated that he used information from the General Staff and fleets to estimate Allied dispositions, but the senior staff officer prepared all action reports.[72] One finds it difficult to imagine that communications officers could afford to devote much time to these duties.

IJN SIGINT and Codebreaking

The IJN had its own history with SIGINT efforts. As early as the Russo–Japanese War, the IJN used radio interception to track the movement of the Russian fleet. The navy began systematic codebreaking efforts targeting the United States and Great Britain in 1929 and successfully intercepted and decoded numerous US diplomatic codes in the ensuing years. In 1936, the IJN established a receiving station in Owada, Japan, which was able to intercept and decrypt communications from the American military attachés in Peking, sent to Washington during the Marco Polo Bridge incident of July 7–9, 1937. The IJN reorganized its efforts in December 1940, removing the SIGINT section of the General Staff from control of the normal departments and placing it under direct control of the IJN chief of staff (as depicted in figure 7). The focus of SIGINT operations, however, remained the acquisition of tactical intelligence materials.[73]

The IJN did garner some important successes in its efforts but also suffered from several limitations. The IJN broke the US diplomatic Brown Code in 1938; but, unlike the IJA, it could not break the American strip ciphers. Furthermore, the IJA did not share its deciphering knowledge with the IJN. To assist with breaking these ciphers during the Pacific War, the IJN established a Special Research Section on the Navy General Staff; the section never succeeded in breaking American ciphers. Amazingly, the IJN did not realize until 1945 that the IJA had broken the ciphers.[74] The USSBS summary of the interrogation of Commander Hideo Ozawa, IJN, who served on the codebreaking operation of the Navy General Staff and was later executive officer of the General Affairs Section within the Special Intelligence Section, indicated that the latter section analyzed ship call signs, radio direction finding, and volume and routing of communications traffic. From the Germans, the IJN apparently received the data necessary to read the BAMS (Broadcasting Allied Movement Ships) basic code for merchant ships. This allowed the Japanese to estimate volume of ship movements but not to locate or track such vessels.[75] Japanese naval intercept stations also "intercepted the communications from the flagships of the US Asian Fleet and Pacific Fleet to Washington, D.C., and the radio transmissions between Honolulu, San Francisco, and the US capital."[76]

IJN Communications Security

The IJN's failings at communication security preceding the Battles of Coral Sea and Midway are well known and materially contributed to the Americans' ability to counteract those Japanese thrusts. This resulted, in part, from Japanese overconfidence and complacency. The IJN's officers believed that their codes were unbreakable; the navy devoted little funding to SIGINT, HUMINT, or counterintelligence.[77]

This lack of emphasis on security not only cost the IJN dearly; it also compromised some of the IJA's activities whenever the two services worked together. In a distinct contrast, by the time of the Japanese attack on Pearl Harbor, the US Navy had a cryptanalytic infrastructure with extensive practical experience against Japanese diplomatic and naval codes, with perhaps forty officers capable of reading Japanese. This groundwork allowed US Navy codebreakers during the opening months of the Pacific War to far outpace their army counterparts. Navy cryptanalysts first penetrated JN-25 (the US designation for the IJN code) in September 1940, while the US Army's initial decryption of IJA ciphers came almost three years later.[78] US intercepts also enabled the interception and destruction of Admiral Isoruku Yamamoto's plane in the Solomon Islands in April 1943, resulting in the death of one of the masterminds of Pearl Harbor and dealing the IJN a severe psychological blow.[79] The Japanese briefly entertained the possibility that their codes were compromised but ultimately decided on an alternate explanation. Admiral Matome Ugaki, nearly killed on the same mission with Yamamoto, attributed the interception to chance, but the Japanese placed the final blame on a lower-level army commander who had presumably transmitted information about Yamamoto's itinerary in a "minor, insecure code."[80] As the war progressed, the cumulative effects of lax Japanese naval security produced a large volume of signals traffic that helped the Americans intercept and rapidly break the Japanese naval code. At the time of Pearl Harbor, Lieutenant Commander Joseph Rochefort and his team of cryptologists could read less than 10 percent of the Japanese code, but six months later they were reading almost all of it.[81] David Kahn described the lax Japanese approach: "Their communications security was as bad as their communications intelligence. Sometimes it seemed as if they didn't care." [82]

Open-Source Intelligence

Open-source intelligence served some of the IJN's needs just as it had with the IJA. Captain Y. Sanematsu, IJN, chief of the "D" section of the 5th Department on the Navy General Staff, was asked where his section got its best information and stated:

> Your radio broadcasts. These were analyzed by us and after some experience we could distinguish between fact, propaganda and attempts to mislead us. Other Departments listened to the broadcasts, transcribed them and sent them to my section which analyzed them.
>
> Newspapers and publications were very helpful. We got few of them physically, but they were analyzed by our men in neutral countries and the gist of them sent by radio to us.[83]

Commander Nobuhiko Imai, IJN, also a veteran of 5th Section, seconded Sanematsu's assertion when asked about the "best source of information for Naval Intelligence," saying that the Japanese tabulated radio news from around the world: "For example, we would hear of a conference between MacArthur and Nimitz in San Francisco, which would mean something important was coming up. Then we would hear of a conference in Pearl Harbor of frontline commanders, and we would try to estimate the direction of the next move."[84] Rear Admiral Ono agreed, citing domestic radio broadcasts as a key source of information for Japan as well as information forwarded from naval attachés stationed abroad.[85] Yet, they seem to have had few sources or agents reading American newspapers. Immediately following the battle at Midway, the *Chicago Tribune* published an article claiming that the US Navy had foreknowledge of the Japanese plan to invade Midway and was therefore able to parry the thrust. The revelation caused much consternation in US naval intelligence circles, but the Japanese apparently never noticed nor drew the appropriate conclusions.[86]

IJN Human Intelligence/Prisoner of War Interrogation

Like its army counterparts, the IJN tried to exploit its naval attachés and use prisoners of war to gather HUMINT on the United States and its allies. The attachés also used OSINT to formulate their reports but were hesitant to trust spies. Rear Admiral Ichiro Yokoyama, IJN, served as a naval attaché in Washington, DC, in the period leading up to war and stated: "You can employ spies and various other means, but one of our primary worries was that spies would turn counter-spy and be picked up by counter-intelligence. America being what it is with freedom of the press, etc., a great deal of material comes out in magazines and newspapers. By this method, we picked up much information. Accordingly, that is where I laid my primary stress."[87] Mr. E. Sone, a member of the Japanese Foreign Office, confirmed intelligence activities of naval attachés in Spain and Portugal and alluded to gathering information from other locations such as Sweden and Switzerland. Other naval attaché offices employed in intelligence operations against the United States included Mexico, Argentina, and Berlin. The USSBS summary of Commander Imai's interrogation states: "Military and Naval Attaches, although a [prolific] source up to 1941, diminished in usefulness as the war progressed, and after the break with Argentina this source virtually vanished."[88]

In contrast, the IJN did not value HUMINT from prisoners of war. Rear Admirals Ono and Takeuchi both stated that they judged prisoners of war as being of only limited utility for intelligence purposes. In fact, the Japanese navy often executed captured Americans after their initial interrogation. This happened to several US aircrew members plucked from the ocean by Japanese destroyers during the Battle of Midway. Despite this attitude, the USSBS report on Japanese intelligence states that certain data about US forces could only have come from POW interrogations.[89]

Front-Line Intelligence and Captured Materials

The IJN also used reports from frontline units to bolster its intelligence estimates. Captain Toshikazu Ohmae, IJN, had operational fleet experience and in January 1945 took over as chief of the 1st Section, 1st Department (War Plans) of the Navy General Staff. When asked about his sources for estimating US capabilities and intentions, Ohmae replied: "Information from the operating forces comes directly here to the planning section. The 5th Section, of course, also receives this. The 5th section collects all information, checks it, makes their evaluation, throws out information which is unreliable."[90] Allied order of battle estimations often depended on information from units at the front, as Commander Imai explained:

> The Order of Battle was estimated from information obtained from our island forces and front line units. We would make plots and graphs and then estimate. When air raids came from carriers, we would tabulate, target, type of plane, length of attack, and could

deduce the strength of the carrier fleet involved in the attack. I based my estimates on a long background of experience. In the field, there might not be people with the necessary background for such an estimation, but I could use reports from the field for this purpose.[91]

In contrast to this explanation, the USSBS report on Japanese intelligence concluded that most combat information reports from the chain of command went to the War Plans Department rather than the 3rd Department.[92] Thus, the war planners of the 1st Department often superseded the intelligence experts and analyzed information without the assistance of the 3rd Department.

Captured materials also played a role in the IJN's intelligence processes. According to the USSBS intelligence report, captured documents, although limited in number, were sent directly to the 3rd Department and were generally considered the most accurate sources of information. Rear Admiral Takeuchi's statement formed the basis of the USSBS report's assertion. Takeuchi said of his intelligence sources: "The most valuable were seized documents. Unfortunately, not many of these were seized," but such documents did come from a variety of sources, including "leaflets [and] documents in destroyed or submerged vessels, including some from Europe."[93] The Japanese captured American strip codes from either Wake Island or Guam early in the war and later seized some aircraft codes from Kiska, but they were unable to put the information to effective operational use.[94] As Japan adopted a defensive posture later in the war, the opportunities for gathering captured material dwindled.

Aerial Reconnaissance and Photo Intelligence

The USSBS report on Japanese intelligence states: "Photo intelligence and flak intelligence were not considered functions of the 3rd Department and no direction whatsoever was exercised over such sporadic developments as were carried out in operational units. In turn, the 3rd Department did not receive information developed on these subjects except intermittently through contact with war plans."[95] Yet, as this statement implies, lower-level operational units were undertaking photoreconnaissance missions. Photographs themselves were often insufficient in quality and quantity and were therefore rarely forwarded, although interpretations of such photos, completed by lower echelons, were often the best source for the Combined Fleet's intelligence estimates.[96] When queried about photo intelligence, Rear Admiral Takeuchi indicated that his 5th Section, 3rd Department, of the Navy General Staff had no role in photo interpretation and that all photographs were taken and interpreted by flying units before forwarding the results to the 5th Section.[97] Captain Ohmae described some of the photo intelligence operations conducted at Rabaul:

> In September of 1943 three photographic interpreters were sent to RABAUL. At that time we could take photographs occasionally of GUADALCANAL, NEW GEORGIA, and BUNA. Later we lost all of our good photographers and the photographic work became very inadequate. It became increasingly difficult to get any pictures at all. The pictures we did get were not given to pilots. They were used for planning. Gun positions and general information [were] marked on charts for the operational fighting and bombing squadrons, and they were instructed in communications procedures.[98]

Clearly, the Japanese valued the photos they received, but they never placed a high priority on photo intelligence.

IJN Intelligence Personnel Selection and Training

Like their IJA counterparts, Japanese naval officers perceived the intelligence career field to be a backwater. Nonetheless, to a greater degree than the army, the navy did try to place officers with appropriate backgrounds into their intelligence billets. Rear Admiral Ono stated that IJN selected men for the 3rd Department of the General Staff based on foreign language proficiency, but he said he and his men had no experience as foreign attachés.[99] The summary of the USSBS interrogation of Captain Taisuke Ito, IJN, who worked in the personnel division of the Naval Ministry for the last year of the war, states:

> The Division of Personnel in the Naval Ministry usually assigned intelligence personnel on the basis of qualifications of: (1) foreign travel, (2) knowledge of foreign languages, (3) personal interest in such work. Often times intelligence officers would be men of rather delicate health. In choosing the intelligence officers for the Naval General Staff, sharpness of mind was emphasized and it was preferred that he be a graduate of the Naval General College. Aptitude in intelligence work was considered in selecting communications officers for lower commands such as small fleets, air groups and flotillas.[100]

Yet the number of personnel they assigned was miniscule. Between December 1941 and spring 1945, the number of officers assigned to the 3rd Department of the Navy General Staff grew from twenty-nine to ninety-seven, while the intelligence staff of the Combined Naval Force grew from one to four. Even these increases occurred only because the dissolution of fleet units afloat late in the war provided a supply of officers.[101] This self-induced manning shortage stemmed in part from the Japanese proclivity to undervalue intelligence.

Naval intelligence personnel received little to no specialized training; the communications school was apparently the only place—beyond rudimentary instruction at the Naval Academy—where intelligence was taught.[102]

Intelligence in the Japanese Naval Air Force

The Japanese Naval Air Force (JNAF) had some of its own intelligence practices. The command structure for the JNAF approximated that of the JAAF, with the navy minister subordinate to the emperor and in a lateral position relative to the chief of the Navy General Staff, while the Naval Air Headquarters (*Koku Hombu*) was controlled by the Navy Ministry. But the operational air fleets (*Koku Kantei*), air flotillas (*Koku Sentai*), air groups (*Kokutai*), and squadrons (*Hikotai*) were under the direction of the Combined Naval Forces, subordinate to the Navy General Staff.[103] As noted earlier, the "D" branch of the 5th Section, 3rd Department, Navy General Staff, was dedicated to the study of American aircraft. The Naval Air Headquarters also had its own branch for technical intelligence. Rear Admiral Ono summed this up: "There was no independent Naval Aeronautical Department dealing with intelligence, but a group which sifted information of a technical nature. One officer did this. Most of the work was handled by the Navy General Staff (Naval Air Corps Intelligence). The 3rd Department was responsible for intelligence of a general nature for the Naval Aeronautical organization, and they handled their own technical intelligence."[104]

From 1943 to 1945, Commander Sashizo Yokura, IJN, served as the air intelligence officer in 5th Section, 3rd Department, representing the one-man show described by Ono above. His duties included examination of US and British aircraft, and he focused the majority of his efforts on the former. Yokura listed radio and written reports from the field, information from 3rd Department, studies of US strikes, POW reports, captured aircraft and documents, and information from attachés as some of his primary sources for evaluation; but he lamented the lack of information from photo and aerial reconnaissance. Commander Yokura described a serious time lag in Japanese technical evaluation of enemy aircraft; it was not until the end of the war that IJN had an accurate understanding of the 1943 performance of US planes.[105] (See figure 9.)

Commander N. Takita, IJN, served in the same capacity as Yokura beginning in June 1945 and confirmed many of the sources claimed by his predecessor, although Takita stressed intercepts of shortwave radio from San Francisco as a particularly valuable source for tracking US air units late in the war. As for the performance of enemy aircraft, Takira indicated that he received no information from a technical group at the air arsenal in Yokosuka.[106] In the course of the war, this arsenal studied a crashed F4F, F4U, SB2C, TBF, TBM-1C, and PB4Y-1 and test-flew a captured F6F, P-40E, and A-20A. The comparable section in the IJA test-flew a captured F2A, Hurricane, PBO, B-17D, B-17E, and PBM.[107] It was indeed unfortunate for the Japanese that this valuable source of technical intelligence on Allied aircraft failed to share much of its information with the intelligence department of the Navy General Staff.

Just as in the surface elements of the IJN, below the levels of Fleet Headquarters and Air Headquarters, intelligence functions lost their independent structure, often being performed as additional duties for an officer assigned to another task. In contrast to American procedures, intelligence officers were conspicuously absent from pre- and postmission briefings. As Commander Y. Terai, IJN, told his interrogators:

> Intelligence officers as such were assigned only to large commands and headquarters. On individual ships and in Air Groups and squadrons, the communications officer handled many of the functions which we think of as duties of the intelligence officer.
>
> Briefing of pilots on carriers was done by several different officers: the aerologist, the air officer of the ship (who had been given most of his "dope" by the communications officer), and the Commanding Officer (of the ship) himself. Interrogation of pilots was handled by having each pilot report to the senior man of his flight and so on up the line until the senior man in the air would report to the air officer and the Commanding Officer.[108]

The interrogation of Commander Masatake Okumiya, IJN, a veteran of the Rabaul–Solomons campaign, confirmed that the air officer, often as-

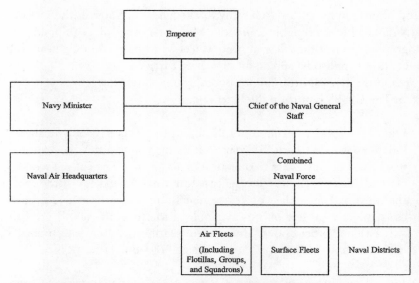

Figure 9. JNAF Air Headquarters and Operational Unit Organization

sisted by the captain and a staff officer, debriefed pilots after a mission; the senior pilot of a flight completed a standard form concerning the mission.[109] In September 1943, the IJN air arm instituted the *Yomushi* program to train various ground roles ranging from personnel to intelligence to athletic instruction. *Yomushi* officers "assigned to air groups and squadrons but not to carriers were the closest thing the Japanese Navy had to intelligence officers in the lower echelons," but "in no sense, however, did they focus solely on intelligence duties."[110] One finds it astonishing that the JNAF put intelligence officers on the same level as athletic instructors—a rather damning indictment of their view of the value of intelligence in war.

JNAF Aerial Reconnaissance and Photo Intelligence

Although the IJN's use of aerial reconnaissance and photo intelligence has already been discussed, some specific aspects of the JNAF's approach to these roles and missions require closer examination. In contrast to American naval aviation, the JNAF, even late in the war, did not operate special photographic reconnaissance squadrons.[111] Rear Admiral Ono lamented the poor quality of cameras available to the Japanese, and Rear Admiral Takeuchi confirmed that responsibility for aerial reconnaissance and photography fell to each individual squadron. Later in the war, the IJN did deploy the capable *Saiun*, or "Myrt," as a specially equipped photographic aircraft that flew at 30,000 feet and operated in eight-aircraft units (not squadrons) spread among three carriers.[112]

As in the IJA, IJN training of photographic interpreters was very limited. The USSBS report on intelligence states:

> Out of the first Navy [photographic interpreter] class (which finished in late 1942) 5 or 6 officers went to Rabaul, 3 stayed at Yokosuka to teach, and the rest went to operational air groups. The entire second class of 20–25 members was sent to Tateyama Air Group. Although the third and final class of 30 members finished early in 1944, because there were few photos available at the time, the whole group was assigned other duties. Thus the entire [photographic interpreter] officer complement of the Navy consisted of from 33 to 38 men.[113]

A limited number of pilots also received some special training for photographic reconnaissance. Commander Yamaguchi stated that photographic pilots received thirty hours of additional training ashore and once they became carrier-based.[114] According to Captain Ohmae, the single Japanese scouting unit used for photographic intelligence at Rabaul often had only three out of twelve aircraft operational. The original pilots had received six months of special training at Yokosuka Naval Air Station, but no replacements ever arrived in Rabaul, making the unit an unpopular assignment in which all the pilots eventually died.[115]

CONCLUSIONS

The Japanese fought the Pacific War with a disjointed intelligence system. Preceding the war and continuing well into 1943, the IJA and the IJN had decidedly different focuses, with the former targeting the Soviet Union and the latter targeting the United States and the Allies. The hostility between these two services is also well known to historians, and that hostility extended to complete noncooperation on intelligence matters.[116] Such divisions could not help but impair Japanese intelligence activities, hampering leaders' ability to garner an integrated and comprehensive intelligence picture of Allied intentions and capabilities.

Neither service emphasized the value of strategic intelligence, nor did the officers in either regard the intelligence function as being important, or assignment thereto a desirable duty. Furthermore, both organizations provided only superficial training in intelligence to the officers assigned to such duties. The USSBS Japanese intelligence report concludes:

> Certain characteristics of the Japanese military mentality tended to nullify the work of intelligence. Corrupted by their own propaganda, military planners, in line with reiterated statements of divinely bestowed Japanese invincibility, overemphasized the importance of the attack at the expense of the preparatory steps necessary for its most effective execution. Being embroiled in internal political administration, suppressing information and bending it to serve political ends became second nature to Japanese militarists, and they became blind to objective intelligence.[117]

Nevertheless, this was the intelligence structure Japan employed throughout the critical phase in which combat raged in the Solomon Islands and on New Guinea from late 1942 until late 1943 and beyond. Despite these fractures in their organization that are visible in hindsight, Japanese intelligence performance should not be prejudged as a complete failure. After all, these same organizations had played an important supporting role in the rapid initial Japanese conquests throughout the Pacific. Although they did not have to be perfect after this initial onslaught, they did have to be effective.

In sum, the intelligence performance of the Japanese in the southern Pacific is a critical element of analysis in determining the shifts in strategic initiative during this critical mid-phase in the war. Armed with the knowledge of the basic components and practices of their system, one can more knowledgeably examine their operational successes, their missteps, and the underlying strategic judgments of both as the war progressed from mid-1942 to early 1943.

5

American Intelligence Organization in the Pacific during World War II

JUST AS THE NATIONAL COMMAND STRUCTURES demonstrated decided differences between the belligerents, the intelligence apparatuses they employed also manifested distinct characteristics. There were, however, some similarities as well. Much like their Japanese counterparts, the US Army and the US Navy each conducted its own independent intelligence activities. Also like their Japanese counterparts, each service had a different focus, with the army favoring the European theater and the navy focused on the Pacific. Unlike the Japanese, however, the Allies made a deliberate effort to synthesize intelligence among and between the Allied nations and their armed services. Cooperation occurred both at the international and national levels with the Combined Chiefs of Staff and the Joint Chiefs of Staff in Washington, DC, as well as in field commands such as the South West and South Pacific Areas. Such cooperative efforts did not, however, always produce superior results. Disagreements existed among allies, armed services, and within the services themselves. Nevertheless, Allied and American intelligence cooperation stands in distinct contrast to that of Japan and often did produce better results. These results, in turn, contributed to Allied battlefield successes and positively influenced both the progress of campaigns and the gaining of strategic initiative.

US ARMY INTELLIGENCE ORGANIZATION, JULY 1942–NOVEMBER 1943

The US War Department stressed the importance of intelligence in many of its publications and field manuals. In accordance with 1942 doctrine, the department divided "military intelligence" into two categories: War Department intelligence and combat intelligence. The General Staff produced the former, which studied possible theaters of operations as well as the military, political, and economic situations in all foreign countries. By contrast, combat intelligence represented intelligence produced in the field after hostilities commenced and included information based on local conditions such as enemy force movements, tactics, weaponry, morale, discipline, terrain, and weather.[1] Thus, the US Army sought to create the structures necessary to meet the challenges of both aspects of military intelligence.

In accordance with President Roosevelt's Executive Order No. 9028, the War Department reorganized on March 9, 1942. This restructuring created four organizations subordinate to the department: the General Staff, the Army Air Forces, the Army Ground Forces (AGF), and the Services of Supply (renamed Army Service Forces a year later). The internal organization of the General Staff remained intact with the now familiar five sections: G-1 (Personnel), G-2 (Intelligence), G-3 (Organization and Training), G-4 (Supply), and the War Plans Division.[2] The Military Intelligence Division (MID) served within the G-2 section. In March 1942, Secretary of War Henry L. Stimson created the Military Intelligence Service (MIS) as the operating arm of the MID and placed a Special Branch for signals intelligence under the MIS's purview. The Signal Intelligence Service (SIS) represented another organization deeply involved in army communications and signals intelligence, but this organization did not reside within the General Staff hierarchy. During the interwar period, the army had formed the SIS under the direction of the Signal Corps to consolidate its cryptological functions.[3] These organizations led the way in "War Department intelligence" at the national level. (See figure 10.)

The army also created an intelligence web in subordinate echelons of command. Section 22 of FM 7-25 Infantry Field Manual: *Headquarters Company, Intelligence and Signal Communication, Rifle Regiment*, dated October 7, 1942, covers "Information Sources and Collecting Agencies." This section delineated intelligence responsibilities for army units from the company up through division level and into higher echelons.

Collection responsibilities started at the company level. The company commander, assisted by his subordinates and his platoons, observed both terrain and enemy activities. The army expected companies to utilize patrols, scouts, and observers and to forward all information, prisoners, captured documents, and captured enemy materiel to the battalion commander. Company commanders could also expect to receive specific intelligence missions from the battalion or higher-level commanders, if those authorities determined an intelligence void had to be addressed. Army doctrine required commanders at all levels to exercise initiative and use

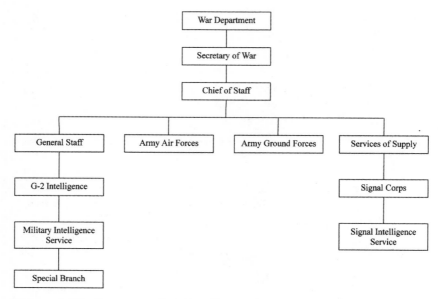

Figure 10. War Department Level Intelligence Organizations

liaisons to collect and forward information, recognizing that troops at the point of contact would often be unable to communicate information in a timely manner.[4]

The battalion commander held similar responsibilities but enjoyed the support of an S-2 intelligence section on his battalion staff, headed by a specifically designated intelligence officer. The intelligence personnel at this echelon received training as scouts and observers; their duties included reading aerial photography and examining enemy prisoners, captured documents, and captured materiel. The army also expected them to begin analysis of the information gained, to conduct counterintelligence activities as required, and to share information with nearby units and up the chain of command.

Intelligence functions expanded even further at the regimental echelon. The regimental commander employed an S-2 section headed by the regimental intelligence officer, and he also had at his disposal an intelligence and reconnaissance platoon that conducted missions at the direction of the S-2. The responsibilities of this platoon varied widely and included (but were not limited to) operating well in advance of the regiment to locate or warn of approaching enemy forces, examining terrain inaccessible to normal combat units, evaluating and disseminating information, assisting with enemy order of battle estimates, maintaining flank protection, and conducting counterintelligence operations as required.[5] While not every battalion and regimental S-2 had the opportunity for specific training in that position, they were dedicated full time to learning and performing their intelligence duties.

The pattern of increasing intelligence assets and capabilities continued as one progressed up the chain of command: divisions and higher headquarters received intelligence from the War Department and from their own collecting agencies and then transmitted this intelligence throughout their command to subordinate units.[6] The US Army thus set up an intelligence structure with dedicated assets at nearly every level of command and attempted to create avenues for proper dissemination of intelligence up, down, and laterally within the chain of command.

US Army SIGINT and Codebreaking

By the time of American entry into World War II, the US Army had years of experience in signals intelligence and codebreaking, which had begun to flourish in the later stages of World War I. During the early interwar years, the army built upon this foundation and enjoyed some success against the Japanese. The story starts with the efforts of Herbert O. Yardley and the MI-8 section of the Military Intelligence Division. MI-8, under Yardley's direction known as the "Black Chamber," broke Japanese naval and diplomatic codes in the early 1920s, which gave the United States an advantage at the negotiating table during the Washington Naval Conference of 1921–1922, a multiparty conference to limit the arms and naval race in the Pacific Ocean. These successes resulted in funding from both the State Department and the War Department. Despite the Black Chamber's manifest value to US security, however, changing political norms worked to its detriment. The election of Herbert Hoover to the presidency resulted in a new emphasis on ethical behavior in Washington. In 1929 Secretary of State Henry L. Stimson was shocked to learn of MI-8's activities; he suspended the operation, believing that it undermined international trust.[7] MI-8 members were dispersed, and Yardley went on to write a best-selling book that both shocked and motivated the Japanese government.

That same year, the army moved all its cryptanalytic functions from MID to the Signal Corps, via the creation of the Signal Intelligence Service under the direction of William Friedman, who would hold the position until 1935. The SIS struggled in this new environment. The Japanese Foreign Ministry reacted to Yardley's revelations with a new cipher system that undermined previous gains, and the Federal Communications Act of 1934 prohibited the interception of foreign messages by US governmental agencies. The army worked around this restriction in very limited fashion by claiming to decipher messages for training rather than for actual intelligence.[8] Despite the limitations, army code breakers pressed ahead with their efforts.

The political situation changed again in 1939 when war clouds loomed on the horizon. The new US Army chief of staff, General George C. Marshall, willingly overlooked the Federal Communications Act, allowing the army and the navy to cooperate in the breaking of the new Japanese diplomatic code dubbed "PURPLE." The two services broke the code in eighteen months; the resulting decryptions fell under the compartmental label "Magic." This breakthrough represented a critical advantage for the Allies during the war.

However, limitations on budgets and personnel meant that the army chose to focus on decryption of a single code—the Japanese diplomatic cipher. The IJA's codes remained unbroken.[9] Indeed, success against Japanese army codes would be a long time in coming, bearing an eerie similarity to the emphasis and results of the IJA's codebreaking efforts. The geography of the Pacific and its effects on the nature of fighting offer a partial explanation in both cases. Unlike the European theater, where large opposing army forces maintained contact with one another for months or years at a time, the Pacific exhibited generally shorter land engagements with smaller units and less consistent contact, the major exception being the Philippines campaign in the final year of the war. Such sporadic contact necessarily diminished opportunities to discern enemy patterns of behavior and break opposing codes.

US Army Communications Security

The army demonstrated awareness of communications security in its intelligence publications, typically including them under the auspices of "counterintelligence." Field Manual FM 7-25 of October 1942 stated that counterintelligence included not only safeguarding documents but also censorship and signals communications security.[10] The manual later stipulated the use of various communications devices in the field and associated communications security procedures for each. For telephones, "conversations must be brief; they must also be discreet since secrecy is never assured." For radios, "due to the liability for hostile interception, messages whose contents may prove useful to the enemy are cryptographed (encoded or enciphered)"; and "coded map grids, prearranged messages, and groups of letters whose meaning are not readily apparent to the enemy are useful in retaining secrecy."[11] In addition, the manual emphasized that radio discipline and security must be strictly monitored, station identities should be prearranged signals and should precede each message, and call signs must be changed and updated regularly to assure security. It is thus clear that the army, through extensive and consistent communications security, sought to inhibit Axis intelligence gathering.

In the main, US Army efforts proved successful against the Japanese army, especially early in the war. Part of that success, as revealed in the examination of Japan's intelligence organizations, may be attributed to the IJA's primary focus on the Soviet threat until the end of the Guadalcanal campaign in February 1943. The Japanese did enjoy some limited cryptographic successes against American and Filipino guerrilla bands in the Philippines, particularly in the first half of 1943.[12] In general, however, the IJA had little success in breaking Allied codes, and certainly not during the early phases of the conflict.[13]

Open-Source Intelligence

The War Department was clearly aware of press and radio as sources of information. Similarly, a 1943 intelligence training memorandum from the Allied Intelligence Bureau (AIB), an element of MacArthur's South West Pacific Area intelligence structure, listed "study of enemy and neutral press, broadcasting, military reports of areas, guide books, gazetteers and similar publications, and the correspondence of prisoners of war" as one of eight possible groups of sources of information.[14]

Intelligence reports indicate that US forces did indeed monitor and utilize open sources of intelligence. MacArthur's air intelligence directorate reported the Japanese Imperial Headquarters's misleading announcements on Tokyo radio declaring a great success in the Midway operation in June 1942. Similar intercepts in late September 1942 allowed the command to identify specific Japanese units operating in other areas such as Formosa and the Philippine Islands.[15] These sources provided another layer of information to enhance the army's estimates of the situation.

Human Intelligence/Prisoner of War Interrogation

The comparative dearth of prisoners taken in combat limited opportunities for the use of human intelligence against Japan. However, some opportunities still existed, and the army recognized the value of human intelligence and information garnered from captured enemy soldiers. The AIB under MacArthur specialized in human intelligence and, in the same intelligence training memorandum mentioned above, directed the exploitation of POWs and enemy civilians and urged the use of agents working behind enemy lines.[16] The army produced an entire field manual, FM 30-15, *Military Intelligence—Examination of Enemy Personnel, Repatriates, Documents and Matériel*, to address the subject of prisoners and captured paraphernalia. The Allies also relied on the Coastwatchers, a network of indigenous personnel working with largely Australian handlers who kept a watchful eye on the island chains in the southern and southwestern Pacific.

Capturing prisoners for interrogation and intelligence was a challenging task for ground forces, and American troops often proved their own worst enemies. A mid-1943 Military Intelligence Division report titled "Problems of Taking Jap Prisoners," which the Marine Corps also used as a reference, indicated some of the difficulties regarding prisoners in the Pacific War. Based on the experiences at Guadalcanal, this report chastised US forces for a "take-no-prisoners" attitude prevalent among many troops on the front lines. The report also related incidents of attempted surrender resulting in the death of potential Japanese prisoners because American soldiers and Marines feared Japanese duplicity.[17] Racial stereotypes and disdain for the "other" had concrete influence on the battlefield, contributing to the "kill or be killed mentality" that pervaded soldiers' and Marines' attitudes.[18] Nevertheless, some Japanese were prepared to surrender after enduring heavy bombardment or starvation; American propaganda broadcasts successfully enticed some of these soldiers and their supporting laborers—Koreans who were more prone to surrender than Japanese combat troops—to cross over into US lines.[19]

Those Japanese the Allies did capture proved valuable to military intelligence. Most answered questions openly, apparently feeling they had already disgraced themselves by falling into enemy hands.[20] A different memorandum—an observer report from the southern and southwestern Pacific forwarded to the War Department by Headquarters, Army Ground Forces—went into more detail on the interrogation of Japanese prisoners and the loyal service of Japanese Americans, or Nisei, in this endeavor. Interrogators checked prisoner statements by including questions to which the answers were already known.[21] This limited resource could and did prove very beneficial on the battlefield.

After-Action Reports and Captured Materials

The discussion of Japanese prisoners in American captivity demonstrates the value of after-action and observation reports. The army also exploited captured enemy materiel for intelligence gain. The Allies often shared these materials among one another so each could gain from the experiences of the others.

There were numerous observer reports from the southern and southwestern Pacific, covering a wide breadth of topics in considerable detail. One such report by Colonel H. F. Handy, consisting of nineteen pages supported by dozens of appendices, covered the period of September 26 through December 23, 1942, in the southwestern Pacific. Colonel Handy examined numerous topics, including training, air transport, fire direction, ammunition wastage, terrain, and weather. His report also included descriptions of Australian methods of direct air support and Australian notes on jungle warfare.[22] Another report by Colonel Harry Knight recounted the difficulties and lessons to be learned from the fighting around Buna, New Guinea, and the challenges posed by tropical disease in such Pacific locales.[23] These reports allowed for adjustments in training and equipment and for the dissemination of lessons learned among the services and Allied militaries.

Captured documents and equipment provided another potential source of information on the Japanese enemy in World War II, and the US Army used such resources when possible. For example, when a Japanese bomber was shot down at Gaille in New Guinea on July 22, 1942, enemy documents recovered from a canvas bag thrown from that aircraft confirmed known information about the enemy's weather reporting code and methods of reporting contacts with Allied forces.[24] Another boon to MacArthur's intelligence came in early 1943 when the Allies captured from a lifeboat a list containing 40,000 names of IJA officers, which later allowed Allied intelligence to correlate individual Japanese officers with specific units in the field.[25] The Americans also used captured Japanese equipment to train their troops to prepare for combat. A training memorandum from the chief of staff of the Americal (23rd Infantry) Division, dated July 27, 1943, mandated the demonstration of Japanese small arms to every combat unit to familiarize the troops with the sound and destructive power of each piece.[26] These efforts to collect and disseminate information from after-action reports and captured materials demonstrate a comprehensive attempt to make use of those intelligence opportunities presented to the United States and its allies.

Photoreconnaissance

When the United States entered the war in late 1941, American photo intelligence remained in its infancy. Earlier in the year, the British had allowed an American, Captain Harvey C. Brown Jr., to receive photo intelligence training at Medmenham, England. Brown then brought his training back to the United States and helped establish a photo intelligence school for the army at Harrisburg, Pennsylvania, to supplement the training already given at another school located in Denver. As the war progressed, American capabilities greatly expanded, but the primary focus of American photo intelligence efforts initially remained the European theater.[27] Nevertheless, the Pacific theater received photo intelligence assets; and photoreconnaissance units operated throughout the South and South West Pacific Areas.

The United States and its allies used photoreconnaissance frequently and quite effectively. The activity is inherently tied to US Army Air Forces activities, and these will be investigated in due course. But the army ground elements also used aerial reconnaissance photos during their operations. The prewar FM 21-26 Basic Field Manual: *Advanced Map and Aerial Photograph Reading*, stated that all military personnel needed to familiarize themselves with aerial photos to supplement or replace large-scale maps in operational areas. This manual discussed the uses of vertical and oblique aerial photographs and lists six different camera/lens combinations used by the USAAF. It went on to describe in detail techniques for the use of aerial photography as a map substitute.[28] The army put these techniques to the test in the South West Pacific Area, where they proved crucial in providing navigational and fire support aids to US forces.

Intelligence Personnel Selection and Training

Like the IJA, though to a lesser degree, the US Army struggled with manning its intelligence units and training its intelligence personnel. The case of the Special Branch is indicative of some of the travails. Army estimates in May 1942 called for a Special Branch staff of fifty-nine officers and eighty-five civilians, but building an adequate staff thereafter became an ongoing struggle for a number of reasons. The exacting requirements of these positions mandated capable individuals of unquestioned loyalty to the United States, which greatly limited the pool of potential recruits. Adding to the difficulty, the army made no allotment for potential use of enlisted personnel, further reducing the pool. This resulted in the direct hire of civilian personnel to fill officer billets, which ran afoul of War Department regulations that limited direct appointments. Finally, bureaucratic impediments from the Civil Service Commission also hampered army efforts to acquire qualified civilian personnel. These restrictions limited Special Branch manning to twenty-eight officers and fifty-five civilians by March 1943, well short of its May 1942 goal.[29]

Nevertheless, the army's intelligence organization grew impressively. During the war, communications intelligence manpower increased thirtyfold from its humble beginnings of 331 people on December 7, 1941. This rapid expansion necessarily limited training and, according to David Kahn, not one student completed the full forty-eight-week course of instruction at the Fort Monmouth, New Jersey, communications intelligence school before the army forwarded them to operational billets. Strength peaked at 10,609 individuals on June 1, 1945.[30] These numbers greatly exceeded those of the Japanese employed in the intelligence field, as discussed in chapter 4.

Counterintelligence

The US Army also recognized the need to protect information as well. The aim of War Department counterintelligence was to destroy the effectiveness of the enemy's intelligence system. Secrecy, censorship, concealment, deception, and counterespionage are among a litany of activities that constituted counterintelligence actions.[31] Technical Manual TM 30–215: *Counter Intelligence Corps*, dated September 22, 1943, addressed the counterespionage and countersabotage aspects of counterintelligence in greater detail for the benefit of theater commanders.[32] This awareness translated into action.

The army recognized the challenge of protecting information and took necessary precautions to do so. The US Army Counter Intelligence Corps, an organization under the Military Intelligence Service, was formed on January 1, 1942. With a training school in Chicago, the corps grew to a strength of 543 officers and 4,431 enlisted members by July 1943. Until mid-1943, its primary focus remained countersubversion within the United States and in base areas. Thereafter, the mission of the Counter Intelligence Corps began to expand, and its assistance to the fielded forces grew more robust.[33]

Operations in the South and South West Pacific Areas demanded significant counterintelligence efforts. In many cases, both the areas of combat and the rear areas contained populations that were potentially opposed to the Allied war effort. The question of loyalty of former colonial subjects on New Guinea, Melanesia, and the Solomon Islands loomed large. Similarly, many of the US bases in the South Pacific Area were on French territory, which implied the possible division of the populace between supporters of Vichy and Free France.[34] The Americans viewed counterintelligence activities as a necessary precaution to suppress the potential Vichy threat and allow for secure operations in the rear areas.

Intelligence in the US Army Air Forces

As a semiautonomous entity within the War Department, the USAAF initially struggled to create an independent intelligence structure for the air war. The USAAF had to develop an effective air intelligence system within its headquarters and to determine its relationship to the intelligence structures of both the AGF and the US Navy. In March 1942, the War Department consolidated air intelligence functions into the Headquarters, Army Air Forces, under the auspices of the Assistant Chief of Air Staff, Intelligence, also known as the A-2, with a staff and an Air Intelligence Service section. Owing to prewar agreements, the General Staff G-2 still had the lead in all army intelligence, which restricted the A-2 to technical and tactical air intelligence unless the G-2 demonstrated a void of knowledge in an area deemed important for the air forces.[35] The agreement was not perfect, but it gave the USAAF some latitude in the air intelligence arena.

Air intelligence training temporarily suffered as a result of bureaucratic battles between the A-2 and the G-2. The Military Intelligence Division initially opposed Air Staff requests for the creation of an air intelligence school, believing all army intelligence training efforts should be unified in one institution.[36] The army chief of staff sided with the Air Staff in late 1941 and authorized the creation of the Army Air Forces Intelligence School at Harrisburg, Pennsylvania. Enrollment quickly expanded to meet air intelligence needs. By the end of the war, the school—which had moved to Orlando, Florida, and been renamed the Intelligence Division of the School of Applied Tactics—had graduated more than 9,000 officers. The USAAF's practice of training intelligence officers before they were sent to combat units contrasted with the AGF's habit of sending its intelligence officers to operational billets before they had completed training. This was apparently because the ground forces were training preexisting National Guard and Organized Reserve divisions, whereas many USAAF units were formed from scratch.

Directives of the prewar Army Air Corps illustrate how aviation units conducted intelligence operations. Information flowed up, down, and laterally within the chain of command. Squadrons represented the smallest administrative air unit. These units were expected to forward their pilots' reports up the chain of command to wing and higher headquarters and, if necessary, to use telegraph printers to forward summaries of these reports rapidly. Wing or equivalent headquarters would send intelligence up the chain via periodic intelligence reports. Units that had been assigned intelligence officers were responsible for informing their personnel about the enemy situation.[37] Intelligence reports and summaries often incorporated information from many of these disparate sources. A-2 intelligence summaries from the USAAF's Gulf Coast Flying Training Center demonstrate the spread of intelligence within the arm. The May 18, 1942, summary discussed the skill and ability of Japanese pilots in combat, and follow-on summaries examined lessons learned from the Battles of Coral Sea and Midway, as well as the experiences of American Volunteer Group pilots in China (the famous unit known as the Flying Tigers).[38] Thus, while still in training, USAAF pilots received up-to-date intelligence from the front lines throughout the Pacific theater. The information flowed up the chain of command from the units at the front and then back down the chain to be disseminated to other commands in the hopes of increasing combat effectiveness. The USAAF hoped the comprehensiveness of this kind of intelligence dissemination would help prepare its pilots for war.

USAAF Aerial Reconnaissance and Photo Intelligence

The US Army Air Forces's photographic intelligence supported its own independent operations as well as those of the AGF and naval forces. Unlike in the European theater, where the American air forces benefited from close cooperation with the British, USAAF photo intelligence operations in the Pacific were conducted on their own. When the war began, the USAAF had no photo intelligence capabilities in the Pacific. The first operational unit to deploy there was the 8th Photo (Reconnaissance) Squadron, which began operations from northern Australia in April 1942, supporting MacArthur's South West Pacific Area command. In the South Pacific Area, the limited means available forced all the services to pool their efforts, first on Guadalcanal and then later with the establishment on June 21, 1943, of the joint Photo Wing South Pacific on Espiritu Santo. When dedicated photoreconnaissance aircraft were not available, the USAAF often improvised with heavy bombers that carried both army and navy photographers on board. Such joint efforts greatly assisted the Allied intelligence picture during the lean years of 1942 and most of 1943.[39]

During the period leading up to war, the United States actively worked to develop a photoreconnaissance aircraft for the looming conflict. Impressed with the performance of the twin-engine British Mosquito, the United States began to look to the twin-engine Lockheed P-38 Lightning as a potential photoreconnaissance platform. The resulting aircraft, designated the F-4 (later upgraded P-38s were designated F-5s), became "one of the most consistently successful (if not spectacular) families of photorecon aircraft of the war." This was not the only airframe dedicated to photoreconnaissance. Among others, the USAAF built the F-7, based on the Consolidated B-24 Liberator; the F-6 family, based on the North American P-51 Mustang airframe; and the disappointing F-9, based on the Boeing B-17 Flying Fortress.[40] The equipment on these aircraft included an assortment of cameras suitable to a variety of conditions and photographic angles.

The limited reconnaissance assets in the southern and southwestern Pacific remained extremely active in 1942 and 1943. Statistics for the 5th Air Force under MacArthur's command indicate that, from February through July 1943, dedicated reconnaissance crews logged more flight hours per crew than did fighter and bomber crews, with March being the sole exception. Intelligence summaries from both the Solomon Islands Air Command in 1943 and Headquarters, Allied Air Forces, South West Pacific Area, in 1942 and 1943 repeatedly make reference to aerial photography and its interpretation for target areas and for estimates of the enemy situation.[41]

Thus both the AGF and the USAAF employed an intelligence system of impressive breadth and depth. The two arms often complemented each other in the intelligence field, as indicated by cooperation with photoreconnaissance. Yet, there were other services involved in the Pacific War, each with its own intelligence system. The US Navy's intelligence system made important contributions of its own and therefore requires close examination.

US NAVAL INTELLIGENCE ORGANIZATION,
JULY 1942–NOVEMBER 1943

Just as the IJN and the IJA had different intelligence priorities, so did America's navy and army, though not to the same degree as was the case with the Japanese forces. The US Navy tended to focus on the Japanese naval threat, while the army focused more on the threats emanating from Europe. Somewhat offsetting this divergence, the US Marine Corps represented a ground force under naval control, which required some Navy Department analysis of Japanese land forces. This structural reality helped alleviate some of the potential for intelligence gaps and oversights in the Pacific.

It is both easy and justified to criticize the IJN's proclivity for developing complex organizations. Yet, the US Navy also demonstrated considerable complexity in its fleet organization and intelligence structures. The March 1942 appointment of Admiral Ernest J. King as both the Commander-in-Chief, US Fleet (CINCUS) and Chief of Naval Operations mitigated for the Americans some of the complexities of high-level naval command.[42] King's appointment contrasted markedly with the situation brought about by Admiral Yamamoto, who, as noted earlier, turned his Combined Fleet into something of an equal to Japan's Navy General Staff, thereby pitting the two powerful entities against each other. King did not have to resort to such bureaucratic chicanery—he was master of both naval administration and naval operations. Nevertheless, the intelligence structures beneath King's two positions require examination. As CNO, King received support from several intelligence organizations within his office (see figure 11). The Office of Naval Intelligence (ONI), or OP-16, fell under the auspices of the assistant CNO for information and security, or OP-11-1. The ONI generally operated as a point of distribution, sending reports and data to naval organizations in need of the information but making no independent analysis of that information. The War Plans Division, known as OP-12, held the responsibility of evaluating the information and estimating enemy intentions. OP-20—Naval Communications—included radio, telegraph, and telephone communications but made the most significant contributions to naval intelligence through signals intelligence and its OP-20-G subsection (Communications Security). The vital role this section played in naval intelligence will be discussed in the section on SIGINT.

King had other intelligence resources supporting him in his role as the Commander-in-Chief, US Fleet (see figure 12). Within CINCUS head-

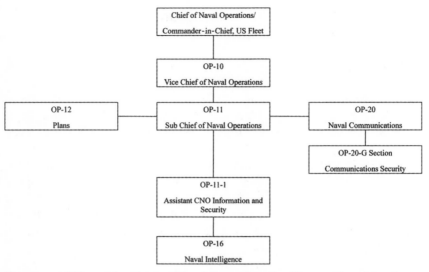

Figure 11. Office of the Chief of Naval Operations Intelligence Flow, March 27, 1942

quarters, the Intelligence Section fell under the purview of the assistant chief of staff (Plans), beneath the Plans Section, along with the Strategic Plans and Joint War Plans Divisions. This office followed operational intelligence, consisting of enemy fleet strength and disposition, and was headed by the fleet intelligence officer, who also served as the head of the Operational Information Section. This awkward arrangement was overhauled on July 1, 1943, with the creation of the Combat Intelligence Division (F-2) as an independent office no longer subordinate to the assistant chief of staff (Plans). This division continued to focus on operational intelligence, while the CNO intelligence organizations handled strategic intelligence.[43]

The US Navy also had several supporting intelligence operations farther afield. OP-20-G placed a radio intercept unit in Hawaii, known as "Hypo," which also worked very closely with the Commander-in-Chief, Pacific (CINCPAC).[44] During the approach to war, the CINCPAC, Admiral Husband Kimmel, began to rely heavily on Hypo and expanded its responsibilities beyond just codebreaking, resulting in an organization with semiautonomous status and a new name, the Combat Intelligence Unit. In April 1942, the Marine Corps commandant, Lieutenant General Thomas Holcomb, argued for the creation of a joint intelligence center at Pearl Harbor, which both Admiral King and Admiral Chester W. Nimitz,

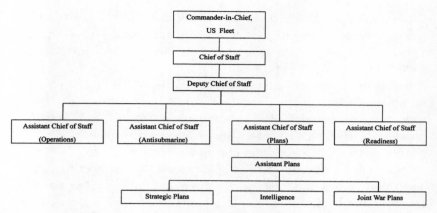

Figure 12. Intelligence Functions under Commander-in-Chief, US Fleet, April 1943
Source: Condensed from Furer's chart covering the entire organization. Julius Augustus Furer, *Administration of the Navy Department in World War II* (Washington, DC: US Government Printing Office, 1959), 139.

the new CINCPAC, endorsed. Nimitz directed the creation of the Intelligence Center, Pacific Ocean Area (ICPOA), with the Combat Intelligence Unit as a subordinate section, in June 1942. Other organizations in the southern and southwestern Pacific also assisted with naval intelligence.

Headquarters, US Marine Corps, operated within the naval hierarchy and depended, in many ways, on naval intelligence for its operations; but it also had its own intelligence structure. The Marine Corps readily adopted the army staff organization within the planning and policy staff section of its headquarters, meaning it had four sections at the start of the war: M-1, Personnel; M-2, Intelligence; M-3, Training and Operations; and M-4, Supply.[45] The headquarters underwent several modifications during the course of the war, but the intelligence section remained intact throughout.

US Navy SIGINT and Codebreaking

The US Navy enjoyed extensive successes in codebreaking and signals intelligence against the Japanese before and during World War II. It had established OP-20-G in 1924, with several intercept stations located throughout the Pacific targeting Japanese transmissions. The navy also received clandestine assistance from the Federal Bureau of Investigation, which periodically broke into the Japanese Consul General's offices in New York during the 1920s and 1930s to photograph naval codebooks.

While working with the army on Japan's diplomatic codes, the navy placed most of its emphasis on Japanese naval codes. As a result, navy signals analysts were well on their way to solving at least some of these codes by the spring of 1942.[46]

Beginning in 1941, the Allies used the code name "ULTRA" to describe information garnered from high-level IJA or IJN codes, such as JN-25, from captured sources, as well as from radio traffic analysis.[47] As the war progressed, naval SIGINT manning multiplied nearly ninefold. The navy employed about 700 people in communications intelligence in the fall of 1941 but by the end of the war increased that number to 6,000.[48] The ability to read the Japanese naval code proved critical to American efforts in the Battles of the Coral Sea and Midway in 1942. A report titled "Narrative, Combat Intelligence Center, Joint Intelligence Center, Pacific Ocean Area" noted: "In the defensive stages of the war, radio intelligence was not only the most important source of intelligence in the Central Pacific, it was practically the only source. There were very few captured documents or prisoners of war. There were no photographs of enemy held positions."[49] Later, during the campaigns in the southern and southwesternPacific, the Allies would come to rely upon a larger variety of intelligence sources.

US Navy Communications Security

The US Navy took communications security seriously and sought to protect its ULTRA breakthrough from Japanese discovery. A very restricted list of senior officers had access to that information, and it was transmitted by special codes. The Allies had to balance the need to protect ULTRA as a source of information with the benefits of exploiting that intelligence. Naval leaders sometimes refrained from acting on ULTRA information for fear of giving away the secret, or they sometimes devised a cover story, such as aerial reconnaissance, to explain actions taken because of intelligence gained via ULTRA intercepts.[50]

The navy and the Marine Corps also educated their personnel on communications and communications security. A Marine Corps "Mailbrief" memorandum from December 18, 1942, discussed CINCPAC requirements that Marine communications officers assigned to the Amphibious Corps and the Third Marine Division increase security training prior to their departure from the United States. The navy also established a six-week communications course at Camp Pendleton, California, in late 1942 to prepare communications personnel for operations in the

Pacific.[51] Through these measures, the navy aimed to maintain effective communications without granting the Japanese the same advantage the Allies enjoyed in ULTRA.

OSINT, HUMINT, and POWs

The US Navy, like the army, monitored open-source intelligence such as Tokyo radio broadcasts. Nonetheless, human intelligence and prisoners of war contributed more to the intelligence picture of naval and Marine forces.

The situation reports and summaries forwarded by units in the Solomon Islands were filled with HUMINT. The sources often duplicated the Coastwatcher network in MacArthur's South West Pacific Command. This network, for example, received almost daily mention in the intelligence summaries of the 1st Marine Division during the fighting on Guadalcanal in late November 1942. Coastwatchers reported on Japanese activity on and around the islands of New Georgia and Santa Isabel in the Solomons, enemy aircraft losses following combat, and the movement of enemy troop barges in the area.[52] Information such as this greatly enhanced Allied situational awareness throughout the Solomon Islands and New Guinea campaigns of 1942 and 1943.

Interrogations of Japanese prisoners also contributed to the Allied naval intelligence picture during these campaigns. A report from Admiral Richmond Kelly Turner dated November 19, 1942, illustrates the usefulness of POW interrogations to naval and Marine Corps efforts. Turner's report includes multiple interrogations of Japanese prisoners, including soldiers, seamen, and aviators. These interrogations revealed important information on a number of topics: the Japanese ground attacks on Guadalcanal in September and October 1942; units operating in the theater; the ships transporting Japanese troops to Guadalcanal; and some of the technical and tactical details of Japanese land-based naval aviation.[53]

After-Action Reports and Captured Materials

The Marine Corps and the navy regularly used information from after-action reports by frontline units and personnel to add to their knowledge of the situation and the enemy. Headquarters, First Marine Amphibious Corps, sent a seven-page report dated April 6, 1943, to two regimental commanders titled "Combat Operations, South Pacific," which discussed lessons learned and frontline reports. The observations specifically addressed Japanese weaponry, the need for supporting artillery, and how to mark one's own lines for the benefit of photographic aircraft, as well as evaluations of American equipment in the challenging jungle environment.[54] In a January 1943 memorandum from Lieutenant Colonel Evan F. Carlson of the 2nd Marine Raider Battalion to the Commandant of the Marine Corps, Carlson proffered a number of suggestions that were intended to improve the combat efficiency of raider battalions. Carlson described his observations about the fighting characteristics of the Japanese, and he stressed the need for superior firepower and effective maneuver and infiltration tactics to counter Japanese methods.[55]

Captured materials also played an important role in naval intelligence. Admiral Raymond A. Spruance, chief of staff to the Commander-in-Chief, US Pacific Fleet, emphasized the importance of captured material in a directive dated February 27, 1943. The directive reiterated the vital importance of both captured equipment and captured documents, and it ordered the rapid forwarding of such materials up the intelligence chain, with specific procedures for anything related to enemy codes and ciphers.[56] In a memorandum dated November 30, 1942, CINCPAC dispatched a list of excerpts from captured Japanese documents pertaining to orders emanating from the Japanese forces on Rabaul, New Britain.[57] Sometimes the exploitation of captured documents and codes provided immediate dividends, as during the naval Battle of Santa Cruz in October 1942 when Japanese aircraft codes recovered from a crashed plane assisted American efforts to decipher Japanese intentions.[58] The US Navy was willing to resort to extensive measures to capture documents with codes and ciphers. In late January 1943, the New Zealand corvette *Kiwi* sank the Japanese submarine *I-1* near Guadalcanal. The navy then salvaged many of the codebooks and cipher keys from the vessel, which, although older, provided a windfall of data for intelligence analysts that added to the Allied understanding of Japanese naval communications security.[59] Captured materials and documents, therefore, significantly aided Allied intelligence in the tactical, operational, and strategic arenas.

US Navy Photoreconnaissance

When America entered the war, naval photographic reconnaissance lagged behind the army's, but over time it improved markedly.[60] Like the army, the navy learned first from the British, when Lieutenant Commander Robert S. Quackenbush Jr., from the Navy Bureau of Aeronautics, paid a three-month visit to Medmenham, England, in 1941. The impetus for this exchange came from Vice Admiral Robert L. Ghormley, future commander of the South Pacific Area. Ghormley had observed the British exploitation of this type of intelligence in the spring of 1941 and pressed the navy to develop similar capabilities, resulting in the Quackenbush trip.[61] The navy's first operational photographic intelligence squadron, Photographic Squadron 1 (VD-1), began operations in early 1943 from Espiritu Santo and shortly thereafter from Guadalcanal, using the naval version of the B-24, the PB4Y-1 "Photo Liberator." Prior to this, naval photoreconnaissance operations relied on shorter-range carrier-based aircraft using handheld cameras.[62]

Following Quackenbush's return from Britain, the navy accelerated its photographic intelligence efforts. Once again, with support from Admiral Ghormley, the navy created a school for photographic interpreters in the Anacostia district of Washington, DC, with Quackenbush as one of its first instructors. The school planned to train 150 interpreters, but this number soon grew; the navy eventually trained 500 interpreters, mostly at Anacostia. In July 1942, the Photographic Reconnaissance and Interpretation Section Intelligence Center began operations at Pearl Harbor with twenty-three officers and four enlisted men. A nearby photo lab with thirty more enlisted troops and eight officers assigned to aircraft carriers augmented the center's operations.[63]

But the process of photo intelligence did not take place solely at major headquarters or ashore. At the end of the war, Chief Photographer Fred Bottomer, US Navy Reserve, recounted his wartime experiences. Beginning in November 1942, Bottomer served aboard the seaplane tender USS *Chandeleur*, which contained a first-rate photo lab. Bottomer also served ashore at Guadalcanal and Munda as part of an army-navy "Crash Intelligence Unit" that scoured the surrounding areas' jungles, even on enemy-occupied islands, in search of downed enemy aircraft to photograph.[64] His account makes very interesting reading, combining photographic intelligence, human intelligence, infiltration, and the capture of enemy materiel—probably a series of events in which a chief photographer never expected to participate.

A memorandum from Admiral King in late October 1942 demonstrated the navy's increasing appreciation of the value of photographic reconnaissance in the South Pacific. King acknowledged that numerous commanders in the South Pacific had urgently requested photographic aircraft. Because the navy had so far been unable to develop suitable carrier-based aircraft for long-range missions, the admiral had asked the Joint Chiefs to allocate an additional eighteen photographic P-38s and eighteen photographic B-25s.[65] This document reinforces the claims made by both Roy M. Stanley and John Prados that the navy had to play catch-up in the photographic reconnaissance arena in 1942 before VD-1 became operational.

Intelligence Personnel Selection and Training

Effective intelligence requires capable, well-trained individuals. The army discovered that acquiring such people is more easily said than done. Service in naval intelligence could also prove detrimental to one's career aspirations, which hampered recruiting. Military promotion systems often appreciate and reward combat duty and combat commands, and the navy as yet had no formal career path for intelligence officers. Such a system often penalized officers who performed important supporting activities. A report on the Combat Intelligence Center at Pearl Harbor is worth quoting at length:

> The career of ***text withheld*** furnishes an object lesson. This officer had the personal misfortune to early exhibit genius in cryptography. This led to repeated assignment to that duty until his career became entangled in the rigidities of the promotion system. He was passed over for selection to Lt. Commander and was finally saved to the Navy by the somewhat dubious and arbitrary action of the Secretary of the Navy in designating him for Engineering duty only. By this means he achieved the rank of Lt. Commander a year after his contemporaries. What this may have cost in personal pride and remuneration can only be guessed.[66]

The problem here is plain to see: the navy valued the products of cryptology but failed adequately to reward those who provided them. This hypocrisy could have been disastrous for the service. Fortunately for the United States, sufficient talented individuals served in the cryptology field despite the navy's skewed reward structure. The US Navy shared this characteristic with the IJN, though perhaps not to the same degree.

The limited horizons of an intelligence career did not mean the navy lowered standards for intelligence officers. On the contrary, standards remained high for these positions. The requirements for photo interpreters provide an instructive example. Recruits needed a "college degree, knowledge of architecture, geology, engineering, or a related field, and good eyesight; they had to meet security qualifications; and be between twenty-one and twenty-nine years old."[67] Such qualification requirements, like those of the army, necessarily limited the recruiting pool.

The navy also needed qualified Japanese linguists. The Naval Language School was formed at Berkeley, California, but later migrated to Boulder, Colorado, and eventually to Minnesota. Intelligence recruits received training from Nisei personnel in Colorado beginning in June 1942; and by 1944 the school included courses in Russian, Chinese, and Malay. Eventually the program produced more than 800 linguists, which included Marines, naval personnel, and even a handful of Royal Navy recruits.[68] As the war progressed, these linguists steadily filled an important void in US naval intelligence.

Counterintelligence

Like the army, the navy also had to address counterintelligence. In 1916, the Office of Naval Intelligence had assumed responsibility for naval counterintelligence operations. The Counterintelligence Branch of the ONI (OP-16-B) in 1939 consisted of several sections: Naval Censorship (B-2); Investigations (B-3); Security of Naval Information (B-4); Commerce and Travel (B-5); Sabotage, Espionage, and Counterespionage (B-7); and Coastal Information (B-8).[69] During 1939–1940, as the war approached, the ONI, at the direction of President Roosevelt, began coordinating counterintelligence activities with the Military Intelligence Division and the Federal Bureau of Investigation. The primary focus for the ONI and the bureau remained domestic security, with a wary eye cast upon Japanese Americans. Proper counterintelligence also demanded restrictions on information flow. The ONI attempted to prevent leaks through a number of activities ranging from discouraging sailors from revealing ship movements to imposing censorship to investigating other agencies, civilians, and journalists.[70] ONI counterintelligence activities also received assistance and support from the naval district intelligence offices, attached to each naval district within the United States and its territories, whose duties included censorship and security.[71]

The office faced a number of counterintelligence challenges during the war. The post-Midway leak in an article published by the *Chicago Tribune*, which could have revealed to the Japanese that the United States could read IJN codes, ultimately passed unprosecuted in large part out of concern for maintaining the security of this radio intelligence advantage. As remarked in chapter 4, the Japanese remained unaware of the article.

The ONI also worked with other governmental agencies to ensure the passage of wiretapping laws and to examine the files of cable and telegraph companies.[72] The navy mistrusted members of the US Communist Party and regularly precluded such individuals from assuming communications duties. Despite the navy's hesitancy, in 1942 President Roosevelt overrode the policy on the basis of the alliance with the Soviet Union.[73]

Intelligence in the US Naval Air Arm

The structure of the US Navy's air arm differed from that of the Japanese Naval Air Force. No US naval air headquarters existed to parallel that of the IJN. The Bureau of Aeronautics, under the secretary of the navy, oversaw the development and sustainment of the US Navy's air component and coordinated with the CNO to meet the readiness needs of the fleet. During the interwar years, this branch relied upon open-source intelligence and the reports of naval attachés to ONI to monitor the development of foreign aircraft. During the war, the system was altered. The Bureau of Aeronautics formed an Aviation Intelligence Branch in late December 1941, a title that changed to Air Information Branch a year later. This branch not only evaluated and disseminated all forms of technical air intelligence but also helped ONI select and train officers for this discipline. The Bureau of Aeronautics also recognized the need for increased intelligence representation in the fleet and began training reserve officers in February 1942 to serve on staffs as well as in all aviation units. Reorganization in August 1943 created the deputy CNO (Air) within the CNO structure, and most of the bureau's intelligence structures transferred to this new office.[74]

Fleet forces received intelligence from the Bureau of Aeronautics and through the normal naval channels of intelligence already discussed. Air intelligence officers provided a key node in the information chain and quickly proved their worth. For example, in December 1942, Captain Forrest Sherman of the carrier USS *Wasp* forwarded an air combat intelligence memorandum. In an enclosure or attachment to this memo, Sherman described how four air intelligence officers had facilitated information flow between the ship's officers and the squadron intelligence officers. Sherman related some of the common air intelligence practices aboard the ship, including post-sortie debriefing of pilots by squadron intelligence officers and the forwarding of the resultant reports to the air intelligence officers. He also articulated some of the many qualifying requirements that should be expected of air intelligence officers and recognized that such procedures were still evolving as a result of actual operations. The captain closed by urging that there be intelligence officers assigned to each carrier, air group, and carrier squadron.[75] In Sherman's eyes at least, the program was proving its worth in combat operations.

Air intelligence also extended ashore in operational areas. The Air Combat Intelligence Center, based at Noumeau, New Caledonia, served the South Pacific Area under the direction of the Commander Air, South Pacific (COMAIRSOPAC) intelligence officer who functioned as a joint intelligence officer, or J-2. The US Marine air wing based on Guadalcanal also established a rudimentary joint intelligence center for air operations with liaison personnel from the Australians, the AGF, and the USAAF.[76] Such cooperation enhanced intelligence awareness for all involved and assisted in conducting effective joint operations.

US Naval Air Arm and Photoreconnaissance

Admiral King's memorandum, cited earlier, indicated the lack of photographic aircraft in the southern Pacific in late 1942, and it requested P-38 and B-25 aircraft to bridge the gap until naval aircraft made it to the region. But the navy did have photographic intelligence assets on Guadalcanal in the fall of 1942. These supporting elements included photographers, laboratory technicians, and photo interpreters but no independent navy photographic lab. The Marines, however, had a photo lab in a trailer and processed pictures taken by naval photographers flying in USAAF B-17s.[77] In this case, resource scarcity forced joint cooperation among the army, the navy, and the Marine Corps.

The June 1943 creation of the Photo Wing South Pacific, headquartered on Espiritu Santo, indicates how far the naval efforts in photoreconnaissance had progressed. This wing included the navy photographic squadron VD-1 and the Marine photographic squadron VMD-154, which also flew the Photo Liberator, as well as several army photographic groups and squadrons.[78] By mid-1943, naval and Marine air efforts in photographic intelligence were clearly maturing.

Examining the army and navy intelligence structures in isolation provides only a partial picture of the intelligence situation for the Allies in the South and South West Pacific Areas. Some of the organizations mentioned above already displayed a degree of joint and combined efforts among the military branches and among the Allies. Just as in the strategic decision-making structures, the Allied intelligence structures, in contrast to Japan's, attempted to cultivate a measure of cooperation among the service branches and among allies. Some of these integrated structures are worth reviewing for the capabilities they brought to Allied strategic effectiveness.

COMBINED AND JOINT INTELLIGENCE ORGANIZATIONS

The Combined Chiefs of Staff received intelligence support from the Combined Intelligence Committee, which consisted of the American Joint Intelligence Committee (JIC), the British Joint Intelligence Committee (also JIC) in Washington, DC, and the British Joint Intelligence Sub-Committee based in London. Given that the Allies designated the Pacific an American area of responsibility, the American JCS structure took the lead in the Pacific War, giving greater prominence to the American JIC. Members of the JIC included: the director of intelligence for the War Department; the director of intelligence for the Navy Department; representatives from the State Department; members of the Board of Economic Warfare; later the director of Strategic Services (of the Office of Strategic Services, OSS); and, after May 1943, the director of the intelligence staff of the USAAF.[79] The JIC received intelligence reports from the British Joint Intelligence Sub-Committee and from the OSS.[80] The OSS, a separate intelligence organization created by President Roosevelt, did not contribute significantly to the campaigns in New Guinea and the Solomon Islands, in part because the South Pacific was a naval command and also because MacArthur had his own, similar organization in the Southwest Pacific. MacArthur, in fact, established an extensive intelligence organization under his G-2, Major General Charles Willoughby, in the South West Pacific Area. This organization included subdivisions such as the Allied Translator and Interpreter Section (ATIS), the Central Bureau, and the Allied Intelligence Bureau mentioned above.[81] ATIS responsibilities included interrogating enemy prisoners and translating captured enemy documents.[82] MacArthur's command endeavored to limit knowledge of the existence of ATIS for security purposes, yet over the course of the war the organization grew from twenty-five officers and ten enlisted men to 250 officers and 1,700 enlisted troops from the wartime alliance known informally as the United Nations. According to a draft history of ATIS, the organization generated intelligence that contributed significantly to both strategic and combat intelligence in the southwestern Pacific, some of which will be detailed in subsequent chapters.[83] By the end of the war, ATIS had interviewed more than 14,000 POWs and had published more than 20 million pages of enemy documents while employing the services of Japanese Americans to interpret and translate.[84] ATIS provides a good example of a combined organization on the Allied side.

The Central Bureau represented another combined organization in MacArthur's intelligence structure. He established the Central Bureau in Australia on April 15, 1942, with a fivefold mission: to provide radio intelligence to MacArthur's command; to provide for Allied communication security; to work closely with the Signal Intelligence Service in Washington, DC; to break Japanese army codes; and to exchange intelligence with the British and the US Navy in nearby theaters. American and Australian personnel worked very closely within the Central Bureau to share data in two ways: Cryptanalytic information concerning the Japanese remained closely held among signals intelligence office, while the results of that codebreaking were disseminated up and down the chain of command. Because of the extreme importance of ULTRA information, the army and navy occasionally engaged in mutual accusations of poor security about their reports.[85] Thus, the organization clearly had some flaws, but despite the tensions it represents another example of cooperation among allies and among military services.

The Allied Intelligence Bureau represented another such structure under MacArthur's command. Its duties included clandestine operations in enemy territory such as sabotage, espionage, and the fomenting of guerrilla resistance movements. MacArthur decided to establish the AIB in June 1942 under the director of military intelligence for the Australian Army, Colonel C. G. Roberts, with support from an American finance officer. The aforementioned Australian Coastwatcher network had existed before AIB and soon became one of the latter's key tools in the clandestine war. The Coastwatcher network also took pains to assist the South Pacific Command with the Australian lieutenant Hugh Mackenzie as Coastwatcher coordinator for the command. The successes of the AIB and MacArthur's desire to maintain close control of the forces in his area led the SWPA commander to refuse a proposal to send OSS agents into his operational area.[86] MacArthur's rejection of the OSS notwithstanding, the AIB provides yet another example of intelligence cooperation on the Allied side, both among nations and across commands.

The navy and the South Pacific Command also created several organizations that demonstrated joint and combined cooperation. For example, the Fleet Reporting Unit, Melbourne (FRUMEL), became the advanced unit for naval combat radio intelligence in the Southwest Pacific. It consisted of American naval communications intelligence refugees from Corregidor in the Philippines and their counterparts from Australia.[87] While functioning as a joint US/Australian naval unit, FRUMEL was also a division of the larger radio intelligence organization, Fleet Radio Pacific (FRUPAC). FRUPAC had succeeded Hypo and then the Central Intelligence Unit in 1943. By the end of August 1943, FRUMEL had four geographically separated intercept stations in Australia. The organization also cooperated with MacArthur's Central Bureau. Yet some tension existed in this liaison relationship, as Willoughby claimed that FRUMEL often withheld information from MacArthur's command.[88]

Nearly all the air organizations in the South Pacific Area demonstrated a joint, cooperative spirit, as suggested above. The Air Combat Intelligence Center at Noumeau functioned as a joint intelligence center, with the COMAIRSOPAC intelligence officer serving as J-2.[89] The Photographic Wing (Composite), South Pacific, also included units from all the services beginning with its formation on June 21, 1943. Colonel William Holden, USAAF, commanded the wing, which included flying units from the navy, the Marine Corps, and the army, as well as photographic interpreters from the navy and the army.[90] Likewise, COMAIRSOLS (Commander Aircraft Solomons) represented a joint organization. Major Victor Dykes, who served on the COMAIRSOLS staff on three occasions, described the extent of that organization's joint character: "There are Army Air Force units and Marine and Navy units operating under his [COMAIRSOPAC's] direction. But these aircraft are not operated by either the Army, Navy or Marine Corps—for tactical use they are loaned to COMAIRSOLS (Commander Aircraft Solomons). COMAIRSOLS, himself, may be either an Admiral or an Army or Marine general and he has a composite staff."[91] Such examples indicate that the South Pacific Area enjoyed a great deal of joint cooperation in air intelligence.

Finally, at Pearl Harbor, intelligence evolved into a joint activity as well. The Intelligence Center, Pacific Ocean Area, created by Admiral Nimitz in June 1942 laid the groundwork for joint integration of intelligence in the future. ICPOA served as a bridge to meet US Marine Corps Commandant Major General Holcomb's suggestion, proffered in April 1942, for a joint organization. In September 1943, ICPOA became the Joint Intelligence Center, Pacific Ocean Area (JICPOA), with Colonel J. J. Twitty, assistant chief of staff for intelligence on the staff of Commander-in-Chief, Pacific Fleet, simultaneously serving as officer in charge of JICPOA.[92] Thus an army colonel became the number-two intelligence officer in the Pacific under Admiral Nimitz. This represented a measure of cooperation unheard of in the Japanese intelligence structures, where interservice rivalries reigned supreme.

CONCLUSIONS

This brief examination of the Japanese and American combatants' intelligence structures demonstrates a number of significant factors that influenced the campaigns in the southern and southwestern Pacific and, therefore, the efforts to retain or to seize the strategic initiative. On balance, the United States and its allies developed a mature and comprehensive approach to intelligence that integrated services and nations much more effectively than did the Japanese. Furthermore, the Japanese tended to focus on immediate tactical matters, whereas the Allies pursued the full spectrum of intelligence from combat information to strategic awareness.

The presence of intelligence officers in command and control headquarters is one measure of the commitment to intelligence. The United States placed trained intelligence officers throughout most of its organizations. The army assigned intelligence officers from the General Staff to the battalion level, and the navy had them from the CNO's staff to its ships and squadrons. For the Japanese, intelligence responsibilities often represented an additional, rather than a primary, duty for officers aboard ships or at the lower end of the military hierarchy. Often these Japanese officers received little or no specific intelligence training.

The foregoing analysis also points to much better intelligence cooperation and integration on the Allied side. The IJA and IJN operated independently in both the intelligence and operational arenas. They may have shared intelligence informally and certainly discussed it when formulating policies and plans at the IGHQ level, but they did not create any joint or integrated intelligence agencies. The Allies, though still at times manifesting service competition and jealousies, formed numerous intelligence organizations that fostered joint and combined cooperation and thereby developed improved intelligence fusion. From the Combined Intelligence Committee to the JIC at the higher levels of command, down to the JICPOA, the AIB, the Air Intelligence Center, and other organizations in the area commands of the Pacific, the Allies created intelligence divisions and agencies that enhanced the flow and exploitation of information and intelligence to all services and all friendly nations.

Early in the war, while expanding its empire, Japan enjoyed some intelligence advantages over the Allies. By dint of conquest, the Japanese had more opportunities for the capture and exploitation of Allied materiel and prisoners of war. And though they took advantage of some opportunities, such as test-flying captured aircraft, they missed others. The IJA did not place much emphasis on POW interrogations; as the IJN's treatment of captured American naval aviators at Midway indicates, prisoners could be easily discarded in short order after revealing immediate tactical information. Rather than retaining these prisoners for further exploitation to learn more about US naval aviation operating procedures, the IJN executed them and unceremoniously committed their remains to the sea.

The Allies also had intelligence advantages in other areas. They clearly held a decided advantage in radio intelligence throughout the war, from prior to Pearl Harbor to Midway and beyond. The US Army struggled against its Japanese counterpart until late in the war, and the navy likewise suffered periods of limited radio intelligence, but the overall results provided a critical advantage. Starting from scratch at the beginning of the war, US photographic intelligence developed into another advantage for the Allies during the campaigns in New Guinea and the Solomon Islands. And while the Allies progressed rapidly in this area, the Japanese stagnated. Human intelligence, in the form of the Coastwatcher network, provided a key Allied advantage over the Japanese in the South and South West Pacific Areas. This network corroborated other intelligence, generated its own valuable information, and helped mask other intelligence breakthroughs such as ULTRA.

In sum, the Allies fought the Pacific War with a more comprehensive intelligence apparatus than did the Japanese. This apparatus more readily stood up to the challenges of a long war than did the Japanese structure, designed primarily as it was for tactical exploitation in a short conflict. The Allied apparatus also adjusted more effectively to the increasing demands of the war. The evolution of joint and combined structures, such as the creation of JICPOA, attests to this fact. The Allies' more inclusive and integrated system helped pave the way for Allied victories in the southern and southwestern Pacific and assisted the Allies in wresting the strategic initiative from the Japanese in late 1942 and early 1943. These organizations gave the Allies enhanced and relatively accurate situational awareness, allowed them to react effectively to Japanese moves, and enabled them to plan and execute successful operations during this critical phase of the war.

6

"East Wind, Rain": The Japanese Seize the Initiative

The epic conflict between Japan and the United States began with Japan's raid on Pearl Harbor and its lightning strike into the Southwest Pacific and Southeast Asia in early December 1941.[1] Japan seized and clearly held the strategic initiative throughout the early months of the war, using that initiative to implement an offensive strategy designed to secure vital resources for the empire. The Japanese hoped to set the stage for later phases to allow them to secure their gains and fight the war on their own terms by protecting the perimeter gained and forcing the Allies to agree to a negotiated peace. In the event, stunning Japanese successes and various American countermeasures caused the Japanese to reevaluate their strategy and make several important adjustments. The course of this first period up to and including the Battle of Midway in June 1942 set the stage for the succeeding phase in which the Allies vied for and eventually wrested the strategic initiative from Japan through campaigns in the southern and southwestern Pacific. Understanding the subsequent shift in strategic initiative requires an examination of this opening phase of the war.

JAPAN'S DECISION FOR WAR

The Japanese war aims included attaining primacy in their chosen sphere of influence in Asia, defeating the Western Allies (and eventually the Soviet Union), subduing China, and creating Japan's Asian "Co-Prosperity Sphere."[2] Japanese military actions in China and Manchuria during the late 1930s and early 1940s had seriously complicated relations with the United States, which steadily escalated economic pressure on Japan and finally embargoed its oil supplies in July 1941. Obtaining unfettered access to critical resources, and to oil in particular, became a paramount concern for Japanese strategy.[3] This placed Borneo, Malaya, the Dutch East Indies, and the Philippine Islands squarely in Japan's crosshairs.

While the Japanese navy looked at Southeast Asia, the IJA had focused and prepared for war against the Soviet Union. The two nations harbored antagonisms dating from the 1904–1905 Russo–Japanese War and had engaged in more recent combat at Lake Khasan in 1938 and at Nomonhan/Khalkin Gol in 1939. Changes in the global situation, not least the 1941 American oil embargo, forced a reevaluation. Other events that reshaped Japanese army calculations included the drubbing that Soviet forces inflicted on the Japanese in the Nomonhan/Khalkin Gol campaign in 1939 and the collapse of France and the Netherlands at the hands of Germany in 1940. After the Japanese had decided on war in the Pacific, peaceful relations with the Soviet Union became an important focal point for Japanese strategy during that war.[4] Documents from the September 6, 1941, Imperial Conference reveal Japanese thinking: "By cooperating with Germany and Italy, we will shatter Anglo-American unity, link Asia and Europe, and we should be able to create an invincible military alignment."[5] This meant a naval war against the United States, which the IJN had long anticipated.

Following the Pearl Harbor raid, the United States developed its own war aims vis-à-vis the Japanese. President Roosevelt held definite ideas about the preferred outcome of the war. Almost immediately he settled on a policy of "unconditional surrender" of the Axis powers, even if the Allies did not formally announce this policy until the Casablanca Conference of 1943.[6] The president also had to keep the Soviet Union engaged in the war against Nazi Germany, which implied that the Soviet Union would be a major player in the postwar world. The United States hoped to destroy Japan's military power but did not seek to subdue Japan to the same degree as it intended to suppress Germany. By itself, however, a weakened and occupied Japan could not provide an effective counterweight to the Soviet Union in the Far East, so Roosevelt intended to cultivate such a counter with a stronger China.[7] All of these considerations shaped American strategy in the Pacific War.

A number of factors influenced this conflict's particular character. Geography dictated a broad maritime war. The vast expanse of the Pacific Ocean also meant that, unlike the European continental war, naval supply lines would be very long and tenuous, while the numbers of troops actually engaged in fighting on either side at any moment would remain relatively small.[8] These geographic factors combined with the airpower capabilities of the day to shape the war's outlines, making airpower the

basis for sea control and air bases a primary consideration for land operations. Strong overtones of racism from both belligerents also characterized the war in the Pacific, with stereotypes and violations of the law of
war being common.[9]

Japanese Strategy at the Outbreak of War

Japan's strategy envisioned three phases for the war: Phase I would be a
rapid conquest of the resource-rich south; Phase II included the fortifica-
tion of a perimeter stretching from the Kuriles to Wake Island, the Marshall, Gilbert, and Bismarck Islands, northern New Guinea, the Dutch
East Indies, and Malaya; and Phase III anticipated consolidation of the
gains, destruction of the inevitable Allied counterattack, and the prosecution of a war of attrition until the enemy tired of war. The Japanese
strategists broke the opening phase into three substages: first, they would
occupy Thailand, land forces in Malaya, and attack the Philippine Islands
and northern Borneo; next, the Japanese would move on Dutch possessions in Borneo, the Celebes, Sumatra, and Java; and finally, they would
stabilize their gains and expand their control in Burma.[10]

Because of its shocking impact, the Pearl Harbor raid has come to
symbolize these preplanned aggressive Japanese moves. Yet, the Japanese
originally formulated their plans without the raid, and only the insistence
of Admiral Yamamoto ensured the raid would open the war. On January 7, 1941, Yamamoto wrote a nine-page summary titled "Views on
Preparation for War," in which he proposed massing the IJN's aircraft
carrier divisions for an attack against Hawaii to annihilate the US fleet.[11]
He later insisted the operation was necessary in order to protect the flank
of the planned Japanese advance into the southern areas.[12] However, the
Navy General Staff opposed Yamamoto's plans, pitting the General Staff
against the Combined Fleet commander and contributing to the command structure divisions described in chapter 3. As already noted, Yamamoto's threat of resignation compelled the Navy General Staff to accede
to the admiral's concept, resulting in the inclusion of the Pearl Harbor
raid as part of the plan to open the war against the Allies.

Japanese naval thinking was dominated by the concept of decisive
battle. The crushing Japanese defeat of the Russian navy at the Battle of
Tsushima Strait in 1905 seemed to confirm the naval theories of Alfred
Thayer Mahan. This focus on decisive battle, with a strong undercurrent
of battleship engagement, shaped Japanese naval strategy and behavior
throughout the war.

Racism also colored Japanese perceptions before and during the war, causing them to underestimate Allied capabilities in many ways. Japanese officers believed that their opponents lacked the will or skill to fight a costly war; they produced biased analyses of US war-making potential and exhibited an overriding, but not unreasonable, expectation that Germany would defeat Britain and the Soviet Union.[13] Early Japanese successes seemed to validate this outlook, but the subsequent course of the conflict demonstrated the severity of their underestimation.

Nevertheless, the Japanese decision to act in 1941 demonstrated both a certain amount of strategic acumen and a shrewd judgment of the international situation. Viewed from Tokyo, the situation appeared as follows: The US embargo had cut off resources; a temporary military balance of power favored Japan; and the Soviet Union was entangled in a fight for national survival against Germany. All of this added up to a fleeting opportunity to force the West out of the Pacific and thereby dominate the Chinese.[14] Masuo Kato strikes a similar chord and reminds the reader of the dominant influence of the Japanese army. According to Kato, "Japan's decision to attack . . . was essentially a now or never decision. It was almost wholly an Army decision, and it represented the Army's best judgment as to the precise time at which the greatest opportunity for success might be expected."[15] Japan based that decision to attack at the most opportune moment on a rational estimate of the situation.

American Strategy at the Outbreak of War

The American strategy for war against Japan in the Pacific depended upon variables in the world situation. American and British coordination began before the war at the ABC-1 staff conference in early 1941 and had serious implications for the conduct of war in the Pacific theater. At this meeting, the two potential allies agreed that if the conflict were to become a global war against Germany, Italy, and Japan, then the effort against Nazi Germany would take priority, a determination that became known as the Germany First strategy. The combined British and American report from the ABC-1 Conference laid the groundwork for this policy when American and Britain (plus Canada) delineated their common strategic objectives:

1. The early defeat of Germany as the predominant member of the Axis, with the principal military effort of the United States being exerted in the Atlantic and European area, the decisive theater. Op-

erations in other theaters to be conducted in such a manner as to facilitate the main effort.

2. The maintenance of British and Allied positions in the Mediterranean area.

3. A strategic defensive in the Far East, with the US Fleet employed offensively "in the manner best calculated to weaken Japanese economic power, and to support the defense of the Malay Barrier by directing Japanese strength away from Malaysia."[16]

A war solely against the Japanese would give the United States more freedom of action to focus on the Pacific. In the event, less than a week after Pearl Harbor, Hitler's declaration of war against the United States ensured a global conflict and spared Franklin Roosevelt a political struggle to persuade Congress to fight Germany. Prior to hostilities, American planners had developed and evaluated a number of different strategies for employment against Japan in the event of war in the Pacific. As early as 1911, Naval War College planners anticipated a possible conflict between the United States and Japan, planting the seeds of War Plan Orange (orange being the designated color-code for Japan). The well-known Rainbow Plans, which envisioned various combinations of friends and foes in the next war, superseded War Plan Orange during the interwar years as the global situation evolved.[17] President Roosevelt eventually gave informal, oral approval to Rainbow 5, the combination closest to what became the Germany First strategy.

Regardless of the overall strategic concept, War Plan Orange continued to provide the basic structure of American strategy in the Pacific. The early versions of Orange envisioned a strong defense of the Philippine Islands in the Far East to provide the time required for the US Fleet to sortie west, fight its way across the Pacific, and relieve the besieged.[18] An update in 1938 aimed to hold a line from Panama to Oahu and on to Alaska, with the expected loss of the Philippines and the launch of an immediate naval offensive. Calculations changed again in 1941. Roosevelt's acceptance of Rainbow 5 reinforced the Germany First strategy, but this did not please former US Army Chief of Staff General Douglas MacArthur, then in the service of the Philippine government. MacArthur realized that he and his command would be sacrificed in the event of war with Japan. In what amounted to a severe contradiction in American strategy, the US Army, at MacArthur's urging, planned to fight stubbornly to retain the Philippines as a strategic base of operations, while the navy still did not envision a sortie to save the islands. The Pearl Harbor attack brought this contradiction into full view, as the navy manifestly lacked the capability with which to attempt a relief of the Philippines.

Like the Japanese, Allied strategic calculations also suffered from the distorting effects of racism. Apparently believing in Anglo-Saxon superiority, Roosevelt and Prime Minister Winston Churchill underestimated both Japanese will and Japanese skill. American naval officers wrongly assumed that the Japanese carrier force was inferior to their own. Similarly, the British held Japanese soldiers in contempt, resulting in a similar eye-opening experience during the battle for Malaya. Indeed, nearly the entire opening phase would provide an education for the Allies in Japanese determination and martial ability. (See map 2.)

JAPAN STRIKES

The choreographed sequence of Japanese aggression began in Malaya and at Pearl Harbor on the morning of December 7, 1941 (December 8 on the Japanese side of the International Date Line) and spread rapidly. The Japanese quickly invaded Malaya, the Philippine Islands, the Dutch East Indies, Hong Kong, Guam, Wake Island, and eventually the Bismarck Islands. They clearly held the strategic initiative while the Allied powers generally reacted clumsily to their rapid onslaught.

The Air Raid on Pearl Harbor

The stunning attack on Pearl Harbor did not materialize out of the blue. Thorough, competent Japanese naval planning, training, security, and execution enabled the operation to achieve most of its short-term objectives and tip the immediate balance of naval power even more in favor of Japan for the opening stage of the war.

In the months preceding the attack, the rapidly expanding American armed forces struggled to establish effective defenses in the Pacific. General Lewis Brereton, USAAF, evaluated Oahu's air defenses while passing through on his way to the Philippines in late October 1941 and wrote: "I was surprised and disappointed to note the incomplete preparations against air attacks, particularly the lack of adequate air warning equipment."[19]

On November 27, 1941, Admiral Husband Kimmel, commander-in-chief of the US Pacific Fleet, received a "war warning" based in part on decryption of Japanese diplomatic traffic. He promptly met with his

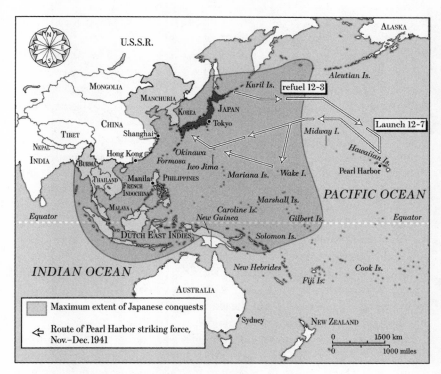

Map 2. Pearl Harbor and Japanese Expansion

aircraft carrier commander, navy Vice Admiral William "Bull" Halsey, and army Lieutenant General Walter Short. They agreed to heighten the alert status for the forces in Pearl Harbor, and two aircraft carriers would ferry aircraft to reinforce Midway and Wake Island, which appeared to be likely Japanese targets. Halsey sailed for Wake aboard the carrier USS *Enterprise* while Admiral John Newton took the USS *Lexington* to reinforce Midway. The third Pacific Fleet carrier, USS *Saratoga*, was already en route to the West Coast of the United States for routine maintenance.[20] As for Hawaii itself, sabotage seemed to be a more likely threat than direct enemy attack. Thus, the defenders took significant precautions but failed to anticipate the daring Japanese strike.

Meanwhile, the Japanese force prepared. Captain Minoru Genda, one of the lead Japanese planners for the attack, first heard of the proposed operation in February 1941. Planning began in earnest with special attention to aerial torpedo attacks in a shallow harbor in June and July, followed with intensive training of the carrier air groups assigned to conduct the attack in September and October 1941.[21] Their preparations paid dividends in the skies over Hawaii in December.

The Japanese accrued excellent intelligence on Pearl Harbor and also succeeded in keeping the operation secure and achieving surprise, despite US successes against their diplomatic codes. Prior to the attack, spies in Hawaii kept Yamamoto and the operation's leader, Admiral Chuichi Nagumo, abreast of the situation at Pearl Harbor.[22] The Japanese used strict radio security prior to the attack, passing orders through courier rather than over the radio, while the strike force maintained radio silence en route to Hawaii. In addition, the task force deliberately sailed on a stormy, northern approach to Hawaii to minimize chances of detection and in the cognizance that the Americans did not patrol north of the islands. The IJN also implemented an effective radio deception plan that led American intelligence analysts to believe that as late as December 1, 1941, the aircraft carriers used in the Pearl Harbor attack remained in or around Japan.[23] On December 7, the first attack wave of 183 aircraft launched from six Japanese aircraft carriers north of Oahu; upon their arrival over the island they found the skies clear of any defending aircraft.[24] The Japanese had achieved total surprise.

The results of the Japanese raid were devastating in the near term for the US Pacific Fleet; but they were not decisive in a longer-term, operational, or strategic sense. In exchange for the loss of 29 aircraft and 5 midget submarines, the raid sank or damaged 18 US ships (including 4 battleships sunk and 4 crippled), destroyed or damaged 288 aircraft, and killed 2,403 Americans.[25] Any chance for an immediate American offensive in the Pacific now rested on the bottom of Pearl Harbor alongside the battleships of the US Pacific Fleet.

However, Admiral Nagumo cautiously withdrew the Japanese strike force after the second wave returned to his carriers, forgoing the opportunity to launch further attacks against Pearl Harbor's port facilities, docks, and fuel-storage tanks.[26] Damage to any or all of these would have diminished the US Navy's ability to recover from the raid and may have forced the US Pacific Fleet to operate from the West Coast of the United States. Yet, contrary to common belief, such facilities were at the bottom of the Japanese target priorities—even if Nagumo had risked a third strike against fully alerted defenses, the Japanese would probably have reengaged the warships rather than attacking fuel tanks.[27] Still, Admiral Matome Ugaki lamented Nagumo's decision to withdraw in his diary entry of December 9, 1941: "This [withdrawal] is open to criticism as sneak-thievery and contentment with a humble lot in life. Since our loss is not more than thirty planes, it is most important for us to expand our results."[28] Furthermore, by sinking the American battleships in the shallow waters of Pearl Harbor, the Japanese made possible the salvage operations that eventually restored all but two (the *Arizona* and the *Oklahoma*) to active operations. Additionally, an element of chance mitigated the success of the raid. American aircraft carriers were noticeably absent from the list of damaged or destroyed ships because, as previously noted, Admiral Kimmel had sent them to sea as part of his precautions prior to the Japanese attack. The Pacific Fleet had been mauled, but the continued existence of its aircraft carriers (along with its excellent fleet of submarines) meant the United States retained potent weapons with which to counter forthcoming Japanese moves. If anything, the temporary setback to American naval power ensured that the war would be so prolonged that American industrial superiority could mobilize to crush Japan.

Perhaps the most important result of the raid, however, was its impact on US resolve to fight and win the global war now enveloping much of the planet. Without the raid on Pearl Harbor, American participation and resolve would have been much more problematic. (See map 3.)

Map 3. Japanese Advances, December 1941–May 1942

The Attack on the Philippine Islands

Pearl Harbor represented the opening act in a sequence of disasters for the Allies. The Americans endured another humiliation in the Philippines nine hours after General Douglas MacArthur's command received word of the raid on Hawaii. Despite the advanced warning that hostilities had commenced, MacArthur's Far East Air Force (FEAF), which included 107 P-40 fighter aircraft and 35 B-17 heavy bombers that the Americans considered a linchpin of the Philippines defenses, was caught off-guard. Some aircraft had taken off when the news of Pearl Harbor reached the Philippines, but these aircraft had landed by the time the delayed Japanese strike arrived.[29]

The first Japanese air attacks caught the Americans unaware at the Clark and Iba airfields, resulting in the destruction of half of FEAF's strength and leaving Major General Brereton, MacArthur's air commander, with only 17 B-17s, 55 P-40s, and 15 older P-35s to resist the continuing air offensive and the forthcoming invasion.[30] The lack of American resistance during the attack stunned the Japanese air ace Saburō Sakai, who also praised the "phenomenal" accuracy of his bomber comrades.[31] The preventable disaster spurred recriminations and blame among MacArthur, Brereton, and MacArthur's chief of staff, Brigadier General Richard K. Sutherland, for years to come.

By December 11, 1941, Brereton's strength had dwindled to 12 B-17s, 22 P-40s and 5 P-35s. One cannot attribute Japanese successes against FEAF strictly to luck. When Brereton assessed FEAF headquarters at Nielson Field, Philippines, in early November 1941, he concluded that the force was numerically insufficient, tactically inexperienced, and lacking in an air warning network.[32] By contrast, the Japanese were well prepared for their offensive. Before the attack, Sakai benefited from photographs of Clark Field that revealed 32 B-17s and 74 other aircraft.[33] The Japanese had also conducted a trial navigation flight from their bases on the island of Formosa to within 20 miles of Luzon. Brereton also claimed that the Japanese had a wide espionage net in the Philippines and had even tapped into the US Army's telephone lines.[34] Poor American security and strong Japanese intelligence collection contributed to the FEAF disaster and helped shape the land campaign that followed.

Smaller Japanese landings hit the Philippines in mid-December, but the main invasion by General Masaharu Homma's 14th Army landed in Lingayen Gulf at dawn on December 22. The fight for the archipelago then commenced in earnest.[35] With 65,000 troops, air superiority, and overwhelming naval support, Homma faced the remnants of FEAF and MacArthur's 130,000 soldiers. Although MacArthur's command enjoyed numerical superiority, it consisted of 22,400 US troops and 12,000 well-trained Filipino Scouts, with the remainder being mostly inexperienced Filipino troops.[36] MacArthur belatedly withdrew to the Bataan Peninsula, where he hoped to hold out until reinforced. MacArthur's ill-advised attempt to stop the Japanese on the invasion beaches had left the defenders of Bataan seriously short of food, ammunition, and other supplies.[37] The Japanese had expected a fight for Manila and ignored intelligence that MacArthur would instead defend Bataan. While this decision slowed the Japanese timetable, it could not prevent the inevitable. After MacArthur's stealthy escape from the islands in March 1942, US and Filipino forces on Bataan capitulated on April 9, sending 12,000 Americans and 64,000 Filipinos into Japanese captivity.[38] The final bastion of significant American resistance, Corregidor Island, fell to the Japanese on May 6, followed thereafter by the remaining US commands in the islands.[39] A numerically smaller Japanese ground force had defeated a larger Allied force in a six-month campaign to secure a strategic geographic position athwart the trade routes necessary to transport vital resources from the Southwest Pacific to Japan.

Malaya and the Dutch East Indies

Nearly simultaneously with the Pearl Harbor attack, the Japanese began landings in Malaya. Advanced elements of Japan's 25th Army landed at Khota Baru and Singora on December 8, followed by the bulk of the army two days later.[40] In an action that put an exclamation point on the results of Pearl Harbor and the vulnerability of battleships to air attack, on December 10 the IJN's 22d Air Flotilla, for the loss of only four aircraft, attacked and sank the British battleship HMS *Prince of Wales* and the battle cruiser HMS *Repulse* as they attempted to counter the Japanese Malayan landings.[41] As in the Philippines, the Japanese established air and naval supremacy to support their army's advance. General Tomoyuki Yamashita, moving adroitly against British and Commonwealth forces that outnumbered his army twofold, soon took all of Malaya and punctuated his victory by capturing the fortress of Singapore in February 1942 after a seventy-day campaign. The Japanese suffered 10,000 casualties but inflicted 38,000 and captured more than 130,000 prisoners in what many regard as the most humiliating defeat in British military history.[42]

The IJA's performance in Malaya shocked the Allies' psyche and demonstrated that the Japanese soldier would represent a formidable foe in the war. In November 1942, as the United States struggled against this same foe in the jungles of the Solomon Islands and New Guinea, the Commander, South Pacific Area, forwarded a report titled "Lessons from Malaya," written by a British battalion commander who had fought the Japanese during this campaign. The author lamented the lack of realistic training of the British troops in Malaya and stressed the particular importance of tactics and quality over quantity in jungle fighting. He also praised the motivation, daring, and alertness of the Japanese soldier, qualities he found lacking on the British side. He found the Japanese maintained a fast tempo, making it difficult for the British to adjust or react effectively. He also noted that the jungle could mitigate a firepower advantage because of the close nature of the combat and that the British command set up unrealistic defensive positions based on the reading of a map rather than the actual terrain and topography.[43] These Japanese strengths and British shortcomings resulted in the unexpectedly rapid loss of Malaya and Singapore and opened the way into the Netherlands East Indies and north into Burma.

In another impressive campaign, the Japanese once again achieved their aims and secured the oil resources in Borneo, the Celebes, and Java. The invaders had already captured British possessions in northern Borneo in December and now looked farther south. The operation proceeded almost like a game of hopscotch, with sequential jumps from one strategic position to the next, using airborne and amphibious operations of the Japanese 16th Army, supported by the IJN's Third Fleet and the 21st and 23rd Air Flotillas.[44] Both air flotillas followed the advance, moving south to a series of new airfields in order to ensure Japanese land and sea operations remained under friendly air cover at all times. By March 9, 1942, the Japanese had taken Palembang, Batavia, and Surabaya when the Allied forces defending the Netherlands East Indies surrendered, sending more than 93,000 soldiers into Japanese captivity.[45]

Several actions in the air and on the sea enabled this Japanese success. Throughout February the Japanese kept up pressure on the Allied air forces in Java, and by February 24 Admiral Ugaki comfortably declared that the Japanese had cleared Allied airpower from eastern Java.[46] The Pearl Harbor carrier strike force supported these operations with air raids on Ambon on January 23 and then on Darwin, Australia, on February 19 to reduce Allied strength and prevent Allied reinforcements from entering the battle.[47] In the Battle of Makassar Strait on February 4, Japanese airpower prevented an Allied force of cruisers and destroyers from engaging a Japanese amphibious force of nearly equal strength. The Allies suffered heavy damage to two cruisers and light damage to a third, but the Japanese force proceeded unmolested. In the Battle of Badung Strait on February 19–20, the Allies forced a Japanese invasion force headed for Bali to return to port and damaged several Japanese ships in the process. But the Allied performance in the battle was unimpressive, while the Japanese destroyers demonstrated skill at night fighting, a characteristic that would soon become familiar to the US Navy.[48] Next, in the Battle of the Java Sea, which started on February 27, a Japanese force of four cruisers and fourteen destroyers tangled with an Allied force of five cruisers and nine destroyers, sinking three Allied cruisers and four destroyers. The next night, at the Battle of Sunda Strait, the Japanese sank two more Allied cruisers.[49] During this campaign, the Japanese had dominated combat, with minor exceptions, on the land and sea as well as in the air.

The Central Pacific, the South Pacific, and the Indian Ocean

Several other Japanese operations completed their initial tide of conquest in the Pacific. The Japanese landed on Guam on December 10, 1941, at 4:25 P.M. in the afternoon, and the island surrendered the next morning at 6:45 A.M. Wake Island alone provided a brief glimmer of positive news for the Americans. US Marines repulsed the first attempt to take the island on December 11, but the Japanese soon returned with a stronger force and captured the island on December 23.[50] Mitsuo Fuchida recounted the Japanese successes as the Philippines campaign progressed, noting that in addition to Guam and Wake, the Marianas, Makin/Tarawa, and the southern anchorages of Rabaul and Kavieng fell to Japan by the end of January 1942.[51] Meanwhile, Admiral Nagumo's carrier force continued its operations in support of Japanese maneuvers and conducted several raids in the Indian Ocean in early April. Nagumo launched a 315-plane raid against Colombo on April 5, then sank the British cruisers *Dorsetshire* and *Cornwall* later that day, and culminated the operation with an attack on Trincomalee and the sinking of the British light carrier *Hermes* on April 9.[52] With the temporary exception of the setback at Wake, the Japanese had rapidly imposed their will on the Allies.

Through early April, the Japanese plan had unfolded on or ahead of schedule, a testament to their judgment of the situation at the opening of the war. In April, May, and June, however, their momentum slowed as the Allies regained some of their footing.

The Doolittle Raid

Following the attack on Pearl Harbor, the remains of the US Pacific Fleet operated with caution. US carrier task forces raided Japanese bases in the Marshalls, on Wake, at Rabaul, and in New Guinea. The Americans, however, soon hatched a daring plan that changed the strategic calculus in the Pacific War. On April 18, 1942, a US carrier task force under the command of Admiral William "Bull" Halsey launched sixteen army B-25 bombers led by Lieutenant Colonel James H. Doolittle for the first American bombing raid on the Japanese homeland.[53] The risks were high, and the physical damage inflicted on Japan was slight. Yet, the raid heartened the American people, and its impact on Japanese thinking shaped the future course of the war. In his diary entry for April 19, Admiral Ugaki wrote:

> In view of this recent success, undoubtedly the enemy will repeat this kind of operation while attempting raids from China. Therefore we must take steps to watch far to the east and, at the same time, always keep a sharp lookout on the threat from the west. As I felt the necessity of drawing up a definite plan now, I expressed my views to the staff officers, hoping they would use them as their guide.[54]

Admiral Yamamoto viewed the American success as a failure on his part and resolved to press for operations that would force the US aircraft carriers into a final, decisive battle for command of the Pacific Ocean. Those Japanese leaders who had previously opposed Yamamoto's plan now relented and agreed to the operation that ultimately led to the Battle of Midway.[55] Thus the Doolittle raid had a pronounced psychological influence on ensuing Japanese strategy, far out of proportion to the physical damage it inflicted.

The Battle of the Coral Sea

The Battle of the Coral Sea represented a portent of things to come for the Japanese. Their opening operations had succeeded at very low cost, and the Japanese now began to adjust to these successes. The drive for further expansion in the New Guinea and Solomon Islands areas originated with the local Japanese forces that had occupied Rabaul in January. They looked to Port Moresby, on the southeastern coast of New Guinea, as a strategic target to protect Rabaul and isolate Australia so the latter could not provide a springboard for an eventual Allied counterattack.

Vice Admiral Shigeru Fukudome, staff officer on the Japanese Navy General Staff, stated:

> After RABAUL was taken and subsequent operations were extended it became more and more clear that a broad area would have to be occupied to secure RABAUL; just exactly who made the original proposal, I do not know, but it is certain that the demand originated at RABAUL, probably on the Navy side, and it [the amphibious occupation of Port Moresby] was approved by Central Authorities. When the decision to take PORT MORESBY was made, the Army reaction to it was that it would be quite simple to occupy PORT MORESBY by sea-borne operation.[56]

This operation resulted in the first American–Japanese carrier engagement of the Pacific War.

Preceding the battle, as the Japanese fleet ran rampant through the Pacific, it generated a large volume of radio chatter that facilitated American efforts to crack the Japanese naval codes.[57] This increased knowledge based on radio intercepts forewarned Admiral Nimitz of the forthcoming Japanese thrust on Port Moresby, detailing much of the timing and strength of the Japanese operation.[58]

Japanese radio intelligence also provided limited information about US movements in the prelude to the battle. Intercepts on April 25–27 suggested that a US task force was headed south, but Japanese analysts were unable to inform the high command of the number or whereabouts of US and Australian warships near Port Moresby.[59] The Americans, therefore, entered the battle with a clearer picture of the enemy situation than did the Japanese.

Between May 4 and 8, the two fleets fought a standoff carrier battle in which aircraft provided the striking power and surface fleets never came into contact with one another. The Japanese lost forty-three aircraft along with the light carrier *Shoho*, while the fleet carrier *Shokaku* was badly damaged. Most significantly, the Port Moresby invasion force was forced to turn back without seizing its objective. The US fleet lost the large carrier *Lexington*, the destroyer *Sims*, the oiler *Neosho*, and thirty-three aircraft, as well as suffering significant damage to the carrier *Yorktown*.[60] Although the Japanese mistakenly believed that they had sunk the *Yorktown*, the carrier was down but not out. The Coral Sea represented the first time in the Pacific War that American forces had thwarted a Japanese offensive.

EVOLVING JAPANESE STRATEGY AND PLANS

Japanese strategy began to evolve following the rapid accomplishment of their initial objectives. The push for more expansion, as exhibited by this first attempt to take Port Moresby, soon reached into the highest levels of the Japanese command structure. The IJA and IJN had significantly different ideas about the future course of the war. The army did not want to expand beyond the initially planned, relatively limited perimeter in the Central Pacific and Southeast Asia. Its desire was to fortify the positions gained and parry the Allied counterattacks. The IJN thought otherwise and pushed for a larger "outer perimeter," especially after the Doolittle Raid made the home islands appear vulnerable. When queried after the war about this divergence and the adoption of the naval view, Admiral Fukudome gave a lengthy response. It is worth quoting in full, as it reveals many of the strategic calculations with which the Japanese had to contend:

> From the very beginning there were two divergent views: namely (1) holding a long line; (2) the other, compact, as you have said; the Navy favoring the former and the Army the latter. The two views in the end, however, came together more or less with the Navy's view prevailing, and I still believe that was the wiser of the two plans because, had we elected to occupy the narrower area, that would have enabled your forces to take the intermediate bases without any opposition so that the greater distance from the UNITED STATES would not enter into the picture as a serious factor. The closer you could come without opposition, the closer you were to the heart of the area which it was incumbent upon us to protect. If you used from these near bases those attacking planes which far outranged ours, it would have placed us at a decided disadvantage, so the Navy's idea of occupying this more expansive area with the hope of getting a chance to strike a heavy blow against your fleet from one of the outlying bases, we felt, gave us a greater chance for continued success, and through that line we intended to gain time.
>
> Time, we felt, was very important. If the war could be continued long enough, we expected there might be slips on your side of which we could take advantage. I believe if we had elected this other line, defeat would have come sooner.[61]

Fukudome's analysis touches upon a number of strategic concerns for the IJN in the Pacific War. The first is the differing approaches to strategy by the two Japanese services. Geography also loomed large in Fukudome's calculations, noting the Japanese desire to strain US logistical lifelines from the United States. But his solution was to expand the Japanese perimeter, which could not help but increase the battlefield's distance from Japan and thereby complicate logistics. Fukudome did not address this seemingly paradoxical aspect of further expansion. His reasoning also demonstrated an appreciation for the importance of land-based airpower in the war and a respect for the heavy bomber, given his reference to aircraft of long range. Additionally, he manifested the IJN's preoccupation with decisive battle, of "striking a heavy blow" against the American fleet.

The Japanese attempted to reconcile these concerns with strategic adjustments in the spring of 1942. The IJN persuaded a reluctant IJA to accede to continued expansion. Attacks on Samoa, Fiji, and New Caledonia sought to interdict an American force buildup in Australia.[62] Yet Japanese plans did not end there. The high command also laid out plans for operations against the Aleutians, eastern New Guinea, Cocos, and India. The IJN even suggested an invasion of the Australian mainland, but the Imperial Army General Staff refused because it could not spare the ten divisions the operation would require.[63]

The IJA did, however, press ahead with preparations to support the further expansion agreed upon. On May 18, Imperial General Headquarters Army Department in its Directive 1152 created the 17th Army for the Fiji–Samoa–New Caledonia operations and for the capture of Port Moresby. Directive 1154 listed the order of battle for the 17th Army and directed the commander of the Southern Army in the newly captured areas to support the new army's lines of communication.[64] But before any moves could be made by the 17th Army, IGHQ made another adjustment to the overall plan.

The results of the Doolittle Raid caused Admiral Yamamoto to insist upon a change of plans. He demanded that the Midway operation take precedence. Army headquarters disagreed, but further negotiations led to a revised plan that made a move on Midway and the Aleutians the next step, to be followed by the drive against Fiji, Samoa, and New Caledonia.[65] In rapid succession, Japan had modified its initial strategy and then quickly amended its own reformulation. The resulting operation would evolve into the momentous and, for the Japanese, disastrous Battle of Midway.

ANALYSIS OF THE FIRST PHASE OF THE PACIFIC WAR

Japan held the strategic initiative throughout the opening stage of the war, dictating the tempo of operations and compelling the Allies to fight

those battles that aligned with Japanese war aims. How, then, did resources, intelligence, strategic acumen, combat effectiveness, and chance
influence possession of the strategic initiative and the course of the war?

Resources

Japan began the war with a large military establishment. Yet, of the fifty-
one established army divisions, forty of them remained tied down in
China and Manchuria.[66] Furthermore, the paper strength of an army in
the Pacific War can be misleading. The geography of this vast maritime
theater often limited the numbers engaged in combat. The Japanese had
conducted some of their largest operations, such as the invasion of the
Philippines and Malaya, with outnumbered ground forces. Despite their
numerical inferiority, the Japanese achieved their objectives relatively
quickly and dealt their adversaries stinging blows in the process.

Pilots represent another important resource. Japan began the war with
2,500 pilots in the IJN and 3,500 pilots in the IJA. These pilots had
received extensive training, and many had benefited from combat experience in the skies over China.[67] By comparison, the US Navy alone began
the war with 3,500 regular pilots and 6,000 reserve pilots, all trained and
with respectable flight experience.[68] The Japanese had crafted their aviation component very effectively for their opening moves and for a brief
war, but they had not prepared their pilot pool or training system for a
long war with high rates of loss.[69] The Japanese simply did not produce
pilots quickly enough for a long, attritional war, nor did they rotate veteran pilots to spread their experience to newer trainees. This weakness
would manifest itself in the later years of the war.

The Allies enjoyed a clear manpower advantage, yet Japan successfully prosecuted its war of conquest despite unfavorable force ratios. The
Japanese had the requisite aviator strength to realize their aims. One must
look to other aspects of their resource base to see what enabled these
Japanese successes.

In material terms, the numbers of aircraft available and the sizes of the
competing naval establishments represent the key areas of comparison
for the opening phase of the Pacific War. Both nations increased naval
construction in the prelude to the war. The Japanese implemented their
Marusan program in 1937, which eventually resulted in the construction of the super-battleships *Yamato* and *Musashi*, while America's Two-
Ocean Navy Act ensured a massive increase in US naval forces that did
not manifest itself until 1943.[70] In 1941 the IJN boasted 10 aircraft carri-

ers, 10 battleships, 37 cruisers, 110 destroyers, and 63 submarines. Total Allied naval forces in the Pacific amounted to 3 fleet aircraft carriers, 11 battleships, 35 cruisers, 100 destroyers, and 86 submarines.[71] Rough parity characterized most categories between the Allies as a whole and Japan, but the aircraft carrier disparity deserves further examination. In addition to the six fleet carriers that had conducted the Pearl Harbor raid, the IJN had four smaller light carriers that were able to steam with the fleet. In these opening months of the war, the US Navy had six fleet carriers between the Atlantic and the Pacific, as well as two older and slower light carriers. While the navy's light carriers contributed markedly less to American operations than did the Japanese light carriers, the Americans could, and did, transfer carriers between the Atlantic and Pacific Oceans. Nevertheless, Admiral Kimmel and Admiral Halsey claimed that the Japanese fleet held an advantage over the Pacific Fleet in "every category of fighting ship."[72] This was not accurate at the beginning of the war, but it soon became so. In the opening days of the war, Japan sank or neutralized eight American battleships at Pearl Harbor and two British capital ships (one battleship and one battlecruiser) near Malaya. The subsequent naval battles in the Indian Ocean and around the Netherlands East Indies also inflicted disproportionate losses on the Allied naval forces. These battles tilted the naval balance in favor of the Imperial Japanese Navy.

In December 1941, the United States had 12,300 aircraft in the USAAF and an additional 5,300 naval aircraft for a total of 17,600 planes. The Japanese initiated hostilities with 4,826 aircraft in the JAAF and 2,120 in the JNAF for a total of 6,946 planes. Production figures for the year 1941 provided a portent of things to come, with the United States making 26,277 new aircraft and the Japanese producing just 5,088.[73]

Yet, as was the case with the army, strength of numbers on paper does not tell the whole story. Many US aircraft were committed in other theaters, and the Japanese achieved lopsided kill ratios in initial air engagements. While conducting their southern operations, the Japanese brought more than 1,500 aircraft from the JAAF and from both land- and carrier-based naval aviation to bear against just 650 frontline Allied aircraft in the Philippines, Malaya, the Netherlands East Indies, and Burma.[74] Despite their overall numerical disadvantage, the Japanese concentrated superior numbers of aircraft over the battlefield when and where it counted during the opening moves of the war.

Even during this early stage of the war, however, Japan's limited aircraft production began to reveal itself as an Achilles' heel. Between December 1941 and April 1942, production struggled to keep pace with naval losses: The fighter pool grew from 660 aircraft to 676, with 300 losses and 316 new manufactures; the carrier strike aircraft pool decreased to 307 aircraft from a start of 330, while land-based strike aircraft increased from 240 to 277.[75] Naval leaders were aware of the problem. Fuchida later wrote that by April 1942 "the vast majority of units not only had no reserve planes whatever but were below normal operating strength."[76] On April 23, Admiral Ugaki noted in his diary: "What we regret most is the insufficient production capacity of aircraft."[77] Production statistics for 1942 reveal the growing discrepancy between the United States and Japan, with the former producing 47,826 aircraft and the latter increasing production only to 8,861 aircraft.[78] The wear and tear on Japanese naval aircraft and lack of replacements did not bode well for the future.

Thus, in material terms Japan held the numerical advantage over the Allies at the point of contact during these early days of the war. It did so, however, mainly because Tokyo enjoyed the strategic initiative and could dictate where and when battles would occur. The IJN began with only a marginal superiority over the Allied naval forces in most categories, but after its successful operations at Pearl Harbor and in the areas around Malaya and the Netherlands East Indies the Japanese advantage increased markedly. The pattern in the air mimicked that on the sea, but the Japanese started with an even larger airpower advantage at the various points of contact during their initial conquests. They pressed their airpower advantage to destroy those Allied air forces that attempted to resist the Japanese advances. These twin advantages on the sea and in the air made possible the capture of the vital resource areas that constituted Japan's initial strategic objectives.

Technology also played a role in Japan's conquests. Man usually designs technology to meet a need, address a problem, or overcome a challenge. Invariably, choices and tradeoffs characterize the development of new technology, often increasing effectiveness in one aspect while perhaps compromising another. Airplanes are no exception, and a strength or advantage in one aspect of combat performance often demands sacrifices in others.

Nevertheless, Japanese combat aircraft demonstrated several technological advantages over Allied aircraft during this phase of the war. Throughout the war, Japanese aircraft engines limited their aircraft's performance and therefore drove some design compromises.[79] To compensate for the limited power of their engines, the Japanese often reduced aircraft weight by excluding the use of armor and self-sealing fuel tanks in their fighter aircraft, both of which reduced combat durability. Japanese designers did work some wonders within these constraints, but they stressed range and agility over sturdiness and survivability. Whereas Allied fighters had an effective range of 150–250 miles, the Japanese could operate out to 350 miles. The Japanese "Zero" fighter operated from both land bases and aircraft carriers. It proved to be a terrifying nemesis of Allied pilots at the beginning of the war, and it boasted an incredible 1,000–1,200-mile range. Additionally, the G4M "Betty" twin-engine land-based naval bomber boasted impressive performance characteristics with a 3,745-mile range and a nearly 1-ton payload. Only in four-engine bombers did the Allies hold the edge, as Japan never produced any operational heavy bombers. Overall, however, Japan benefited from a technological edge in the air at this point of the war, due in part to the Allied priority given to the European theater and in part on the Allies' dated aircraft designs (which would soon be replaced by newer models).

Japanese army technology was on the whole not as impressive. Throughout their conquests, Japanese small arms proved effective and generally reliable even if not overpowering. Japan's subjugation of Malaya involved the use of dozens of tanks, while the British defenders had none. Japanese armor at the beginning of the war included the Type 95 light tank and the Type 94 and 97 medium tanks; all were slow and only lightly armed.[80] These Japanese tanks generally did not measure up to the newer Allied models, but this disadvantage was not of great significance. Although more important than some anticipated in jungle war, armor was nowhere nearly as important in the Pacific as it was in Europe.

The Japanese produced ships with a specific goal in mind. Japan's naval strategists understood that they could not outmanufacture the United States, so they focused instead on offsetting their presumed quantitative deficiency with qualitative superiority. Accordingly, they attempted to launch ships that were individually superior to their enemies' ships, with an emphasis on maximum offensive capabilities and speed. In particular, the IJN focused on night combat practice and torpedoes and guns that could outrange the enemy.[81] The battleship *Yamato*, launched in late 1941, was the largest in the world and carried 18-inch guns; Japanese cruisers outgunned their contemporaries with up to ten 8-inch guns and multiple torpedo launchers; and the Japanese *Fubaki*-class destroyers, designed for night torpedo attacks, represented a major offensive addition to the fleet. The Japanese, lacking radar capabilities, developed excellent optics to assist in their night fighting, and they developed the remarkable oxygen-fueled Type 93 "Long Lance" torpedo with its tremendous range, hitting power, and stealth through lack of a wake.[82] The United States

held an important edge in radar technology on its ships and for air warning ashore; but, as Admiral Halsey admitted, it often struggled to employ
such equipment effectively early in the war.[83] American torpedoes often
failed miserably, missing their targets, running too deep, and not deto-
nating upon contact because of multiple design flaws.[84] These torpedo
problems plagued the Americans well into the war.

On balance, Japan possessed an overall technological edge at the beginning of the war. Japan employed superior aircraft and superior naval technology to expand its empire. Those advantages the Americans enjoyed in
heavy bombers and in radar technology did not play a sufficiently large
role in early combat to tip the technological balance in their favor.

In the category of resources as a whole, Japan also barely edged out
the Allies at the beginning of the war, but this superiority would not last.
Japanese advantages in materiel and technology helped to offset the disparity in manpower in the opening campaigns of the war. However, like
a hockey team playing short-handed with exceptional players, qualitative
advantages would bring victory only if Japan could hold on to the puck
known as strategic initiative.

Intelligence

The intelligence struggle began before the shooting war. Prewar preju-
dices distorted both sides' impressions of the capabilities of the other.
Germany's successes against the Western powers caused the Japanese to
underestimate British Commonwealth forces' capabilities and also contributed to a superficial analysis of American war-making capacity.[85] On
the Americans' side, racial stereotypes shaped perceptions of their Japanese foes by discounting the capabilities of the Japanese carrier force as
inferior copies of the American model.[86] Pearl Harbor rudely corrected
that fallacy.

Japanese intelligence effectively supported the initial operations. Spies
in Hawaii provided the Pearl Harbor planners with accurate information about the status of American defenses and the US Pacific Fleet.[87]
Japan had complete information on US forces in Hawaii in large measure
from open-source intelligence such as newspapers and other publications,
in addition to personal observations.[88] General Brereton, as previously
noted, lamented the reach and effectiveness of Japanese espionage in the
Philippines; and Sakai confirmed the contribution of Japanese photo intelligence prior to the air raid on Clark Field. Indeed, photo intelligence
revealed that a previous estimate of 900 American aircraft in the Philip-

pines was wildly high of the mark, enabling the Japanese to plan the Philippine campaign with a relatively accurate assessment of the opposing air strength.[89] In November 1941, Japanese assessments of Allied strength in Malaya and the Netherlands East Indies amounted to 60,000–70,000 troops and 320 aircraft in the former and 85,000 troops and more than 300 aircraft in the latter.[90] These Japanese calculations tended to underestimate Allied manpower, as prisoner hauls revealed, while overestimating Allied air strength. Japanese signals intelligence knew of the departure, but not the composition, of the American task force destined to partake in the Battle of the Coral Sea.

The United States and its allies derived the vast majority of their intelligence from radio intercepts and decrypts. Yet, despite the remarkable success of the Magic decrypts beginning before the war, the Americans failed to anticipate the Pearl Harbor raid and tended to focus most of their energies on the Philippine Islands.[91] Signals intelligence clearly enabled the American resistance at Coral Sea and at the forthcoming Battle of Midway in June 1942. Yet, the Americans often struggled with more conventional intelligence means during this phase. Brereton, for example, lamented his lack of knowledge about the enemy air forces on Formosa before those forces destroyed his command in the Philippines in December.[92]

The Japanese clearly held an edge in intelligence collection and analysis during this first phase of the war. They pieced together a more realistic, if not entirely accurate, appraisal of the situation for each of their operations than did the Allies, and they reaped the corresponding rewards. The Allies had just begun to exploit their strategic advantage in radio intelligence at Coral Sea but would extend this advantage in the coming months. The changing relative capabilities of Japanese and American intelligence services played a major role in the shifting of the strategic initiative from the Japanese to the Americans in late 1942 and 1943.

Both sides also worked to protect their operations with counterintelligence and security measures. The Japanese guarded their Pearl Harbor plan zealously, and the success of that operation attests to the effectiveness of their security. However, the Japanese did not know that the Allies had broken their naval and diplomatic codes, a devastating security breakdown. American efforts also stuttered. Safeguarding the secret of the Magic breakthrough dominated American concerns, and they did this successfully. Yet, they failed to secure their defenses in the Philippines and Pearl Harbor from Japan's prying eyes, with devastating results.

Thus, the overall intelligence picture favored Japan during this opening stage. Tokyo had a clearer picture of the situation at the front, while the United States failed to capitalize fully on its greatest advantage—radio intelligence—to identify the enemy's main objective.[93] Despite the picture the United States pieced together, the Allies still misread their intelligence and underestimated Japan's abilities to conduct military operations and wage a war of conquest in late 1941 and early 1942.

Racism and cultural blinders contributed to the intelligence challenges for both sides and no doubt influenced the way the Allies underestimated the Japanese military threat. Western nations had been conditioned by decades of colonial rule over Far East lands to take for granted a racial and cultural superiority over Asians. During the first few months of the war, these attitudes undermined the US intelligence picture. Americans had assumed the Japanese to be inferior warriors and underestimated the effectiveness of the Japanese carrier force and Japanese pilots, thereby contributing to their intelligence shortcomings at the opening of the war. Similarly, the Japanese view of their *Yamato* race engendered similar feelings concerning their own superiority. The Japanese exaggerated their own spiritual strength and social cohesiveness while denigrating the material strength and moral fiber of the Allies.[94]

Strategic Acumen

Japanese strategic acumen at the beginning of the war represents something of a paradox. The Japanese military services rapidly achieved their initial goals, validating their planning and their assessment of the military balance at that time. Yet, this success also revealed an underlying vulnerability in their planning. According to Fuchida, "Japan's strategy-makers had been so engrossed in the immediate problem of acquiring oil resources that they had formulated no concrete strategic program for the ensuing course of hostilities after these resources had been won."[95] In January 1942, Admiral Ugaki felt that Japan must press its advantage through an attempted invasion of Hawaii to force a decisive naval battle.[96] In the subsequent strategic debate between the IJA and the IJN, the two forces eventually agreed to take advantage of their early dominance and extend the perimeter. This reformulated strategy, with the addition of new outer-perimeter operations directed at Fiji, Samoa, New Guinea, the Solomons, and Midway, triggered the subsequent campaigns that would eventually yield the strategic initiative to the Allies.[97]

At the beginning of the war, the Japanese strategists outclassed their American counterparts. The belated, mid-1941 American decision to revert to earlier plans to hold the Philippines with a forward defense on the beaches disintegrated under Japanese bombs at Pearl Harbor and Clark Field, exacerbated by MacArthur's poor operational decisions. The Allies could not mount effective counteractions to stem or reverse the enemy onslaught and save their possessions in the Far East. Thus, the strategy had to be significantly altered to fit the new conditions, seeking to maintain a few footholds for future operations.[98] This focus on Australia and locations south meant that Japanese plans to extend the perimeter in that same area threatened the new American strategic priorities.

Opportunities seized or lost remain a corollary of the strategic acumen discussion. Japan missed two significant opportunities during the opening hostilities. First, Admiral Nagumo's prudent decision to withdraw from Pearl Harbor after the second wave of his attack returned, as noted, left American dry docks and oil farms in commission, allowing for both a more rapid recovery from the raid and continued US naval operations from Hawaii. Second, the Japanese did not commence, and would never initiate, unrestricted submarine warfare against the Allies' vulnerable shipping resources because they remained focused on destroying enemy combat vessels rather than merchantmen. In contrast, the United States did not miss this opportunity, declaring unrestricted air and submarine warfare against Japan six hours after the attack on Pearl Harbor.[99] Later in the war, America would reap great rewards from this decisiveness.

The Japanese certainly bested the Americans and their allies in achieving surprise. Pearl Harbor, aided by some radio deception to keep the United States thinking that the Japanese carriers remained in home waters, clearly stunned the Americans and altered the strategic balance at the beginning of the war. The Japanese also achieved surprise in the Philippines and elsewhere as they secured their coveted resource areas. The United States achieved one notable surprise with the Doolittle Raid, and this had strategic consequences for the next phase of the war; but its immediate effects did not significantly alter the Pacific situation.

In short, the Japanese demonstrated superior acumen to that of the Allies at this stage in the war. Their plans more closely matched reality, and they secured their initial aims rapidly, demonstrating a good balance of ends, ways, and means for the first six months. They were not perfect, missing some critical opportunities, and their strategic decisions in early 1942 set the stage for the Allies to vie for and then take the strategic initiative in the conflict. Yet, with the arguable exception of their decision to expand the initial perimeter, during the opening phase of the war the Japanese proved as superior in judgment as they did in execution.

Combat Effectiveness

When measuring combat effectiveness in terms of accomplishing one's assigned mission with the least expenditure of resources in the shortest amount of time, the Japanese forces reigned supreme during this first phase of the war.[100] On land, sea, and air, Japan, with the temporary exception at Wake Island and the more significant exception in the Coral Sea, imposed its will on the Allies.

In late 1941 the IJA was an experienced, disciplined force, largely composed of light infantry forces that always preferred the offensive to the defensive. This army demanded near-suicidal bravery from its troops to compensate for lack of technology and firepower. The IJA held a long tradition of attacking at night that predated the invention of firearms; and, realizing it could not stand up to the growing industrial power of the Soviet Union, it returned to the tactics of night attack in the 1920s.[101] The Japanese answered the challenge of fighting a superior power with an emphasis on tactical surprise through night attacks unsupported by heavy weaponry, and they trained extensively in this mode. This night training paid handsome dividends when applied to amphibious operations early in the war. Adding the darkness of night to the already complex maneuver of amphibious attack did not slow Japanese landings in the Philippines, Malaya, Wake, Guam, or the Netherlands East Indies. The pattern continued with another successful night landing near Salamaua, New Guinea, in March 1942. The Japanese tactics, training, and discipline also served them well on land, where they rapidly and impressively overran larger Allied armies.

The IJN demonstrated similar skill and discipline in its early operations. Naval leaders sensed the coming war in the late 1930s, and the Combined Fleet's training and maneuvers were not conducted with peacetime safety limitations, but rather with full wartime intensity and risk.[102] The IJN swept aside Allied resistance in the southern operations as easily as the IJA did. From Pearl Harbor to Ceylon, the Japanese carrier force operated with impunity until checked at the Battle of the Coral Sea in May 1942. Part of the Japanese skill lay in the concerted use of multiple aircraft carriers, something the US Navy still struggled to master, due in part to the efforts and insights of their commander then, Minoru Genda. The Japanese skill in night fighting and their ships' superior armament also contributed to their successes.[103]

The Battle of the Coral Sea broke the string of Japanese naval victories. This battle requires closer scrutiny, as it revealed several strengths and weaknesses of both navies in the carrier warfare that would characterize the next stage of the Pacific War. Most noticeably, American carrier pilots proved to be more formidable foes than much of the resistance previously encountered by Japan's naval aviation elite. American naval aviators sank the Japanese light carrier *Shoho* with an estimated eleven bomb hits and five torpedo hits, also scoring three bomb hits the next day on the fleet carrier and Pearl Harbor veteran *Shokaku*. American pilots noted that the supporting Japanese ships scattered during their attack rather than forming a ring of defensive firepower around the *Shoho*.[104] The veteran Japanese pilots scored bomb hits on both American carriers present at the battle, sinking the *Lexington* and severely damaging *Yorktown*. Despite their apparent skill and success, the American attacks also manifested several faults. American torpedo bombers performed remarkably well against the *Shoho*; but in the next day's engagement against *Shokaku*, Japanese observers noted that the American aircraft launched their slowly running torpedoes too far away from the target, allowing the ship to maneuver and either avoid or outrun the threat. Yet, in his May 7, 1942, diary entry while the battle still raged, Admiral Ugaki lamented the loss of *Shoho* and wrote: "A dream of great success has been shattered. There is an opponent in war, so one cannot progress just as one wishes. When we expect enemy raids, can't we employ the forces in a little more unified way? After all, not a little should be attributed to the insufficiency of air reconnaissance."[105] In these remarks, Ugaki recognized some important areas of concern for the IJN in future operations. To this point in the war, Japan had been able to act at will, but the Allies were now regaining their balance.

Japan's naval and army air forces also demonstrated their combat effectiveness against their Allied counterparts, and Japanese airpower assisted the Japanese domination on land and sea. The IJA and IJN conducted exceptional prewar training, and their air forces followed suit. Prewar Japanese naval pilot training demanded stringent qualification standards and experienced a 60–70 percent attrition rate. In 1941 the average Japanese frontline pilot had 600 flight hours, with 50 percent of the army pilots and 10 percent of the navy pilots having combat experience.[106] At the beginning of the war, Japanese naval pilots received 700 hours of flight training compared to a respectable, but much lower, 305 hours for American naval pilots.[107] The Japanese training and experience paid off in combat. Allied pilots did not impress Saburō Sakai in the first few months of the war: "I am firmly convinced that in those early days of the war the individual skill of our pilots was definitely superior to that of the men flying the Dutch, Australian, and American fighters."[108] Several statistical indicators confirm Sakai's assessment of these opening stages.

While attacking Colombo in the Indian Ocean on April 5, 1942, 91 Japanese bombers escorted by 36 fighters tangled with 40 Royal Air Force fighters, with the latter losing 19 aircraft to the former's 7. During the entire foray into the Indian Ocean that April, the Japanese carrier strike force lost only 17 aircraft, while sinking 23 Allied merchant vessels.[109] Throughout the course of its destructive sweep from Pearl Harbor to Darwin and the Indian Ocean, the Japanese carrier strike force's moderate losses amounted to 50–60 aircraft in combat and 20–30 operational losses, leaving approximately 300 aircraft intact. The 21st and 23rd Air Flotillas also suffered only light to moderate combat losses of between ten and twenty aircraft each while conquering the southern resource area.[110] Sustaining these limited losses, the Japanese naval air force destroyed much of the American land-based airpower in Hawaii and, in conjunction with the JAAF, neutralized Allied airpower in Malaya, the Philippines, and the Netherlands East Indies—a perfect example of achieving one's aims rapidly with limited expenditure of resources.

But this early combat also exposed several weaknesses in Japanese methods. Although it represented an advantage during the opening phase of the war, the stringent selection standards and high failure rate of the IJN's pilot training system did not bode well for a long war with heavy pilot attrition. Furthermore, while Japanese fighter pilots bested their Allied counterparts in the close-in maneuvering engagements known as dogfights that characterized the opening months of the war, the Americans soon learned to avoid such engagements. Over time, the Allies developed tactics that neutralized the Japanese strengths.[111] During their rapid advance to the south, Japanese construction of forward air bases proceeded more slowly than anticipated, contributing to high operational losses on rough airfields. Finally, the advance to the south also demonstrated that the Japanese had much work to do in aircraft logistics if they were going to meet the other important aspect of combat effectiveness: endurance. By March 1942, the 23rd Air Flotilla's aircraft losses to all causes amounted to eighty-eight aircraft, but the flotilla received only forty replacement aircraft.[112] The swiftness of conquest in this first phase, however, temporarily masked these Japanese deficiencies.

Japan clearly held an edge in combat effectiveness throughout this opening phase of the war. Its forces dominated the Allied armies, navies, and air forces while extending Japanese conquests. The Battle of the Coral Sea checked this run of success, but on balance the Japanese achieved nearly all of their aims in a timely fashion and at low cost. Nevertheless, Japanese forces demonstrated weaknesses that would threaten their longer-term prospects.

Chance

Chance interceded in the first phase of the war in several instances. First and foremost, none of the US Pacific Fleet's aircraft carriers were in Pearl Harbor on the morning of December 7 because the Americans were taking steps to reinforce other points. Had the carriers been in port, there is little doubt they, like many of the battleships, would have been resting on the bottom of the harbor. The loss of the aircraft carriers would have left the United States with no means of countering the Japanese save submarines—a weak option given what we now know about the deficiencies of the American Mark 14 torpedo—and so Japanese plans to isolate Australia by taking Port Moresby would have stood a much greater chance of success. The carriers' survival ensured that the United States still had some means to resist Japan.

Nagumo's decision to leave Pearl Harbor after the second wave represents an example of human interplay with chance in this phase. He had already achieved a great victory and likely understood the importance of his carrier strike force to the Japanese war effort. From that standpoint his decision was sound and reflected the Japanese focus on attacking combatant vessels. It seems fair to say that Nagumo would have been justified in taking a calculated risk and pressing the attack further, with much potential for gain. That he did not do so represents the working of chance much in favor of the Americans.

On the other side of the coin, Generals MacArthur and Brereton missed a similar opportunity in the Philippines. When weather over Formosa delayed the departure of Japanese aircraft designated to strike the Far East Air Force, American commanders balked instead of launching their own strike. Whether the Americans could or would have caught the Japanese aircraft on the ground is moot. Had they launched a strike against Formosa, American aircraft would not have been caught and destroyed on the ground that afternoon. The overall outcome of the campaign would not likely have changed, but resistance in the Philippines may well have been more effective and durable if American air assets had not been halved on the first day. Fog at Formosa presented MacArthur with an opportunity, but hesitation in the face of the "fog of war" took that opportunity away.

CONCLUSIONS

The Japanese seized the strategic initiative on December 7, 1941, and held it throughout the first months of the Pacific War. They had superior resources overall, with strengths in technology and materiel offsetting deficiencies in manpower. Japanese intelligence supported their operations and strategic planning while shielding the timing and location of Japanese raids and amphibious landings. The Allies, despite important successes against Japanese diplomatic and naval codes, had major intelligence blind spots in this first phase of the war. Japan's opening moves caught them flat-footed despite awareness that war loomed. Japan's opening moves also proved to be well grounded in reality: the Japanese matched their ends, ways, and means for a rapid conquest of the resource areas they deemed necessary for the sustenance of their empire. Allied plans to hold Malaya, Singapore, and the Philippines shattered under the hammer blows of the Japanese army, navy, and air forces. In terms of combat effectiveness, the Japanese bested the Allies on the land and sea, as well as in the air. The Japanese achieved their objectives rapidly with minimal expenditure of resources, and any weaknesses in the endurance of their military forces were not made manifest by June 1942. Thus, Japan held advantages in four of the five underlying foundations of strategic initiative; these advantages allowed it to seize and maintain and exploit that initiative throughout the opening months of the war. Only in the matter of chance was the United States more effective (or lucky).

Nevertheless, Coral Sea served as a possible portent of the future. The US Pacific Fleet had regained some of its balance, and the Japanese had amended their strategy to incorporate a new outer perimeter to defend their conquests. Continued Japanese expansion and the renewed determination of the United States to resist that expansion led to a momentous battle near the tiny island of Midway. The results of the June 1942 Battle of Midway would do much to shape the course of the war for the next year and a half. All eyes now turned toward the Central Pacific.

7

Midway: The Initiative in Dispute

The Battle of Midway in June 1942 followed closely on the heels of the Battle of the Coral Sea. The second of the carrier engagements between the US Navy and the IJN, Midway reshaped the strategic calculus in the Pacific. The dramatic American victory captured the American public's imagination and has become a legend in US naval history. Yet, Midway neither decided the war nor granted the United States naval dominance in the Pacific theater. Instead, it opened a period in which the two sides disputed on more equal terms. Japan's loss of four of the six carriers that had struck Pearl Harbor returned some balance to the comparative naval strengths in the Pacific. As a consequence, Japanese strategic choices necessarily narrowed, while American freedom of action increased. The results of Midway allowed the United States and the Allies to challenge Japan's hold on the strategic initiative. June 1942 marked the end of Japanese free rein in the Pacific. In the battle's immediate aftermath, the Allies were still reacting to previous and ongoing Japanese operations in the southern and southwestern Pacific, but Midway allowed them to do so forcefully and to dispute the strategic initiative held by the Japanese since Pearl Harbor.

JAPAN'S DECISION TO STRIKE MIDWAY IN JUNE 1942

Since January 1942, Admiral Yamamoto and his chief of staff, Admiral Matome Ugaki, had focused on plans for taking Midway as a means with which to threaten Hawaii and force a decisive fleet battle. Yamamoto faced opposition from the Navy General Staff and the IGHQ. He continued to press for support for his plan to attack Midway and in April—as he had before Pearl Harbor—used the threat of resignation to secure grudging approval for the operation.[1] The Doolittle Raid that followed less than a fortnight later reinforced the decision and may have advanced the timeline for the operation. The IJA reluctantly agreed to postpone the Fiji, Samoa, and New Caledonia operations in favor of Midway, but at a cost. The compromise between the army and navy stipulated that while Midway would take priority over the Fiji operation, the navy had to divert forces from Midway to assault the Aleutian Islands.[2] This compromise substantiates the judgment of Jonathan Parshall and Anthony Tully, who maintain that the Aleutian thrust did not represent a psychological diversion from the main effort against Midway but was actually an important objective in the eyes of the Japanese high command.[3]

Timing played a key role in the Midway campaign. The advance of the start date placed Midway immediately on the heels of the Battle of the Coral Sea. That battle had cost the Japanese the use of the carriers *Shokaku* and *Zuikaku*. In effect, with the Midway operation and the Aleutian push occurring so closely to the attempt to invade Port Moresby, Japanese strategy was overreaching by trying to expand the perimeter in the Pacific in three places nearly simultaneously.[4] Timing also affected the Midway invasion tactically and operationally. The Japanese had trained for and succeeded in conducting night amphibious operations and, quite reasonably, intended to employ the tactic against Midway. Such landings demanded a full moon, which meant attacking no later than June 8, 1942, or delaying the operation until July.[5] This target date necessarily dictated the timing of the supporting naval and air operations, constraining the freedom of action for the Japanese carrier strike force commander, Admiral Chuichi Nagumo.

Yet, despite these constraints and the consequent dispersion of effort, Yamamoto judged that he retained sufficient strength to achieve his aims. Japanese planners were obviously aware that two of their own carriers were unavailable after the Battle of the Coral Sea. However, the weakness of their intelligence procedures prompted these same planners to believe pilot reports that they had sunk both American carriers that had participated in the battle.[6] Such a trade appeared to ensure continued Japanese superiority in aircraft carriers in the Pacific and, more specifically, for the operation against Midway. On the eve of battle, the Japanese expected the Americans to be unprepared to defend Midway, having lost heavily at Coral Sea and being most concerned with defending Australia.[7]

Admiral Nimitz Reacts to Japanese Plans

Throughout early 1942, the US Pacific Fleet's radio-intelligence capabilities grew steadily. As the Battle of Midway approached, the American network intercepted approximately 60 percent of the IJN's message traffic and read about 40 percent of what it took in. American officers pieced together Japanese plans for the attack on Midway and its supporting operations, such as "Operation K" for the reconnaissance of Pearl Harbor. Accurate intelligence allowed Admiral Nimitz to plan his own countermoves, such as thwarting the planned aerial reconnaissance.[8] There remained vastly different opinions of the Japanese objectives among US intelligence agencies and officers from Pearl Harbor to Washington, DC. Admiral King at first feared another Japanese strike to the south until intelligence from codebreakers in Melbourne confirmed the opinion of those at Pearl Harbor that Midway was the target. Nimitz, with some of his own staff officers still expressing skepticism about the presumed Japanese attack, committed his three remaining aircraft carriers, including the damaged but usable *Yorktown*, to the defense of Midway Island.[9]

In so doing, Nimitz took a calculated risk based upon his interpretation of the enemy's capabilities and intentions. General Delos Emmons, the army commander responsible for the defense of Hawaii, remained concerned about Japan's possible moves and cautioned Nimitz that the Japanese still held the capacity to strike at Oahu. Nimitz nevertheless chose to concentrate most of his forces for a "fleet-opposed invasion" of Midway, with a small naval surface force to counter the anticipated strike against the Aleutians. He also increased the aircraft, ground forces, and antiaircraft artillery defenses on Midway Island. With the intelligence he had on hand, Nimitz hoped to surprise the Japanese aircraft carriers at their most vulnerable moment. Nimitz directed his carrier task force commanders, Admirals Frank Fletcher and Raymond Spruance, to operate under the theory of calculated risk in which they did not expose their forces to attack by superior enemy forces unless they had the prospect of inflicting greater damage upon the enemy.[10] Nimitz's actions preceding the battle demonstrated a willingness to trust his own judgment, thereby manifesting the coup d'oeil so lauded by Carl von Clausewitz. His decision to oppose Yamamoto and Nagumo set the stage for an epic naval showdown north of the tiny island of Midway.

BATTLE JOINED

On paper, the resource balance for the Midway operation appeared daunting for the Americans. The Japanese armada included eleven battleships, four large aircraft carriers, one light aircraft carrier, one seaplane carrier, thirteen cruisers, and fifty-eight destroyers. The American force opposing them included just three aircraft carriers, eight cruisers, and fourteen destroyers. Japan also dispatched two light aircraft carriers, one seaplane carrier, six cruisers, and fifteen destroyers in the simultaneous attack on the Aleutians. The Americans mustered six cruisers, five Coast Guard cutters, and eleven destroyers to oppose these assault forces.[11] The Japanese heavy and light carriers expected to embark a total of 367 strike and fighter aircraft.[12] The three American carriers had a total of 233 operational aircraft, with an additional 96 combat aircraft and 31 long-range PBY Catalina patrol planes on Midway Island.[13] On paper, the Japanese enjoyed a staggering advantage in ships and a potential advantage of 38 combat aircraft for the coming battle.

The paper strength of the forces proved to be illusory. The Japanese plan dissipated carrier and aircraft strength among numerous, widely separated task forces, with two light carriers out of the main battle supporting operations in the Aleutians. The Americans concentrated their carriers in two groups, Task Force 16 and Task Force 17, operating in close proximity to one another and to the island of Midway. This division of forces was necessitated by the fact that *Yorktown* was delayed in Pearl Harbor undergoing repairs for damage suffered at the Coral Sea and could not join the others until the eve of battle. In addition, the Japanese carrier air groups operated below strength, leaving Nagumo and his four carrier strike groups with a total of 248 aircraft, not their nominal strength of up to 261. Taken together with the absence of the *Zuikaku* and *Shokaku* as a result of Coral Sea, the Japanese carrier strike group entered the Midway battle at only 60 percent of the airpower strength (412 aircraft) it had used at Pearl Harbor. Therefore, in the battle area north of Midway, Japan pitted 4 aircraft carriers, a total of 20 other warships, and 248 aircraft against 3 American aircraft carriers, 25 warships, an unsinkable island airfield at Midway, and nearly 330 strike and fighter aircraft.[14] Where it mattered most, the Americans outnumbered the Japanese, at least in the air. This fortunate condition was the product of both Nimitz's foresight and Japan's divided purposes.

Prelude to Combat

The United States dominated the Japanese in intelligence throughout the battle. Surprise had benefited early Japanese operations from Pearl Harbor to the Philippines and Malaya. American radio intelligence, however, precluded Japanese surprise at Coral Sea and again at Midway. Unlike the Coral Sea, off Midway the Americans exploited their radio intelligence to achieve surprise, hoping to attack the Japanese carrier strike force when it

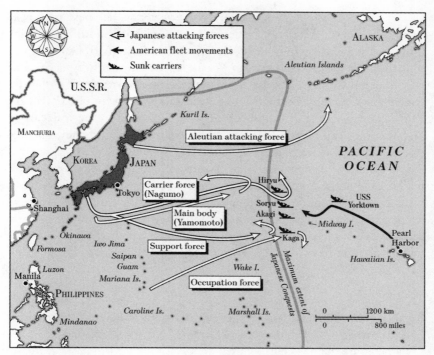

Map 4. Midway

was most vulnerable. Nimitz also employed a deliberate deception effort to make the Japanese believe the American focus remained on the South Pacific. In the prelude to battle, Nimitz ordered Vice Admiral Bull Halsey to expose Task Force 16, then consisting of the carriers *Enterprise* and *Hornet*, to Japanese detection near the Solomon Islands before it sailed for Hawaii. Admiral Ugaki's diary confirms that the ruse attracted Japanese attention when, on May 15, 1942, a flying boat from the island of Tulagi spotted and reported the location of the American task force.[15] (See map 4.)

Moreover, Nimitz's efforts required additional security measures to ensure the Japanese did not detect US preparedness for the invasion of Midway. Radio intelligence revealed Japanese plans for Operation K, an aerial reconnaissance flight over Pearl Harbor using flying boats with submarine support staged in the French Frigate Shoals, located 500 miles northwest of Hawaii. This operation commenced the last week of May, but Nimitz, armed with foreknowledge of Japanese plans, dispatched US vessels to the preplanned Japanese rendezvous point, forcing the Japanese to cancel the mission. This maneuver deprived the Japanese of timely intelligence on the American fleet on the eve of the battle. Further contributing to the Japanese blindness of US fleet dispositions, IJN submarines sent to scout the waters between Pearl Harbor and Midway arrived at their stations too late. The Japanese plan assumed, erroneously, that the American fleet would sortie from Hawaii only *after* the initial attacks on Midway. In fact, US radio intelligence permitted the two American carrier task forces to sail from Hawaii in late May, before the Japanese submarines could establish a picket line.[16] According to Fuchida, who was present at Midway, the Japanese "had not the slightest idea that the enemy had already sortied, much less that a powerful enemy force was lying in wait, ready to pounce upon us at any moment."[17] Thus, the Japanese entered the battle unaware of the location or intentions of the US aircraft carriers, while the US carrier task force commanders had a much clearer picture of what to expect and when to expect it.

The Carrier Forces Engage

Regardless of American advantages in these preliminaries, the battle still had to be fought, and its outcome was anything but foreordained. The actions taken by the on-scene commanders and the performance of American and Japanese aircrews on June 4, 1942, would settle the issue and set the stage for the next phase of the Pacific War. On June 3, two events confirmed the American intelligence appreciation of Japanese moves and validated Nimitz's trust in Hypo, his Pearl Harbor intelligence station. An alert naval patrol aircraft from Midway detected and shadowed the Japanese Midway invasion task force, with its troop transports, about 600 miles west of the island. That afternoon B-17 bombers from Midway attacked the troopship convoy but caused no damage. Meanwhile, the northern Japanese task force commenced its operations in the Aleutians with an air attack on Dutch Harbor.[18] The main event would open closer to Midway the next morning.

The Japanese initiated the action as planned in the early-morning hours of June 4. The day commenced with the predawn launch of search aircraft to scour the area to the northeast of Nagumo's carrier task force for any American naval presence and the launch of the 108-aircraft strike force against Midway. The Japanese reserved the remainder of their strike aircraft to counter any unexpected appearance of US warships. Once again, naval patrol aircraft from Midway spotted the Japanese, in this instance Nagumo's carrier force. Midway's radar detected the incoming Japanese air strike, allowing all the operational American aircraft to take off and avoid destruction on the ground. The Japanese pilots conducted the attack with their usual skill, but the escape of the American aircraft and the limited size of the strike force meant that the Midway airstrip remained operational.[19] Meanwhile, events to the north of the island began to unfold, much to the detriment of Nagumo's force.

Nagumo and his carrier strike force expected a busy morning but surely nothing along the lines of what transpired between 7:00 and 11:00 A.M. American patrol aircraft spotted Nagumo's carriers shortly before 6:00 A.M.; armed with the location of these carriers, American commanders launched a series of strikes against the enemy force. US Navy and US Army bombers armed with torpedoes and launched from Midway commenced the first attacks against the Japanese between 7:00 and 7:30 A.M.[20] The Japanese who saw these first aerial torpedo runs watched a performance that would characterize American torpedo attacks throughout the battle: the aircraft launched their torpedoes too far from their targets, and the torpedoes ran too slowly, making evasion easy.[21] As these attacks took place, Nagumo ordered his reserve aircraft to be rearmed for the second attack against Midway, a land target, as opposed to their existing state of readiness to strike against naval targets. Shortly thereafter, at 7:30 A.M., one of the Japanese search aircraft spotted an American naval task force but did not report the presence of aircraft carriers until fifteen minutes later when the search crew reported a single carrier. At that time Nagumo ordered the rearming of his aircraft reversed to deal with the unexpected shipborne threat. Unknown to Nagumo, *Hornet* and *Enterprise* began launching their aircraft to attack the Japanese carriers at 7:00 A.M. and *Yorktown* followed suit an hour later.[22] Events soon began to cascade out of control for the Japanese.

Midway's aircraft continued to pressure Nagumo's fleet, with two groups of dive-bombers and another series of attacks from high-level B-17 bombers disrupting the Japanese fleet from about 7:55 to 8:35 A.M., which delayed the recovery of the Japanese aircraft that had earlier struck Midway.[23] In a repetition of the previous day's attack against the Japanese transports and setting a pattern for future operations in the Pacific, the high-level B-17 bombers scored no hits against the maneuvering vessels below.[24] Between 8:35 and 9:15 A.M. things seemed to settle down for the Japanese strike force, which had yet to suffer any damage. Nagumo's carriers recovered the waiting Midway attack aircraft and continued to prepare to attack the recently located American carrier. Nagumo did not realize that this temporary lull represented the eye of the storm and that the onrushing second half of that cyclone would soon swamp his cherished carriers.

American attacks, this time consisting of carrier-borne aircraft, resumed shortly after 9:15 A.M. Torpedo Squadron Eight, from *Hornet*, followed by Torpedo Squadron Six, from *Enterprise*, attacked between 9:15 and 10:10 A.M. Torpedo Squadron Eight fell to the last man; Torpedo Squadron Six lost all but four aircraft to Japanese fighters and antiaircraft fire, scoring no hits against the Japanese ships. Despite the Americans' horrendous losses and poor results, these torpedo attacks prevented the Japanese carriers from launching their rearmed strike aircraft and drew the Japanese fighter cover down to sea level. Throughout the morning, American attacks had been strung out and sequential, making them easier for the Japanese to counter than a coordinated, multidirectional attack including both dive-bomber and torpedo aircraft. The next attack changed that dynamic to the detriment of Nagumo's carriers. Yet another American torpedo squadron, Torpedo Squadron Three, from *Yorktown*, began its run on the Japanese task force at 10:10 A.M., joined in part through happenstance by several other squadrons—Bombing Three, Scouting Six, and Bombing Six—within ten minutes.[25] After a series of inconclusive attacks by other aircraft, the American dive-bomber squadrons finally broke through the Japanese defenses. In rapid succession, American bombs holed the flight decks of the carriers *Akagi*, *Kaga*, and *Soryu*, with only *Hiryu* escaping unscathed to carry on the battle.[26] *Hiryu*'s captain chose valor over discretion in characteristic Samurai tradition and elected to continue to fight against what was now, with three Japanese carriers out of action, a clearly superior American carrier force.

Fight on *Hiryu* did, and for a brief time it engaged effectively. Shortly after the devastating American attack, *Hiryu* launched its first counterstrike: eighteen dive-bombers and six escort fighters—a meager package compared to that employed by both sides earlier in the morning. This relatively small force penetrated Task Force 17's defenses and scored three bomb hits and two near misses on *Yorktown*, another testament to the skill of Japanese naval pilots. *Hiryu* snuck in a second punch that afternoon, sending another small strike force of ten torpedo planes and six fighters that mistook the still afloat *Yorktown* for an as yet undamaged American carrier. The small force scored two torpedo hits on the already battered American vessel, putting it out of action (to be sunk later by a Japanese submarine as it was being towed back to Pearl Harbor). The remaining American carrier aircraft found and savaged *Hiryu* with a dive-bombing attack shortly after 5:00 P.M. that afternoon.[27] As the day drew to a close, the Japanese continued to maneuver and plan for an attempt to salvage victory at Midway. In fact, the loss of Japan's four carriers had decided the issue in the US Navy's favor.

Losses

Japan suffered a devastating defeat at the Battle of Midway. A cruiser and all four aircraft carriers in Nagumo's strike force ended up on the bottom of the Pacific, with the associated loss of all their aircraft and thousands of men. Japanese personnel losses included over 120 skilled aircrew—not a crippling loss but nevertheless significant—and more than 720 difficult-to-replace aircraft mechanics.[28] The Americans also paid a price. *Yorktown*, struggling with its recent wounds from Midway and the lingering effects of damage from Coral Sea, and the destroyer *Hammann* both sank as a result of a successful torpedo attack by the Japanese submarine *I-168* on June 6 as the vessels made their way back to Pearl Harbor. In addition to those two vessels, the Americans also lost some 150 aircraft and a total of 307 men.[29]

Performance in Battle

How did the Americans achieve such a complete victory? A brief examination of the combatants' performances in these actions offers some explanation for the final outcome and Japan's defeat.

Intelligence efforts before the battle enabled the Americans to begin the contest with a decided advantage in situational awareness and to surprise Admiral Nagumo with their carrier presence near Midway. In comparing the performance of the two sides' aerial reconnaissance efforts, the American efforts helped them maintain a situational advantage throughout the decisive morning of June 4, proving that Admiral Ugaki's observation following the Coral Sea—that the Japanese needed to pay particular attention to this area—was indeed prescient. During his postwar interrogation, Captain Y. Watanabe, a gunnery officer on Yamamoto's staff, cited Japanese search failures as the cause of the loss at Midway.[30] Fuchida agreed, lamenting the poor Japanese search plan employed during the battle.[31] In addition, a number of factors inhibited effective Japanese reconnaissance on June 4: Japanese doctrine left the majority of scouting to the floatplanes attached to their cruisers and provided for few search units aboard their carriers. Moreover, some of the floatplanes employed at Midway were older Type 95 aircraft with very limited range, the Japanese search plan employed only seven aircraft to cover an area the size of Sweden, and the Japanese cruisers launching the search aircraft experienced delays that put the aircraft behind schedule. One of the scout aircraft, in part because of the delay, spotted an American task force at 7:40 A.M. but misreported its position by 60 miles and initially failed to inform Nagumo that the force included a carrier.[32] In contrast, American patrol aircraft from Midway located the Japanese invasion task force on June 3, enabling a bombing attack, and then re-located Nagumo's carrier strike force the next morning. This allowed strike aircraft from Midway and the American carriers to attack that force repeatedly.

Technology also played an important role in the battle. Unlike the Americans, the Japanese had no radar on their ships at Midway; furthermore, they lacked radio-controlled fighter direction with which to vector their combat air patrols toward the attacking American planes.[33] The American carriers and Midway had both radar and radio-based fighter direction, which increased their situational awareness and allowed them to react quickly to the situation as events unfolded.

The primary US torpedo bomber employed at Midway was the TBD Devastator. This aircraft was the first all-metal carrier monoplane used in the US fleet and had been in service for five years when the war started. By the time of Midway, the TBD was obsolete. It had limited range, slow speed, and only light defensive armament; it also lacked self-sealing gas tanks, making it very vulnerable.[34] During the battle, only six of the forty-one TBDs that attacked the Japanese carriers survived.[35] The Nakajima B5N2 "Kate" torpedo bomber represented the Devastator's Japanese counterpart. This aircraft was large, relatively fast, and capable of carrying a heavy armament load, making it arguably the finest torpedo bomber in the world in 1941.[36]

The opening phase of the war had already revealed the merits of the Japanese fighter, the Zero. The US Navy countered at Midway with two versions of the Grumman F4F Wildcat. Lieutenant Commander John S. Thach, a Wildcat pilot who participated in the battle, lamented that the newer version of the Wildcat, the F4F-4, couldn't come close to matching the Japanese Zero in climb, maneuverability, and speed. Yet another Midway fighter veteran, Lieutenant Commander James Flatley, stressed the strengths of the Wildcat as excellent armament (either four or six .50-caliber machine guns, depending on the model) and survivability, while also pointing out that teamwork in the air could compensate for the aircraft's deficiencies.[37] In other words, the F4F had to hold its own until newer aircraft arrived in 1943.

Each navy also used dive-bombers during the battle. The Aichi D3A1 "Val" was a reliable and effective dive-bomber that the Japanese had planned to replace, but production delays forced the Vals to remain in frontline service.[38] The American dive-bomber, the SBD Dauntless, represented America's top performer at the battle. Bombs from this aircraft destroyed all four Japanese carriers, and it had good range, durability, defensive armament, speed, and carrying capacity.[39] The SBD, like the F4F, continued to serve the United States well into the next phase of the war. One final but significant note: the vaunted American B-17 high-level bomber, a technological marvel for its time with no Japanese equivalent, inflicted no damage against the Japanese fleet. Despite the USAAF's protestations (and numerous fistfights between navy and army officers after the battle), the B-17 was clearly designed for high-altitude strategic bombing of industrial centers, not for attacking enemy fleets that could take evasive action.

Technology can be beneficial, but it still must be employed properly by commanders and operators. Coral Sea provided both sides with their first experiences in standoff carrier warfare, but it occurred so close in time to Midway that there simply was no time for in-depth analysis of that battle's lessons or for more than basic modifications to carrier operating procedures.[40] When the meticulous Japanese plan, based on the expectation of achieving surprise at Midway, ran afoul of the unexpected American carrier presence, Admiral Nagumo struggled to adjust to the situation. In their groundbreaking reassessment of the battle, Parshall and Tully accuse the Japanese of "plan inertia," in which Nagumo's and his staff's overriding concern for adhering to doctrine and for maintaining the timetable of the operation prevented a more flexible and effective reaction in the face of the unanticipated threat.[41] The American commanders, in contrast, exploited the advantages intelligence and reconnaissance afforded them and handled their task forces competently in accordance with Nimitz's directive for assuming calculated risk. The results speak for themselves, with Japan suffering devastating carrier losses while inflicting only limited damage on the American fleet.

Operational performance was mixed for both sides. As was now customary, the Japanese launched an integrated attack against Midway using aircraft from multiple carriers, a feat the United States could not yet duplicate.[42] Yet, because of the ensuing flow of the battle, the Japanese never got the opportunity to launch such a coordinated attack against the American carriers. The Americans struggled to mount a coordinated attack from a single carrier, with their different squadrons locating targets in a staggered stream rather than a massive strike. The sequential nature of the earlier American air strikes on the Japanese fleet eased the Japanese task of defense. Experience, where they had it, showed for the Americans. *Yorktown*, having just fought at Coral Sea, was the only American carrier whose air group attacked in unison, aided by chance by bombers from *Enterprise*, and delivered the deathblows to three Japanese carriers. In marked contrast, *Hornet*'s air group suffered a nearly 50 percent rate of attrition on the morning strike, with many aircraft never sighting the enemy and no damage inflicted on the Japanese fleet.

Tactically, both sides demonstrated both skill and shortcomings. Japanese fighters savaged American torpedo bombers and successfully escorted three attacks that inflicted damage upon the Americans; but due to poor positioning and bad luck, they failed to protect their carriers from the American dive-bombers. Japanese pilots demonstrated impressive skill, attaining multiple hits against the *Yorktown* despite the small size of their strike forces. American fighters stood up to the mighty Zero but failed to protect their obsolete torpedo bombers and allowed small numbers of Japanese aircraft to damage one of their carriers severely. American strike aircraft performed in mixed fashion. No American carrier torpedo bombers scored any hits against the Japanese fleet, yet the dive-bombers demonstrated their skills by destroying four Japanese carriers.

Endurance contributed substantially to American combat effectiveness and thereby to the victory. The United States took an important edge in this arena even before the battle had begun. *Yorktown* arrived back at Pearl Harbor on May 27 needing an estimated ninety days of work to repair the damages suffered at Coral Sea. Nimitz demanded the carrier be made ready for action within three days; *Yorktown* sailed for Midway on May 30.[43] In contrast, both the Japanese carriers engaged at Coral Sea missed the Midway battle: *Shokaku* suffered significant damage that could not be repaired in time, and *Zuikaku*, although not physically damaged, could not reconstitute its depleted air group in time to make the sortie with the rest of the fleet. The same dichotomy in staying power was revealed on June 4. Excellent American damage control kept the *Yorktown* in action despite multiple bomb hits and induced the Japanese to strike the carrier a second time inadvertently, thinking it a different, undamaged American vessel. By contrast, the Japanese carriers present at Midway never recovered once damaged by American aircraft. A number of factors conspired to render Japanese damage-control efforts far inferior to those of the US Pacific Fleet, costing Japan its four best carriers for the remainder of the war.[44]

Chance

Chance and the human capacity for dealing with it influenced the battle on several occasions. Chance and the fog of war befuddled Nagumo when his search aircraft detected an American task force but made no mention of the presence of a carrier. Part of Nagumo's dilemma and hesitancy could be traced back to Japanese experiences in the Coral Sea, where they had launched an errant strike against an American oiler and destroyer, believing them to be a carrier force.[45] Nagumo's flat-footedness this time cost him the opportunity to inflict greater damage on the American fleet. Another chance event, related to poor navigation and execution by a search aircraft, meant that Nagumo missed the opportunity to detect an American carrier task force between 6:15 and 6:30 A.M. and possibly avert the ensuing disaster. The third significant example of chance involved the *Enterprise*'s dive-bomber group under the command of Lieutenant Commander Clarence Wade McCluskey. At 9:55 A.M. on June 4, with gas in their tanks dwindling, McCluskey's group nearly missed out on the action, until they sighted the Japanese destroyer *Arashi*, which had separated from Nagumo to chase an American submarine, racing north to rejoin the Japanese fleet.[46] This chance sighting enabled McCluskey's group to locate and attack Nagumo's task force at the same time as *Yorktown*'s air group, and from a different axis, thereby overwhelming Japanese air defenses. Moreover, the previous torpedo-bomber attacks had pulled the defending Japanese fighters down on the deck, out of position to intercept McCluskey.

A CHANGED NAVAL BALANCE IN THE PACIFIC

May and June 1942 were not kind to the IJN's carrier force. Losses at Coral Sea and Midway, which totaled five carriers, forced the Japanese navy to reorganize.[47] The United States suffered as well, losing both *Lexington* and *Yorktown*. The Japanese navy now sailed a hodgepodge of aircraft carriers: the modern and effective fleet carriers *Shokaku* and *Zuikaku*; the recently commissioned but less reliable *Junyo* and *Hiyo* (converted from ocean liners); and the light carriers *Hosho*, *Ryujo*, and *Zuiho*.[48] Less than a week after the battle, the carrier *Wasp* passed through the Panama Canal to augment the US Pacific Fleet's three remaining carriers, *Enterprise*, *Hornet*, and *Saratoga*.[49] The numbers were still skewed, at 7:4 in Japan's favor; but in reality the four large American fleet carriers matched up well against the heterogeneous collection operated by Japan, of which only the first two could be considered true fleet carriers. Despite Japan's continued numerical advantage in battleships, this shift in the carrier balance really meant a shift in the naval balance—and an evening of the odds.

STRATEGIC REACTIONS TO THE NEW NAVAL BALANCE

Japan's dramatic reversal at Midway thus altered the strategic initiative in the Pacific from having been clearly in the Japanese favor to being now in dispute. Both sides reevaluated their strategies to match their views of the new situation. The decisions made in the wake of Midway determined the future course of the war and set the conditions either for the Allies to seize the strategic initiative or for the Japanese to regain it.

Japanese Reaction and Reevaluation of Strategy

Following Midway, the Japanese attempted to conceal the extent of the disaster from their own public. In an active cover-up assisted by Emperor Hirohito, the wounded remained quarantined in hospital wards in Japan, the uninjured survivors of the lost carriers were quickly and quietly dispersed to other commands without receiving any shore leave, and the press reported Midway as another glorious victory for the imperial forces. More important for future strategy, the Japanese navy also concealed the full extent of its losses, and therefore the impact on its operational capabilities, from the IJA.[50]

As the Japanese strategic gaze again turned southward, the effects of the Midway battle immediately altered their plans, although their plans to expand in New Guinea and the Solomons remained intact. A week after Midway, however, the IGHQ ordered the 17th Army commander temporarily to delay the planned operations against both Port Moresby and Fiji–Samoa–New Caledonia. The next IJA directive, dated June 12, 1942, instructed the 17th Army commander to coordinate plans locally with the naval forces at Rabaul, initiating an overland operation to capture Port Moresby after securing positions on the northern coast of New Guinea. By the end of July, the Japanese commanders decided to cancel the Fiji–Samoa–New Caledonia operation altogether and to focus on their advances in New Guinea and in the lower Solomon Islands.[51] They thus planned to continue to expand their perimeter through offensive action, but in a more limited fashion.

US Reaction and Reevaluation of Strategy

Coral Sea had already demonstrated that the IJN was not invincible, and the Americans recognized the opportunity that their excellent intelligence provided them at Midway. The June 3, 1942, entry in Admiral Nimitz's command summary stated: "The whole course of the war in the Pacific may hinge on the developments of the next two or three days."[52] A follow-up entry the next day, after the battle had commenced, stated: "CincPac [message] 051225 generally records the start of what may be the greatest sea battle since Jutland. Its outcome, if as unfavorable to the Japs as seems indicated, will virtually end their expansion. We lost a large percentage of highly trained pilots who will be difficult to replace."[53] Before the battle had even ended, the US Pacific Fleet began to consider its implications.

In reality, the thoughts of the Joint Chiefs of Staff preceded the battle as they also turned their gaze southward. A JCS memo to the Combined Chiefs on May 24, 1942, assessed the current state of affairs in the Pacific and revealed deep concerns over the Japanese threat to Australia, citing Japanese force superiority and their geographically advantageous position of interior lines.[54] A week later, Admiral King followed up this report with a message to Nimitz discussing the importance of destroying advanced Japanese bases, such as that located at Tulagi in the Solomon Islands, in order to protect Australia.[55] The results at Midway provided the Americans with an opportunity to act on these thoughts, a topic of much strategic debate at the highest levels of the command structure.

Admiral King and General MacArthur both recognized the window to act afforded by the victory at Midway. A June 8, 1942, memorandum from MacArthur to Marshall argued that an offensive against the New Britain–New Ireland area, using a Marine division, two US Army divisions, and an Australian division supported by two aircraft carriers, stood an excellent chance of success if implemented quickly. King recognized Midway as a "golden opportunity" but had his own ideas for action in the South Pacific Area.[56] He replied to Marshall regarding MacArthur's proposal, stating the US Navy already had plans for operations in the area that would be predominantly naval and amphibious in character, and he felt operations aimed directly at Rabaul premature.[57] These differences in opinion soon led to infighting over who should command any upcoming operation in the southern Pacific.

As plans crystallized, Marshall and King exchanged a series of pointed memoranda discussing the question of command, with Marshall favoring

MacArthur and King favoring Nimitz. Marshall emphasized the need for unity of command and stressed that the major objectives of the upcoming action lay in the area afforded to General MacArthur, the South West Pacific Area. King responded aggressively, arguing that the initial portion of the operation must be conducted predominantly by forces from the South Pacific Area and that MacArthur's forces could provide little in the way of support and—startlingly—threatening to move ahead with the operation with or without US Army support. Marshall took exception to the threat and hoped to resolve the issue through direct, personal discussion.[58] The two continued working toward a solution until they reached a satisfactory compromise that granted naval command for the first portion of the upcoming offensive, occupying portions of the lower Solomon Islands.

The concept of this offensive, agreed to by the JCS on July 2,1942, laid the groundwork for the future course of the war. The "Joint Directive for Offensive Operations," signed by King and Marshall, stipulated three sequential tasks for the offensive: seizure and occupation of the Santa Cruz Islands, Tulagi, and adjacent positions under the command of CINCPAC; occupation of the remainder of the Solomon Islands, Lae, Salamaua, and the northeastern coast of New Guinea under the command of General MacArthur; and the seizure and occupation of Rabaul and adjacent positions in the New Guinea–New Ireland areas.[59] The JCS set the target date for the first task as August 1 and reserved to themselves the timing of the remaining tasks and the transfer of command. Task one represented a limited offensive in reaction to Japanese incursions in the south, designed to secure the lines of communication to Australia and set the conditions for later, more substantial, advances when conditions allowed.

Roosevelt and the Impact of Grand Strategy on the Pacific in Mid-1942

While King and Marshall haggled over the command structure of the forthcoming counteroffensive, they also participated in another debate involving global strategy. This exchange had even greater influence on the course of the Pacific War and the Allied seizure of the strategic initiative therein.

Competition for resources between the Pacific theater, particularly the South Pacific, and the European theater had already required presidential intervention. Roosevelt sent a memorandum to Marshall on May 6, 1942, in response to memos from both King and Marshall concerning resource allocation among the theaters. Roosevelt clearly expressed his preference to focus on Operation Bolero, the buildup of forces in England in preparation for a second front against Germany to relieve pressure on the Soviet Union, over sending too many resources to the South Pacific, despite the Japanese threat to Australia.[60] If the president believed this memo had settled the matter, he was mistaken.

Plans for a counteroffensive in the Pacific coincided with strategic debates between the Allies, as the members of the JCS began to sour on the strategic judgment of their British cousins. Roosevelt's decision in May 1942 pleased Marshall because of his belief that Germany represented the bigger threat and had to be defeated as quickly as possible. Yet in July, the British began backing away from their earlier commitment to a second front in Europe in late 1942 or 1943. The British instead proposed an Allied invasion of North Africa to complement British operations in Egypt and Libya. Such an operation would undoubtedly postpone Operation Roundup, the planned 1943 invasion of continental Europe. Marshall balked at what he considered a dangerous diversion of American resources and argued, with King's backing, that, should the British abandon Bolero and Roundup, the United States should turn its full attention against the Japanese threat.[61] Roosevelt, intent on keeping the American focus on the European theater, called the officers' bluff. He ordered Marshall and King, along with presidential adviser Harry Hopkins, to proceed to London and confer with the British for the next move in the European theater.[62] Roosevelt issued his guidance to these representatives in a July 15, 1942, memorandum that stipulated they should attempt to remain in compliance with the initial agreements for operations in Europe but that, if no agreement could be reached, they could accept a North African operation as proposed by the British. He again emphasized his rejection of the plan to focus on Japan. In this memorandum, pointedly signed "COMMANDER-IN-CHIEF," Roosevelt again expressed his concerns regarding the possible collapse of the Soviet Union; listed the myriad dangers he associated with the loss of the Middle East and the Suez Canal; and stressed that the defeat of Germany, in his view, "means the defeat of Japan, probably without firing a shot or losing a life."[63] The president made clear his position as commander in chief and his expectations on strategy for 1942 and beyond. Roosevelt's determination to focus on Germany necessarily came at the expense of resources to the Pacific and would make seizing the strategic initiative in that theater more difficult.

CONCLUSIONS

The Japanese suffered a stunning defeat at Midway. Nimitz had capital-
ized on his intelligence superiority and taken a calculated risk that paid
handsome dividends, revealing his strategic acumen. His subordinates
performed effectively, though not flawlessly, and delivered the firepower
necessary to cripple the Japanese carrier strike force. The Japanese performed well tactically, but American carrier endurance and durability,
both before and during the battle, helped offset the Japanese tactical skill
at both Coral Sea and Midway. The Japanese were inflexible in the development of their plan, and Nagumo struggled in his efforts to operate
in a confusing, swirling battle. The United States benefited from radar,
which helped with American situational awareness and gained time during combat. The Japanese had superior torpedoes, torpedo bombers, and
fighters, but the flow of the battle, in no small part attributable to the
surprise appearance of the American fleet, undermined the potential of
these weapons. As a result, Japan lost four of its best fleet carriers, while
the Americans lost only one. This changed the naval balance in the Pacific
in terms of carrier striking power, placing the United States on a more
equal footing with Japan.

The change in carrier balance, in turn, shifted the strategic calculations
of each side. The Japanese looked south and planned to continue their
advance on New Guinea overland and in the Solomons via short island
hops. They canceled their ambitious operation to attack Fiji–Samoa–New
Caledonia. The Americans sensed that Midway provided them a fleeting
opportunity to counterattack. They, too, looked to the southern Pacific.
MacArthur envisioned his own ambitious plan to take the entire New
Britain–New Ireland area. King thought that proposal too ambitious and
planned a limited offensive in the southern Solomons. If successful, the
Solomons attack would protect sea lines of communication to Australia
and establish the conditions for future advances up the Solomon Islands
chain. The JCS had to work out their command disagreements. In the
event, they developed an acceptable internal compromise while at the
same time conducting a debate with their British allies over Atlantic strategy. Roosevelt rejected JCS plans to focus on the Pacific in the event the
British insisted on a North African campaign, thereby ensuring that the
Allied struggle to wrest the strategic initiative from the Japanese would
take place without a large influx of resources.

Despite the lopsided results of the battle, Midway did not hand the strategic initiative to the Allies. Instead, this battle placed the initiative in dispute. The Japanese, however, thought otherwise. Unaware of the magnitude of the Midway defeat, the IJA sought to exploit that initiative by attempting an overland attack on Port Moresby, New Guinea.[64] The Combined Chiefs of Staff, in a memorandum dated July 7, 1942, also noted its assessment that Japan retained the strategic initiative, and it anticipated an advance in the southern Pacific as a possible enemy course of action.[65] In reality, the Americans now enjoyed a freedom of action they had not experienced since Pearl Harbor. King's plan to hit the lower Solomons amounted to a limited offensive designed to check the Japanese plan to further expand its defensive perimeter.[66]

Roosevelt would not allow a full-blown focus on the Pacific, but the Americans felt compelled to do what they could to protect the sea route to Australia. Midway afforded them the chance for a counterpunch and enabled them to contest the strategic initiative. The counterpunch soon evolved into a brawl and ensured that the course of the Pacific War would run through the southern and southwestern Pacific until late 1943.

8

New Guinea and Guadalcanal, July–October 1942: The Initiative Remains in Dispute

Following Midway, both combatants focused their strategies on the southern Pacific, placing them on a collision course for an epic eight-month struggle in two intertwined campaigns: one in eastern New Guinea, also known as Papua, and the other on Guadalcanal. Historiography often examines the two campaigns separately, in part because the two opponents viewed them as such: both the IJA and MacArthur's army-dominated Southwest Pacific headquarters focused on New Guinea, while the IJN and Nimitz's navy-centric Pacific Ocean Area headquarters became locked in conflict over the Solomons. Yet, the combined results of these two parallel campaigns enabled the Allies to seize the strategic initiative from the Japanese.

In the opening stages of these campaigns, the outcome remained very much in doubt, and in both campaigns the Allied actions initially represented reactions to the Japanese strategy of continued advance. The Japanese aimed to cut off Australia, while the Allies fought desperately to keep the lines of communication open between the South Pacific and the United States.

IMPLEMENTATION OF THE OPPOSING POST-MIDWAY STRATEGIES

The authorizations for the Japanese advances in New Guinea and the Solomons reveal much about the Japanese command structure. The Japanese army had no detailed plans for the Pacific War following its initial conquests. It had instead planned to focus on the continental concerns of China, Burma, and the Soviet Union.[1] However, in mid-1942 IGHQ began to analyze the possibilities of an overland advance from northeastern New Guinea to capture Port Moresby. In June and July, the IJA studied the feasibility of an advance from Buna, on the northeastern coast of New Guinea, over the imposing Owen Stanley Mountains via the Kokoda Trail to seize the vital Allied outpost at Port Moresby. The commander of the South Seas Detachment, General Tomitaro Horii, felt success was unlikely without the construction of better roads. Nevertheless, on July 17, 1942, Lieutenant Colonel Masanobu Tsuji, a staff officer from IGHQ sent forward to coordinate, authorized the overland advance on his own authority. At this point, IGHQ was leaning toward an overland attack but was waiting for an assessment from the 17th Army before issuing further orders.[2] Not unlike events in China and Manchuria during the 1930s, a midlevel army officer acting on his own initiative wielded undue influence on Japanese actions, prompting the 17th Army to press ahead with the overland attack.

Meanwhile, the advance in the Solomon Islands furthered IJN aspirations. Having seized Tulagi in the southern Solomons earlier in the year, the IJN aimed to convince its army counterpart that further advances were necessary to secure Rabaul, prepare for continued action to isolate Australia, and prevent the Allies from using the Solomons as a base for counterattacking Japanese possessions in the southern Pacific. The IJN's vision of future operational activities included the construction of additional air bases in important locations on New Guinea and in the Solomon Islands chain.[3] Thus, the IJN began examining the possibility of placing an airfield on Guadalcanal in the lower Solomons in late May 1942, and the Navy General Staff authorized its construction on June 13.[4] This activity did not escape Allied notice.

These two operations—the advance over the Kokoda Trail and the construction of the Guadalcanal air base—had commenced with the IJA's tacit approval but without specific agreements or additional army resources. The army did not anticipate a significant drain on its resources to the southern Pacific and kept its eyes on continental Asia. But when these operations began, they quickly drew the IJA into two desperate struggles in some of the most difficult and formidable environments in the world.[5]

The Allies' Move to Implement Their Planned Counteroffensive

The Allies remained intent on the Germany First grand strategy, which President Roosevelt forcefully reaffirmed in July. Nevertheless, the Allies, prompted by Admiral King, fully intended to seize the opportunity presented by their victory at Midway. The July 2, 1942, declaration by the JCS served as the basis for the upcoming counteroffensive, and the Americans prepared to move on Task One: the seizure of the Santa Cruz Islands, Tulagi, and adjacent positions, including Tanambogo, Gavutu, and Guadalcanal. Admirals King and Nimitz, with the US Army's agreement, assigned the task to Vice Admiral Robert T. Ghormley and his recently activated South Pacific Command. Nimitz had advised Ghormley that one of his chief duties as Commander, South Pacific would be to prepare a major amphibious offensive against the Japanese positions.[6]

Ghormley, however, hesitated in implementing King's directive. On July 11, 1942, he sent a message to both King and Nimitz stating the operation was feasible only if MacArthur provided the land-based aircraft needed to interdict the Japanese in the northern Solomons.[7] MacArthur shared Ghormley's doubts about the forthcoming operation, and both felt that the Allies should delay a counteroffensive until they had the strength to accomplish all three tasks envisioned by the JCS in rapid sequence.[8] The Joint Chiefs recognized the risks involved, but it also knew the world situation meant that sufficient resources would be a long time in coming and believed the rapid accomplishment of the first task "absolutely essential."[9] The operation, code-named "Watchtower," would proceed as planned despite its risks and the objections of the two area commanders appointed to carry it out. The result was a frantic series of improvisations that cost the American forces dearly.[10]

THE CAMPAIGNS BEGIN

Both the Japanese offensive advances in New Guinea and the US moves against the lower Solomons occurred over the objections and pessimistic estimates of the local commanders. The drawn-out struggles in both areas validated many of the concerns expressed by those appointed to carry out these hasty operations. The campaigns hung in the balance for some time, with neither side sure who would emerge victorious. In July 1942, the Japanese moved first.

Buna, Gona, and the Kokoda Trail

In preparation for the overland advance on Port Moresby, the Japanese moved on Gona and Buna in northeastern New Guinea in late July. The initial elements of the invasion force departed Rabaul Harbor on July 20 and landed near Buna and Gona during the late afternoon and early evening the following day.[11] Allied intelligence had anticipated a Japanese move to New Guinea. Japanese aerial reconnaissance of the Buna and Kokoda areas telegraphed their intentions, while radio intelligence and documents captured by an Australian guerrilla force near Salamaua indicated the future deployment of several Japanese units to New Guinea.[12] The Allies responded to the landings with a series of fifteen air attacks against Buna and Gona, ranging from single fighter aircraft to groups of heavy and medium bombers. Despite this Allied reaction, which damaged one transport and one destroyer, the landings proceeded apace, and Buna quickly fell to the Japanese.[13]

After securing Buna and Gona, the Japanese advanced rapidly south on the Kokoda Trail, moving at night to avoid attacks by Allied aircraft.[14] Japanese construction units completed a rudimentary airfield at Buna by August 18, which enabled the arrival of the main body of the South Seas Detachment on that date.[15] A harrowing struggle against Australian troops along the Kokoda Trail soon developed.

MacArthur and the senior Australian commander, General Thomas Blamey, had anticipated the possibility of a Japanese advance on Port Moresby from the Buna area and had taken steps to prepare for this eventuality.[16] The Japanese, buoyed by their successes to date, nevertheless proceeded with confidence. The words of Vice Admiral Fukudome provide some insight into the thinking of Japan's strategists at this point in the war and help explain the course of events in the Solomons and on New Guinea:

> The [Japanese] Army thought that the [Owen Stanley] mountains could be very easily crossed. Back of that thought was an erroneous impression on the part of the Japanese Army that the U.S. Army presented no serious problem, in other words the Army estimated the U.S. Army much too lightly; that applies also to the Australian Army. Our Army learned this truth only after the reverses at GUADALCANAL and the SOLOMONS. This under-estimation of U.S. and Australian Armies led to the belief that even after we lost GUADALCANAL [in early August 1942] that that position could be easily recovered with perhaps as small a force as 500 crack troops. The same idea was behind the Army belief that the crossing of the OWEN STANLEY range would be a simple operation.[17]

The battle along the Kokoda Trail began almost as soon as the Japanese secured Buna. It was anything but simple. (See map 5.)

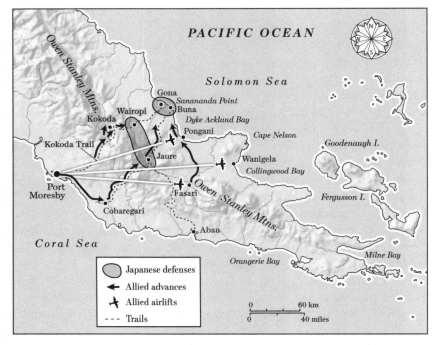

Map 5. The New Guinea Campaign

By mid-August 1942, more than 14,000 Japanese had landed in the Buna area to support the overland march on Port Moresby via the Kokoda Trail. Among them were 2,000 soldiers of the 41st Infantry Regiment, selected for the operation by General Horii because of its jungle-fighting experience gained in Malaya. Little did they know that the veterans of the Australian 7th Division, with two years of combat experience in the Middle East, were racing to meet them. Following their pattern in Malaya, the Japanese made good progress in August and early September, pushing the Australians back to Imita Ridge within 40 miles of Port Moresby.[18] However, the rudimentary logistical infrastructure strained to support the Japanese advance, greatly limiting the ammunition available for their machine guns and supporting artillery. Japanese planning, based in part on photoreconnaissance, erroneously assessed that forces could be supplied via motorized transport from Buna to the village of Kokoda. This faulty presumption contributed to the Japanese supply difficulties. By mid-September, the Australians had dug in at Imita Ridge and held their ground, while the Japanese halted to rest, resupply, and reinforce their efforts with elements of the 2nd Division prior to a final push on Port Moresby.[19] Those reinforcements never arrived, and the Japanese would advance no farther.

The Australians, fighting over the same terrain and under the same conditions, faced their own sustainment difficulties. They met the formidable supply challenge through the combined use of motorized transport, horses and mules, native carriers, and air-dropped materiel.[20] The Australians were able to recover only 75 percent of the latter. Despite its best efforts, the Australian 7th Division remained logistically constrained. In mid-September, the Australians estimated that they outnumbered the Japanese on New Guinea by 30,000 troops to the enemy's 10,000, but they also believed the Japanese had superior forces at the point of contact because of their own difficult logistical situation.[21]

The supply situation, the Australian position on Imita Ridge, the Allied position at Milne Bay (see next section), and events in the Solomons altered the New Guinea campaign in September 1942. Toward the end of August, the Japanese army had ordered Horii to limit his advance and then, on September 23, directed the South Seas Detachment to abandon its advance on Port Moresby and fall back toward Buna.[22] Meanwhile, the Australians started to advance cautiously in late September.[23] Throughout October, the Japanese withdrew gradually with the Australians close on their heels, maintaining pressure and demonstrating jungle-fighting skills of their own. Some of the Japanese troops soon resorted to cannibalism to make up for their lack of supplies, and the Australians continued their advance to the town of Kokoda by the beginning of November.[24]

Battle of Milne Bay, August–September 1942

While conducting the overland attack on Port Moresby, the Japanese also turned their attention farther east to the Allied position and airfields near Rabi and Milne Bay, New Guinea. On August 25, 1942, the Japanese landed the Kure 5th Special Naval Landing Force, a battalion-size formation, via a cruiser, destroyer, and subchaser flotilla in the face of stout Allied resistance near Milne Bay.[25] Allied air attacks soon destroyed the Japanese stores of food and ammunition, placing the landing force in a precarious situation. On August 29, the Japanese reinforced their efforts by landing the Kure 3rd and Yokosuka 5th Special Naval Landing Forces, but Allied airpower continued to ravage the invaders. Allied air attacks forced them to move at night and hide during daylight hours. Furthermore, reinforcements sent from Buna lost all of their landing barges to

Allied air attacks and became stranded for two months on nearby Good-enough Island.[26]

MacArthur's intelligence helped the Allies stay ahead of the Japanese moves. General Headquarters, South West Pacific Area, Situation Report No. 347, dated August 25, 1942, recorded the air attack by twelve P-40 aircraft that contributed to the marooning of the Japanese on Goode-nough Island and further noted tracking of the Japanese convoy that landed the assault force at Milne Bay.[27] Prior to these actions, Allied in-telligence anticipated a possible Japanese move against Milne Bay based on observations of Japanese aerial reconnaissance and on captured docu-ments that indicated Milne Bay as a target.[28] The Allied presence at Milne Bay grew accordingly. On August 8, the force consisted of nearly 6,200 men, and by the 22nd it had increased to more than 8,800 men.[29]

The Japanese did not have a clear picture of the Allied situation at Milne Bay, estimating that the area was being held by a much smaller force of up to three companies and 20–30 aircraft. They initially landed a force of 1,170 naval assault troops with some limited tank support and on August 28 reinforced them with 770 more troops. These combined forces ran into strong resistance from the Allied troops defending the area. The Japanese soon realized that they had no hope of achieving their objectives and taking the surrounding airfields. Admiral Gunichi Mikawa, the 8th Fleet commander at Rabaul, decided to evacuate the force; the surviving Japanese returned to New Britain by September 6. The Japanese had lost nearly 600 killed in the operation to the Allied losses of 322 killed and 198 wounded.[30] Having preceded Horii's retreat along the Kokoda Trail, the Japanese defeat at Milne Bay represented the first significant Japanese defeat on land in the Pacific War.

Guadalcanal: A Struggle on Land, on Sea, and in the Air

The Japanese occupation of Tulagi in May 1942 initially attracted Allied attention to the lower Solomon Islands, but soon Japanese activity on the nearby island of Guadalcanal began to garner even greater interest. The Allies monitored the area through a variety of means. A South West Pacific Area situation report from May 20, 1942, noted that a Japanese Kawanishi four-engine flying boat made a thorough reconnaissance of Guadalcanal three days earlier over an area suitable for the rapid con-struction of a fighter airfield. A month later, another report noted mul-tiple destroyer visits to the same area and fires on the plains, indicating Japanese preparations for airfield construction.[31] The Australian Coastwatcher network, including the detachment under the famous British operative Martin Clemens, monitored the construction of the airfield and estimated a Japanese strength of 3,000 on the island.[32] These reports and the danger this airfield represented to the American lines of communication with Australia explain the importance the JCS placed on expediting the operations against Tulagi and surrounding areas despite the objections and hesitations of Ghormley and MacArthur.

The operation proceeded in early August, representing the first Allied counteroffensive of the Pacific War. The Japanese knew the Americans had something in the offing, but they did not know the objective or the scope of the forthcoming effort. The 8th Signals Unit of the 8th Base Force at Rabaul and the Navy Department of the Imperial General Staff both noted changes and increases in American signals communication in July and anticipated the changes as a precursor to a forthcoming operation. Admiral Shinzo Onishi of the 8th Fleet anticipated a potential move against Guadalcanal, but on August 4 the Imperial Navy Department issued a memorandum predicting an upcoming American operation to reinforce New Guinea.[33] On August 7, the American force, centered on the hastily cobbled-together 1st Marine Division (reinforced), landed at Tulagi and Guadalcanal, surprising the Japanese, much to the chagrin of Admiral Ugaki of the Combined Fleet.[34] A grueling six-month campaign had begun.

Local Japanese forces at Rabaul reacted rapidly and violently to the landings. On August 7, fifty-three aircraft from Rabaul attacked while planes from several American aircraft carriers attempted to defend and support the landings. From Rabaul, Admiral Mikawa sortied five heavy cruisers, two light cruisers, and a destroyer to attack the American fleet the following evening in a night engagement.[35] Meanwhile, the Marines seized the smaller islands of Tulagi, Tanambogo, and Gavutu after fierce fighting and, by their second day ashore on Guadalcanal, had taken the nearly completed Japanese airfield, encountering little resistance. (See map 6.)

The ensuing naval engagements off Savo Island on the night of August 8–9 and Cape Esperance on October 11 had serious ramifications for the course of the campaign and for the forthcoming naval struggle. Savo Island was an unmitigated disaster for the Allies, but it could have been worse. As in the opening stages of the war, Japanese training in night fighting and their remarkable Long Lance torpedoes allowed the IJN to dominate its foe. The Allies lost four cruisers, with another cruiser damaged, and more than 1,000 dead, without inflicting any serious damage

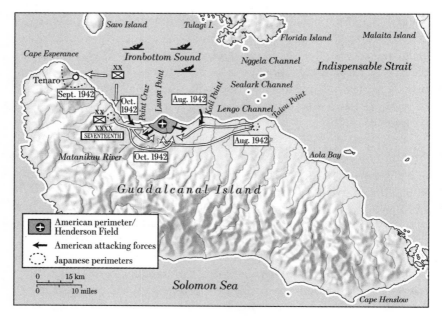

Map 6. Guadalcanal, August–October 1942

on the Japanese.[36] Admiral Mikawa did not press on to attack the US transports farther to the south, missing a great opportunity to send valuable Allied shipping to the bottom of the sea and to stop the Allies in the opening phase of the operation to reduce Rabaul.[37] Nevertheless, the battle established Japanese dominance in the waters around Guadalcanal, at least during the hours of darkness. The Allies did not contest this control until the Battle of Cape Esperance two months later. The Americans acquitted themselves well in this latter engagement, sinking one Japanese cruiser and one destroyer while damaging another cruiser for the loss of one destroyer and damage to another destroyer and a cruiser. The Japanese, however, still managed to get some of their destroyer transports through to land more troops and artillery to reinforce their forces on Guadalcanal.[38]

These major night surface engagements alternated with two carrier battles: the Battle of the Eastern Solomons on August 24–25 and the Battle of Santa Cruz on October 25–26. In the first encounter, two American carriers attempted to stop the landing of Japanese reinforcements at Guadalcanal, distantly screened by a protective force that included three Japanese carriers. When the battle ended, the Americans had lost twenty aircraft and had one carrier, the *Enterprise*, heavily damaged by three bomb hits, but they had turned back the Japanese reinforcements, destroyed ninety Japanese aircraft, and sunk one light carrier and one destroyer while also damaging a cruiser and a seaplane tender. Having frustrated Japanese aims, the battle was a clear American victory. The October battle was not as clearly decided; and between the Eastern Solomons and Santa Cruz battles the US Navy lost the carrier *Saratoga*, damaged on August 31, and the carrier *Wasp*, sunk on September 15, both to Japanese submarines.[39] At Santa Cruz, the Japanese fleet sortied to support a major concurrent air and land effort designed to retake the airfield on Guadalcanal and evict the American forces from the island. Tactically, the Americans suffered more damage, losing one carrier and one destroyer sunk, receiving damage to another carrier, a battleship, a cruiser, and a destroyer, and losing more than seventy aircraft. The Japanese lost no ships but nearly a hundred aircraft while sustaining damage to one fleet and one light carrier, one cruiser, and two destroyers.[40] The American fleet, however, remained in operation around Guadalcanal, and the Japanese offensive failed to recapture the key island, thus thwarting Japan's larger objectives.

The battle for Guadalcanal also flared up repeatedly on land. The Japanese made almost monthly thrusts at the American perimeter around the airfield, now christened "Henderson Field" by its Marine owners in honor of one of their own aviators lost in the Battle of Midway. The first attempt occurred on the night of August 21, with the assault carried out by the Ichiki Detachment, a regiment-size formation hurriedly rushed to Guadalcanal to counter the American landing. The Japanese, not knowing the strength of the American force and assuming the forces landed at Guadalcanal were withdrawing to the island of Tulagi, ordered the Ichiki Detachment to recapture the airfield.[41] Ichiki's ill-advised night attack against a numerically superior foe ended in disaster for the Japanese force, with 800 Japanese soldiers from this elite detachment killed while inflicting only ninety-nine casualties on the Marines and never threatening the airfield.[42] The next Japanese thrust came on September 12 to 14 with an attack by a reinforced brigade at "Edson's" or "Bloody" Ridge. Once again, the Japanese attacked based on faulty intelligence, as General Kiyotake Kawaguchi led this effort against what he thought amounted to 5,000 American defenders. On September 13, Kawaguchi attacked the American perimeter from the jungle to the south, launching 2,400 troops against a ridge held by 600 Americans under the command of Marine Lieutenant Colonel Merritt A. Edson, but again the Americans held and inflicted heavy losses on the attacking Japanese.[43] The Japanese, having learned in August and September that rushing into the attack would not dislodge the Americans from Guadalcanal, prepared for a more coordinated assault in late October.[44] However, they still underestimated US strength, anticipating an enemy force of 10,000 while the Americans actually had more than twice that number on the island.[45] The Japanese attacks in divisional strength using the 2d Sendai Division from October 23–25 once again ended in failure and in disproportionate losses for the assaulting force.[46] Thus, between August and October, the Japanese attempted to take back the Guadalcanal airfield with three separate attacks, all of which resulted in severe losses to the attacking force. Neither side knew it at the time, but the October attack represented the last serious land assault by the Japanese to retake this vital facility.

Throughout the campaigns on New Guinea and Guadalcanal, combat also raged in the skies over the battlefields. Indeed, securing bases suitable for airfields to support the next push often drove the operations of both sides. The Japanese pushed toward Port Moresby and Milne Bay to gain use of the airfields there to isolate Australia, while the Americans landed on Guadalcanal to prevent the Japanese from establishing an air presence there. Rabaul, with its complement of Japanese land-based naval aircraft, served as the hub for the Japanese air war effort, supported by the Combined Fleet's aircraft carriers. The Allies operated predominantly out of airfields on New Guinea and, after mid-August, on Guadalcanal, supported by carriers when available.[47] The character of the maritime environment in the South and South West Pacific Areas enabled the side with air superiority to restrict significantly the operational flexibility of its opponent by hampering the movement of reinforcements and supplies. The battle for control of the air, therefore, resulted in a sustained battle of attrition. At this stage of the war, no major Japanese Army Air Force formations were committed to the southern Pacific. Japanese naval aircraft carried the fight in the air and focused the majority of their efforts on Guadalcanal at the expense of operations in New Guinea.[48] The Allies had independent air commands in the South and South West Pacific Areas, and both remained active supporting the operations in their geographic areas of responsibility; aircraft from the SWPA often struck directly at Rabaul as well.

At Guadalcanal a pattern soon emerged. The defeat of the Allied naval force at the Battle of Savo Island had yielded nighttime control of the waters around Guadalcanal to the Japanese. But the establishment of Allied aircraft on Guadalcanal, often assisted by supporting aircraft carriers, meant the Allies controlled those waters during daylight. As early as August 23, a Japanese convoy destined for Guadalcanal turned back because of Allied air pressure; the Japanese soon resorted to the less efficient method of making high-speed night runs using destroyers, rather than transports, to land troops, equipment, and supplies on the island (these operations becoming known as the "Tokyo Express").[49]

While statistics do not tell the whole story, they do reveal some of the character of the air war in the southern Pacific around Guadalcanal. In the struggles for control of the air in the southern Solomons between August 1 and November 16, 1942, including two carrier battles, the Japanese lost just over 500 aircraft to all causes, while the Americans lost 480.[50] These figures demonstrate the heavy attrition taking place. Both sides maintained capable air forces in the fight despite their losses, but the disparity in aircraft production meant the American air forces could replace losses and continue to grow. The Japanese, in contrast, struggled to sustain their force. The ramifications of this production disparity played out from late 1943 onward.

Just as they had on land and sea, the Japanese made a concerted effort in the air to dislodge the Americans from their position on Guadalcanal. The 11th Air Fleet escalated its operations against Henderson Field on October 21 and sustained increased efforts for the next five days, when the attacks ceased after it was clear the ground offensive had failed to capture the airdrome.[51] Despite the Japanese efforts to reduce and destroy the joint American air force on Guadalcanal, the "Cactus Air Force" as it now regarded itself still operated from Henderson Field to defend the island.

After the completion of nearly three months of battle on land, sea, and in the air around Guadalcanal, the issue remained undecided. Three Japanese ground attacks against the American perimeter had failed to retake the airfield. Four naval battles shaped the pattern of reinforcement and resupply but did not establish clear sea control for either side. The constant battle in the air bled both sides, but both air forces remained in the fight.

ANALYSIS OF THE STRATEGIC INITIATIVE

The strategic initiative also remained in dispute. The battles in eastern New Guinea and in the southern Solomon Islands resulted from the Japanese advances to the south to isolate Australia. The Allies had countered these moves with what they believed would amount to a limited counter-offensive to protect their lines of communication. The ensuing confrontation, however, evolved into two independent but closely intertwined campaigns that became the primary locus of the Pacific War for both sides. How, then, had the elements of strategic initiative influenced events during this period of disputed initiative?

Resources

The mobilization and use of manpower between July and October 1942 followed a pattern similar to that of the opening months of the war. Despite the large size of the IJA, its commitments in China and Manchuria—as well as the geography of the Pacific theater—limited the numbers engaged at the points of contact. Meanwhile, the United States, despite the Allied grand strategy focused on defeating Germany first, had deployed just enough resources into the Pacific to stem the rapid and unexpected Japanese advance. By June 1942, the US Army had more than 300,000 troops in the Pacific theater, compared to only 60,000 in the Atlantic; between July and September these numbers would grow to nearly 400,000 and 200,000, respectively.[52] But the United States also fell victim to the constraints of geography and to the need to defend a line of outposts protecting the sea route to Australia, resulting in limitations on the number of troops available for action on the front lines.

The Allies typically had manpower advantages at the various points of contact. Nonetheless, as in their earlier conquests, the Japanese did not shrink from engaging superior forces. On New Guinea, the invaders attempted to take Port Moresby against a larger American and Australian force. The Japanese also attempted to dislodge 8,000 Allied soldiers with a force of just 2,000 at Milne Bay, although here they believed the Allied force to be much smaller. On Guadalcanal, the Japanese operated from a position of numerical inferiority throughout the battle.[53] Unlike the opening operations of the war, in these battles the Japanese failed to take their objectives.

The material competition between the combatants also continued. To wage the air war in the southern Pacific following the American landing on Guadalcanal, the Japanese had the 25th and 26th Air Flotillas in Rabaul, with a nominal combined strength of ninety-six fighters, eighty-seven bombers, and six flying boats.[54] Japanese naval airpower in the Solomons remained at this peak level through October.[55] By contrast, in July the Allies had only two squadrons of fighters at Port Moresby in New Guinea and several bomber groups based in Australia.[56] Allied land-based fighter and attack aircraft from the South Pacific Area did not have the range to support operations in the Solomons until they moved to Guadalcanal and operated from Henderson Field in late August. The arrival of aircraft at Henderson Field represented a seminal event in the Guadalcanal campaign. Between August 20 and September 21, the American South Pacific Command fed 153 aircraft to Henderson Field and on September 22 the field held 87 serviceable planes.[57] The strength of the Cactus Air Force waxed and waned throughout the battle, but the Japanese never fully eliminated the American air presence on Guadalcanal.

Midway had narrowed the gap between the combatants in aircraft carriers, but the IJN still remained a potent force that had suffered only negligible damage in other combat ship categories thus far in the war. The four large naval battles between August and October involved varying force levels. At Savo Island, seven Japanese cruisers and a destroyer engaged a force of five Allied cruisers and six destroyers. The Japanese employed three carriers, eight battleships, five cruisers, and eighteen destroyers against the Americans at the Battle of the Eastern Solomons. The Americans countered with a smaller force of two carriers, one battleship, four cruisers, and ten destroyers.[58] As was the case for each standoff carrier battle, the number of aircraft on the carrier decks represented the real striking power of the fleets, with 173 Japanese aircraft pitted against 154 American planes.[59] The battle at Cape Esperance pitted four Japanese cruisers and a destroyer against four American cruisers accompanied by five destroyers. In the final encounter at Santa Cruz, another carrier battle, Japan had four carriers, four battleships, ten cruisers, and twenty-eight destroyers against an American force of two carriers, one battleship, six cruisers, and fourteen destroyers.[60] Once again the Japanese had an edge in shipborne aircraft: 199 to 136.[61] Overall, with the exception of Cape Esperance, the Japanese marshaled equal or superior resources for the four naval encounters occurring between August and October 1942.

Thus, the material disparity between the Allies and Japan tightened during this period. Japan had a strong naval air force at Rabaul and maintained that strength through October despite grueling losses. Yet, that force focused predominantly on the Guadalcanal operation at the expense of other priorities. This gave the Japanese an advantage in land-based aircraft in the struggle for Guadalcanal but ceded the same advantage to the Allies in the campaign on New Guinea. The IJN, however, still held a quantitative superiority over its Allied foe, particularly in the large carrier battles of the Eastern Solomons and Santa Cruz.

No really significant technological changes in the air war affected the two forces between July and October, although forthcoming changes on the Allied side were in the offing. The Japanese continued to rely on their mainstays: the Zero fighter, G4M "Betty" land-based bomber, "Val" dive-bomber, and "Kate" torpedo bomber. The vast majority of Allied aircraft remained familiar to the Japanese as well: Royal Australian Air Force Hudson bombers, as well as American P-40s, B-17s, F4F Wildcats, and Dauntless dive-bombers. Others had also made some minor appearances earlier in the war, such as the B-26 Marauder medium bomber and the TBF Avenger carrier-borne torpedo bomber that had participated in small numbers at Midway, and the B-25 Mitchell medium bomber that had taken part in the Doolittle Raid. Some new American aircraft did make their first appearances. P-38 fighters began arriving in the South and South West Pacific Areas, and A-20 Havoc light bombers also operated from some of General George Kenney's Fifth Air Force bases in Australia and New Guinea. Both of these aircraft would play a significant role in the continuing battle for New Guinea and the Solomons, but the first P-38 aircraft suffered teething troubles with fuel leaks, and the A-20s arrived in theater without bomb racks or machine guns.[62] Other new American aircraft included the P-400, an export version of the P-39 Airacobra with reduced armament, and the B-24 Liberator heavy bomber. This variety of Allied aircraft indicates two aspects of the air war in the South Pacific at this point: both the army and navy aviation units were heavily involved, opposed only by IJN aircraft, and the Americans had begun to field improved aircraft, which did not bode well for the Japanese in 1943. But, in mid- to late 1942, the Allied aircraft did not match the Japanese in either range or performance, with the notable exception of heavy bombers. Radar, which was operational on Guadalcanal even before any American aircraft had arrived, remained an important advantage because it allowed Cactus's fighters to reach their attack positions in time to intercept Japanese raiders before they struck the airfield.[63]

The Japanese navy continued to exploit the technological advantages it had used to complete its conquest of the southern area: fast and powerful cruisers and destroyers, excellent night optics, and the Long Lance torpedo. American torpedoes, in contrast, continued their unreliable performance. The US Navy's use of its radar advantage remained spotty. Despite the potential advantage of radar, its poor employment and overreliance on it at Savo Island contributed to the significant Japanese victory in that battle.[64]

Technology in the land battles did not differ significantly between the two combatants, particularly early in the Guadalcanal campaign. Much of the Japanese infantry's equipment was obsolescent if not obsolete, such as the 1905 rifle that was slow to fire and accurate only at short distances, the 1914 Hotchkiss model heavy machine gun, small artillery pieces of 75mm or smaller dating from 1905 or 1922, and the 1922 model light machine gun.[65] Reports from the field still found such weapons to be formidable. In one such report, Lieutenant Colonel Louis A. Walsh Jr., US Army, offered a more positive appreciation of enemy weaponry. According to Walsh, the small caliber of the Japanese rifle meant that its discharge was hard to spot, which served well in darkness, jungle, and camouflaged positions. Walsh also praised the Japanese light machine gun as being more portable and better suited to the jungle environment than its US counterpart, and he referred to the Japanese 50mm knee mortar as "the Jap's most effective and most accurate weapon."[66]

Turning his analytical eye on American equipment, Walsh found the .30-caliber heavy machine gun too bulky for effective jungle operations but thought the Browning Automatic Rifles and canister rounds fired from 37mm antitank guns to be very effective.[67] During these early stages of the fighting on Guadalcanal the Marines also fought with old weaponry, such as the model 1903 Springfield rifle. The former Marine turned journalist/historian Ore Marion pointed out that the Springfield 1903 represented a good weapon but was a slower, bolt-action rifle, unlike the Army's newer M-1 Garand semiautomatic rifle; Marion also backed Walsh's positive evaluation of the Browning Automatic Rifle.[68] Clearly, neither side yet had a significant technological advantage in the ground war.

The technology gap, like the resource gap, had narrowed slightly between July and October 1942, but Japan retained a slim advantage. The Japanese still enjoyed a slight superiority in aircraft, but newer American models had begun to arrive in the South Pacific; the American advantage in heavy aircraft remained, and radar early warning proved a significant boon in combat. The Japanese also retained their naval superiority, although the Americans gained some experience with the use of radar in surface combat at Savo Island and at Cape Esperance. On land, the challenging character of jungle warfare with its limited visibility and close-quarter combat prevented either side from having a significant advantage in its infantry weaponry.

The overall resource element, including manpower, materiel, and technology, still favored the Japanese, though much less so than in the opening phase of the war. The Allies outnumbered the Japanese on land, while

Tokyo's forces held a very slight edge in materiel in the air and a larger edge in naval power. The Allies began to gain on, but not yet surpass, Japan technologically by putting their own advantages of heavy bombers and radar to better use, while also introducing newer aircraft like the TBF Avenger and the P-38 Lightning into combat in increasing numbers.

Intelligence

The intelligence war changed in the South Pacific because of a number of factors. The Japanese were now operating farther afield and in more remote areas with which they had little contact prior to the war. This stands in contrast to their earlier operations that focused on the Far East and on Hawaii, with its significant Japanese population, where the Japanese had more time and resources to assist in planning prior to the actual outbreak of war. The Allies, however, operated in areas with which they were more familiar than the Japanese and where they had established relationships with indigenous people, allowing for the creation of the Coastwatcher network. Additionally, the geography of the area enabled extensive aerial reconnaissance and photography, unlike the operation at Midway in the open spaces of the Central Pacific. Finally, the Japanese had recently changed their naval codes; the Americans could no longer decrypt Japanese radio traffic but instead had to rely more on analysis of radio traffic to anticipate enemy activity.[69] The Allies, therefore, entered a critical period of the war without their most important advantage to date, which in many ways had been their only source of reliable intelligence.

Despite the loss of efficacy in decryption of naval codes, the Allies generally maintained an accurate estimate of Japanese intentions and capabilities during this period of the war. Japanese aerial reconnaissance of Buna and the Kokoda Trail forewarned MacArthur of the coming Japanese effort to cross the Owen Stanley Mountains and attack Port Moresby by land. MacArthur's intelligence apparatus also deduced the attack on Milne Bay by integrating intelligence from aerial reconnaissance, captured documents, and patterns in Japanese aerial reconnaissance. Radio traffic analysis monitored Japanese aircraft carrier activity based out of Truk Harbor on August 23, 1942, the eve of the Battle of the Eastern Solomons.[70] Admiral Nimitz's personal diary entry for October 23 reveals he was well aware of the forthcoming Japanese push on Guadalcanal and that he anticipated a "supreme test" in the offing.[71] Throughout both campaigns on New Guinea and in the Solomons, the Coastwatchers provided intelligence to the Allies that warned of Japanese naval and troop movements, as well as impending air attacks launched from airfields at Rabaul. Coastwatchers on Bougainville regularly provided Henderson Field with forty-five minutes of warning for Japanese aircraft flying from Rabaul down the Solomon Islands chain, supplementing radar and allowing the Cactus Air Force to scramble aircraft in time to fight off the attack.[72] Throughout this period, the integrated Allied intelligence efforts prevented the Japanese from achieving strategic or tactical surprise.

Japanese efforts did not yield the same results. Despite information based on analysis of radio traffic that indicated a forthcoming Allied operation, the Japanese failed to anticipate the landing at Guadalcanal. The Japanese had also underestimated the strength of the Allied force defending Milne Bay and, partly as a result, landed insufficient forces there with which to accomplish their objectives. The Japanese continually fell into the trap of underestimating the quantity and quality of Allied forces facing them on Guadalcanal. Colonel Kazuji Sugita, an intelligence officer with the Japanese 2nd Division on Guadalcanal in September and October, later lamented his inability to get accurate information on the American forces from his superiors at 17th Army headquarters on Rabaul. He also faulted poor Japanese army and navy cooperation as a contributing factor to poor Japanese intelligence in the Solomons. Sugita noted that the Japanese struggled at estimating the number of Allied reinforcements landed on the island and that they captured very few documents and little equipment.[73] Throughout this period, the Japanese pieced together only a hazy picture of the Allied situation.

Intelligence collection and analysis clearly favored the Allies at this point in the war. The Allies anticipated Japanese moves and judged Japanese strength relatively accurately. The Japanese often underestimated Allied strength and failed to anticipate the landings in the Solomon Islands, despite indications of a forthcoming Allied operation.

The Allies also bested Japan at security during this phase. They protected the secrecy of Operation Watchtower and the attacks on Tulagi, Gavutu, Tanambogo, and Guadalcanal. They also effectively masked their strength at Port Moresby, Milne Bay, and around Henderson Field. The Japanese made one significant improvement in security by changing their naval codes, eliminating the major source of intelligence for the Allies in previous months. However, the Japanese failed to nullify the Coastwatcher network or to prevent extensive Allied reconnaissance and photo intelligence. The Japanese often tipped their coming moves with their own aerial reconnaissance, which astute Allied analysts used to anticipate the landings at Buna and at Milne Bay and the march over the Kokoda Trail. These failures in operational security allowed the Allies to stay abreast or ahead of Japanese movements in the southern Pacific.

Overall, the intelligence competition favored the Allies between July and October 1942. The Allies developed a clearer picture of the Japanese capabilities and shielded their own intentions more successfully than did their foe.

Strategic Acumen

The Japanese premised their strategic approach on a fundamentally flawed assumption that colored the opening phases of the overland advance on New Guinea and the battle for Guadalcanal: they judged the United States incapable of launching any kind of counteroffensive until 1943.[74] The results of this thinking are plain to see. Most Japanese commanders and staff officers initially believed the landings at Guadalcanal represented a small reconnaissance in force, not a major amphibious effort to take the airfield.[75] This assessment, consistent with the assumption that no significant counterattack would occur until 1943, caused the Japanese to divide their forces with simultaneous advances in late August against Port Moresby and Milne Bay, while also landing the small Ichiki Detachment on Guadalcanal. They achieved none of their objectives and would have been better served to prioritize their operations and concentrate their resources. By contrast, the Allies benefited from this situation in part by design. Admiral Nimitz regarded the two campaigns as being mutually supporting, designed to increase the pressure on Japan and complicate both its strategic and operational situation.[76] The Japanese division of forces, manifested both on the ground by the three August attacks and in the air, where the available naval aircraft focused almost exclusively on Guadalcanal at the expense of New Guinea, demonstrated the wisdom of the Allied approach.

The situations in both campaigns, however, remained precarious throughout these trying months, especially on Guadalcanal. Here, Nimitz made another important decision that demonstrated the validity of his strategic assessment and that would have positive ramifications for the American efforts in the coming months. On October 17, 1942, Nimitz relieved Ghormley of command in the South Pacific Area, replacing him with Admiral William "Bull" Halsey. In his handwritten diary, Nimitz noted the hours of "anguished consideration" he devoted to the decision, writing: "Reason (private) Ghormley was too immersed in detail and not sufficiently bold and aggressive at the right times." The timing of this decision, only one week before the major Japanese offensive to retake Guadalcanal, makes it particularly courageous given Nimitz's expression of trepidation about the situation.[77] Ghormley, a man whom Nimitz respected, had remained pessimistic and hesitant throughout the Guadalcanal struggle, but Halsey soon seized the reins and reinvigorated the command in the South Pacific. On October 20, Halsey met with Major General Archer Vandegrift, the Marine commander for all the US forces on Guadalcanal, and asked the latter if the Americans could hold, to which Vandegrift responded: "I can hold, but I've got to have more active support than I've been getting."[78] Vandegrift did hold against the Japanese attacks that month, and Halsey infused his South Pacific Area command with a new, aggressive spirit. Nevertheless, the campaign on Guadalcanal remained in doubt for several weeks to come.[79]

The Americans achieved greater surprise than their adversaries during this period. None of the Japanese operations caught the Allies fully unprepared. The amphibious landings in the Solomons, however, hit the Japanese in an unexpected area, creating surprise and mental dislocation. In his August 7, 1942, diary entry, Admiral Ugaki noted of the American attack on Guadalcanal: "That we failed to discover it until it [the force] attacked deserves censure as extremely careless. A warning had been issued two days before. Anyway, we were attacked unprepared."[80]

The Japanese also missed a crucial strategic opportunity at the very beginning of the Guadalcanal campaign. Despite winning a significant victory against the Allied covering force at the Battle of Savo Island, Admiral Mikawa did not exploit that success to destroy the Allied transports supporting the landings, an action that might have defeated the American attack at its start. Mikawa's decision was probably due to the IJN's "Decisive Battle Doctrine" that viewed the destruction of the enemy surface fleet as granting automatic debilitation of his command of the sea, an attitude that ignored the impact of modern aircraft that could invalidate surface warfare success.[81] Japanese sensitivity to the loss of major combat vessels, such as heavy cruisers, surely factored in as well. As the battle unfolded, aircraft based at Henderson Field ensured that the Allies controlled the sea by day, while the Japanese operated only at night. Mikawa had unwittingly let slip a golden opportunity to inflict a serious setback on the Allies.

Thus, during this period the Allies demonstrated a more refined strategic acumen than did the Japanese. Japanese plans did not match reality, and they did not balance their ends, ways, and means on either New Guinea or Guadalcanal. The Allies balanced ends, ways, and means effectively on New Guinea, although they cut things very closely and nearly overreached in the Solomon Islands. Nevertheless, they held Henderson Field, with the issue remaining in doubt until the end of November. In sum, by the end of October 1942, the Allies had seized the opportunity afforded by the results of the Battle of Midway to check the Japanese advance and to dispute the strategic initiative the Japanese had held before the battle.

Combat Effectiveness

The Japanese ground units employed on New Guinea and Guadalcanal retained the discipline and experience that represented the hallmarks of the Japanese army in the first stage of the war. Their Allied opponents consisted of a more heterogeneous mix, from the battle-hardened Australian 7th Division, with its previous Middle East service, to untested US Army and US Marine Corps units. The ensuing combat revealed much about both sides.

The Japanese started their Kokoda operations with an offensive success similar to that initially experienced in the jungles of Malaya. Yet, the campaign soon bogged down and eventually stopped at Imita Ridge, within sight of the Japanese objective of Port Moresby. The Japanese attack on Milne Bay resulted in abject failure and heavy loss of life. The three major Japanese night assaults in August, September, and October on Guadalcanal pressed the Americans at times but did not achieve their objectives and resulted in disproportionate losses to the attackers. In defense, however, the Japanese resisted with a stubbornness on Tulagi, Gavutu, and Tanambogo that foreshadowed the bloody fighting that would come later in the war.[82]

Each side assessed the reasons for the Japanese failures despite their using the previously successful tactic of night attack. The Japanese believed that US air superiority over Guadalcanal and their own ignorance of the topography of the island forced long marches in the jungle that weakened the attacking forces; this, combined with heavy American firepower and an effective warning system, enabled the Allies to resist their attacks.[83] An operations report from the 1st Marine Parachute Battalion related the effectiveness of the American artillery barrage against the Japanese night assaults on Edson's Ridge on September 13–14, 1942. General Vandegrift himself also credited the effectiveness of Marine 105mm artillery in this battle while praising the Japanese soldiers' skill and determination.[84] Similarly, the postwar Japanese accounts laud the training and mental attitude of the Marines on Guadalcanal.[85] Vandegrift's unorthodox decision to organize a cordon defense with a continuous perimeter around the airfield represents a key to the American success. Analyzing Japanese capabilities and propensities, as well as his own force's strengths and weaknesses, Vandegrift went against conventional military wisdom with this decision but, in so doing, took a calculated risk that paid handsome dividends and deprived the Japanese of one of their favorite tactics: night infiltration around the flanks of an opponent.[86] Thus, the American and Australian troops facing the Japanese in mid- to late 1942 had the discipline, equipment, training/experience, and leadership with which to repel the fearsome Japanese night assaults.

Japan struggled to sustain its troops in the field. The IJA generally expected its troops to gather the majority of their provisions from their local area of operations, but the Owen Stanley Mountains and the jungles of Guadalcanal could not provide sufficient food. Japanese troops along the Kokoda Trail, despite meager and ineffective attempts to keep them provisioned through airdrops, resorted to cannibalizing Australian corpses.[87] The Japanese *Senshi Sōsho* flatly acknowledges that resupply for the South Sea Force on New Guinea had failed by late September.[88] The situation for the Japanese Kawaguchi Detachment and 2nd Division on Guadalcanal was not much better. Postwar Japanese accounts state that the dependence on destroyers for resupply instead of transports meant "it was impossible to supply sufficient quantities of materiel essential for ground action," making the equipment of both units "totally inadequate and even their food supplies . . . dangerously low."[89]

The Allies also struggled with logistics but to a lesser degree. Vandegrift noted the paucity of supplies and the short rations that characterized the Marines' first two weeks on Guadalcanal, but he said the troops made light of the hardships and maintained high morale.[90] Like the Japanese, the Allies also used airlift to sustain and reinforce their positions, providing some additional sustenance. In one example, between September 18 and 24, as the Australians made their stand on Imita Ridge, General George Kenney and the Fifth Air Force flew four thousand men of the 128th Infantry Regiment, US 32nd Infantry Division, from Australia to reinforce Port Moresby on New Guinea.[91] Airlift also supplied thousands of pounds of food, shoes, ammunition, and clothing to sustain the Australian and American forces fighting in the New Guinea jungles.[92] Through such efforts the Allies remained fit to fight.

The Allies demonstrated better combat effectiveness on the land between July and October on both New Guinea and in the Solomons. Allied ground forces took and held their objectives, while the Japanese army and Special Naval Landing Forces failed to complete their missions, in large measure due to poor tactical performance and insufficient numbers. In addition, the Japanese suffered disproportionate losses in their failed efforts. Throughout the period, both sides struggled to keep their forces equipped and fed, with the Allies enjoying somewhat greater success.

On the sea, advantages were not as clear-cut. In two major nighttime surface engagements, each side could claim one tactical victory: the Japanese clearly won at Savo Island, and the Americans did better at Cape Esperance. In both cases, however, the losing side still managed to land forces and supplies on Guadalcanal despite the unfavorable engagement. In terms of shipping sunk or seriously damaged, the Japanese came out ahead. The Japanese lost one cruiser and one destroyer sunk, with one cruiser seriously damaged. Recent scholarship explains the disproportionate losses. According to Jeff Reardon, during the 1920s and 1930s the US Navy consciously focused on "big guns" for a presumed daylight fleet engagement against the IJN, while ignoring the potential hitting power of the surface-launched torpedo. The Japanese, recognizing their likely material inferiority in war against the United States, planned differently. They too focused on "decisive battle" but planned to wear down the American fleet using torpedoes in nocturnal attacks prior to the decisive engagement. The American deficiency revealed itself at Savo Island, while the marginal tactical victory at Cape Esperance masked continued inferiority to the Japanese in night tactics.[93] For this period, in operational terms, the Japanese came out slightly ahead, as the victory of Savo Island granted them sea control at night, which allowed them to contest the American lodgment on Guadalcanal.

The carrier war also generated mixed results. Despite significant losses, the Americans at the Battle of the Eastern Solomons had turned back the Japanese attempt to land reinforcements on Guadalcanal. At Santa Cruz, the IJN punished the American fleet but failed to support the Japanese effort to retake Guadalcanal. Thus, on the whole, the US Navy, despite its losses, achieved its objectives while the IJN did not.[94]

One other aspect of the sea war demands brief mention. Although the Japanese never implemented unrestricted submarine warfare against the Allied merchant fleet, Japanese submarines effectively stalked their warship prey around Guadalcanal. During this critical period, Japanese submarines damaged the carrier *Saratoga* and sank the carrier *Wasp*. In the most notable US submarine success against warships during this period, on August 10 an American submarine sank the cruiser *Kako* near Rabaul.[95] This differential—one Japanese cruiser in exchange for two American carriers either disabled or sunk—clearly favored the Japanese and noticeably reduced American naval strength during these trying months.

Naval combat effectiveness was a close-run competition during this phase of the war. The United States retained a very marginal edge and more successfully accomplished its naval missions supporting New Guinea and Guadalcanal between July and October. The Japanese, however, secured sufficient freedom of operation during the night hours and vied for more control during the daylight hours to sustain a determined effort to retake Guadalcanal.

The air battle, in which Japan no longer dominated, also taxed both sides. The air struggle over Guadalcanal represented almost a statistical dead heat in terms of losses between August and early November. Still, the continued survival of the Cactus Air Force remained the key factor in the campaign. The marvelous performance and long range of the Japanese aircraft enabled them to attack Henderson Field regularly in their efforts to gain air superiority over Guadalcanal, but they could never wrest that control from the Americans. The Japanese encountered several of the same problems the Germans had experienced against the British in the Battle of Britain in 1940. The Americans had an early-warning net that included radar and the Coastwatcher network, which allowed them to meet the attackers in the air, rather than being caught on the ground as had happened at Pearl Harbor and in the Philippines. Additionally, the long flight from Rabaul to the target area meant that the Japanese fighters had limited fuel for combat and that any damaged aircraft or downed aircrews stood a much greater chance of perishing than American crews who operated much closer to their base. Japanese ace Saburō Sakai also credited the Americans with improved performance, stressing their teamwork and improved tactics.[96] In addition, the Americans used airlift to help their air force endure the rigors of combat. During the struggle for Guadalcanal in October, the Americans arranged for the airlift of badly needed fuel drums to keep the Cactus Air Force in operation.[97] The effort succeeded at a critical juncture in the campaign and ensured that daylight operations for the Japanese around Guadalcanal would remain costly.

The campaign over New Guinea differed substantially at this juncture. The Japanese navy and naval aircraft at Rabaul focused on Guadalcanal. The IJA's focus on New Guinea lacked air support, as no Japanese army fighter or bomber aircraft operated in theater. This allowed Kenney and the US Fifth Air Force to interdict Japanese supplies, strike at Japanese beachheads, and launch attacks against Rabaul to support both the New Guinea and Solomons operations. Allied air efforts contributed greatly to the aforementioned breakdown of Japanese logistical support for the South Seas Detachment, and air attacks destroyed much of the food and munitions the Japanese had landed in support of their Milne Bay attack.

Thus, during this period the overall air war favored the Allies. The various Allied air components accomplished their most important missions and contributed to the Allied successes in both campaigns. The Japanese naval air forces effectively ceded air control in one campaign and failed to achieve their goals in the other.

Chance

Chance intervened during this period on several occasions, both in the form of happenstance and in the form of command decisions made in the face of uncertainty. First, the US invasion force at Guadalcanal advanced under the cover of bad weather, which contributed to the inability of Japanese reconnaissance aircraft on Tulagi and Rabaul to detect the covering fleet and enabled the Americans to surprise the Japanese on land and at sea.[98] Second, on August 8, Admiral Fletcher, who was in charge of the carrier force supporting the invasion, decided to withdraw his carriers to the south because heavy Japanese air attacks had depleted his fighter defenses.[99] This decision left the invasion force exposed and revealed Fletcher's hesitancy to operate in the unknown, perhaps stemming from his experiences of losing the carriers *Lexington* and *Yorktown* in earlier battles and his awareness of the strategic value of the remaining American carriers.[100] Third, Admiral Mikawa, after achieving his victory at Savo Island, did not press his attack on the Allied transports farther to the south, unwilling to risk his force after this victory.[101] Fourth, chance deprived each side of another aircraft carrier in the two carrier battles. In the Eastern Solomons, the American carrier *Wasp* and its sixty-two aircraft unwittingly missed the carrier battle while refueling, which cost the United States an opportunity to employ superior numbers in that engagement. Two months later, at Santa Cruz, the Japanese carrier *Hiyo* missed the battle with engine trouble but transferred some of its aircraft to another carrier and thence to Rabaul.[102] Finally, a rain squall at Cape Esperance obscured the Japanese vision but not the American ships' radars, allowing the Americans to gain tactical surprise in that battle.[103] In previous night surface engagements, the Japanese sighted the Americans first and initiated combat with an unexpected barrage of Long Lance torpedoes.

Four out of the five important examples of chance listed above favored the Allies. To be sure, Fletcher's flinch in the face of strong Japanese resistance at Guadalcanal represented a real danger to the operation, but the Japanese missed the opportunity to take advantage of the withdrawn American carriers. Indeed, Mikawa's hesitation that evening largely nullified the opportunity presented by Fletcher's withdrawal. The Allies dodged a bullet that could have ended the first counteroffensive in the Pacific less than forty-eight hours after its beginning. In all, chance during this period of the war favored the Allies.

STATE OF THE STRATEGIC INITIATIVE

Borrowing H. P. Willmott's analogy, the strategic initiative now lay "like a gun in the street" at the end of October 1942. The Japanese still held an edge in available resources writ large, but shifts had occurred in the other categories underlying possession of the initiative. During this period, the Allies had better intelligence in terms of collection, analysis, and security. They also demonstrated better judgment and strategic acumen, matching their ends, ways, and means and achieving surprise in a manner the Japanese failed to emulate. Combat effectiveness on the land, sea, and in the air ebbed and flowed but generally favored the Allies. Finally, chance and the fortunes of war generally favored the Allies. The advantages they held in four of five areas analyzed allowed them to place the strategic initiative firmly in dispute.

CONCLUSIONS

The combatants were well aware of the dynamic situation as this period progressed. In late August, Admiral Ugaki realized that Guadalcanal would be a "prolonged" battle. At the end of September, he wrote: "Looking back, I find nothing has been accomplished this month." Then, at the end of October, despite the Japanese navy's success at Santa Cruz, Ugaki admitted that his focus remained on the army's failure to recapture the airfield on Guadalcanal even as the carrier battle raged. His last diary entry for October foretold continued operations against the island in a coming general offensive the next month.[104] At the same time, Emperor

Hirohito celebrated the naval victory of Santa Cruz but urged his soldiers and sailors to intensify their efforts to retake Guadalcanal.[105] The struggle was far from over. Nimitz knew this as well. His diary entry for October 30, 1942, written at 3:45 A.M., is worth quoting:

> I am not so busy as I am mentally churned up. My imagination is very vivid and I realize my helplessness so far away. No one knows better than I do the difficulties that confront Halsey and Vandegrift and the superiority enjoyed at present by the Japs. I am so aware of what might happen that it keeps me very much preoccupied. Our forces are doing grand work with less strength than our opponents and if matters continue until next summer we hope to see our strength considerably built up.[106]

The October victory around Henderson Field, Nimitz was well aware, bought more time but did not settle the issue on Guadalcanal.

MacArthur also chimed in with an emphatic request for more resources of every kind to save the situation in the Solomon Islands and thereby preserve his South West Pacific Area command. Meeting the far-ranging demands of MacArthur's message would have required canceling or postponing the upcoming invasion of North Africa, something President Roosevelt remained unwilling to do.[107] The South and Southwest Pacific theaters continued to receive only limited support, despite the possibility of once again ceding the initiative in the Pacific to the Japanese.

At the end of October, both sides remained determined to gain control of Guadalcanal.[108] The campaigns on Papua New Guinea and on Guadalcanal would reach their denouement in the period between November 1942 and the end of February 1943. Another large battle around Guadalcanal loomed in November. Allied forces prepared to push back at the Japanese on the northeastern shore of New Guinea. There remained a great deal of fighting to decide which side would come out on top in each campaign and who would therefore gain possession of the strategic initiative—and with it the ability to dictate the future course of the war.

9

New Guinea and Guadalcanal, November 1942–February 1943: The Allies Seize the Initiative

The failed Japanese attack on Henderson Field in October 1942, accompanied by large-scale air and sea actions, set the stage for yet another push on Guadalcanal by the Japanese in November. Both sides steeled themselves for the forthcoming confrontation. In eastern New Guinea, the Allies had halted the Japanese thrusts at Port Moresby and at Milne Bay, but the invaders remained ensconced along the northern portions of the Kokoda Trail and in the Buna–Gona–Sanananda area of the northern coast. MacArthur prepared his forces to launch a two-pronged counterattack to displace this Japanese lodgment. Both campaigns were far from over. Between November 1942 and February 1943, however, the Allies secured their position on Guadalcanal and, after bloody fighting in the jungles of New Guinea, seized their objectives there as well. In winning these two campaigns, the Allies also claimed the strategic initiative in the Pacific War. As a result, they wielded greater influence over the remainder of that war until its conclusion in August 1945. How did they manage to close out these hard-fought battles successfully and reap the corresponding rewards?

CAUGHT IN EACH OTHER'S GRIP: CONTINUING CONFRONTATIONS IN THE SOUTH PACIFIC

Neither side had launched its operations in the South Pacific intending to fight long and large-scale confrontations that would evolve into attritional battles, but that is exactly what occurred. The Japanese had aimed to isolate Australia to prevent its development as a base for potential Allied counteroffensives. The Allies sought to protect the lines of communication to the same in order to defend Australia and eventually use it as a base for offensive operations. However, the Japanese southward moves

forced an Allied reaction, which in turn resulted in increased Japanese efforts to achieve their ends. After October both sides remained committed
to accomplishing their strategic goals.

The leaders of the Japanese high command reevaluated the situation
at the end of October 1942. In their view, the "Southeast Pacific," as
they called the Guadalcanal and New Guinea areas, represented the most
likely point for an Allied counterattack. This potential avenue of attack
seemed to allow the Allies to concentrate strong land, sea, and air forces
to threaten Japanese sea control in the West Pacific and then retake the
southern resource area; in turn, this would offer bases from which to
launch air attacks against the Japanese homeland from the south. These
calculations spurred the Japanese army high command to reorganize for
the coming fight and create the 8th Area Army to oversee the entire area,
with the already established 17th Army to focus on Guadalcanal and the
Solomon Islands, while a newly formed 18th Army operated on New
Guinea. The Japanese planned to strengthen their forces by sending additional army divisions to the area, by moving JAAF units to Rabaul, and
by making yet another effort to capture the airfield on Guadalcanal.[1]

The Allies also continued to focus on the South Pacific, anticipating the
Japanese would do the same. In Honolulu, the Pacific Ocean Areas headquarters estimate of the situation on November 1, 1942, expected continued Japanese pressure in the Solomons and on New Guinea but did not
predict another Japanese "grand offensive" because of the losses they had
suffered in the late October battles. Two days later, Nimitz's staff noted
the general situation on Guadalcanal "is not unfavorable" and that there
had been no real interruption of logistical support or reinforcements to
the island since the October confrontation.[2] Meanwhile, MacArthur prepared to act on New Guinea. Despite the Australians' continued progress
along the Kokoda Trail, MacArthur had temporarily postponed plans to
shift to offensive operations in late October to await the outcome of the
critical situation on Guadalcanal. The successful repulse of the Japanese
effort there enabled MacArthur to authorize a larger offensive against
enemy positions near Buna, slated to begin in mid-November.[3]

During this period there were fewer identifiable, pivotal battles than
in the previous four months, although the ground and air forces of both
sides remained in almost constant engagement. MacArthur's offensive
against Buna and Gona encapsulated the end of the struggle on eastern
New Guinea, although it lasted from November 1942 until late January 1943. The final struggle for Guadalcanal resulted in two additional
naval confrontations, the Battles of Guadalcanal and of Tassafaronga,

and the fighting there on land would hereafter be characterized by the steady advance of the Americans, particularly after the Japanese decided to withdraw their forces from the island. Although perhaps less dramatic and not punctuated by definable confrontations as in the period of August through October, the combat remained difficult and bloody in both locations.

Pushing the Japanese Out of Papua New Guinea

The Allies commenced their offensive against the Buna positions on New Guinea with a misplaced confidence. The defeats inflicted upon the Japanese along the Kokoda Trail and at Milne Bay seemed precursors to the rapid eviction of the Japanese and the Allied occupation of the northeastern coast of New Guinea.[4] The supply situation for the Australians, now advancing north over the Kokoda Trail, improved drastically with the capture of Kokoda village and its airfield, which enabled reliable airlift support with which to continue the attack to the northern coast. By November 13, the Australians had pushed the Japanese farther north, with heavy fighting, making them fall back onto their positions in the Gona area. The Americans also used an air bridge to assemble elements of the 32nd Infantry Division at Pongani, 30 miles southeast of Buna.[5] These maneuvers set the stage for the coming battle. (See map 7.)

The Allied plan of attack against the Japanese Buna/Gona beachhead envisioned a three-pronged advance, with the Australians hitting from the southwest and the Americans working from the south and southeast. On November 16 these forces began to advance. Two weeks later, despite heavy fighting and repeated Australian attacks, the village of Gona remained in Japanese hands.[6] The Americans also struggled against Buna. Two weeks after the start of this attack, the village remained in Japanese hands. General MacArthur ordered the I Corps commander, Lieutenant General Robert L. Eichelberger, to proceed to the Buna area, relieve Major General Edwin F. Harding, commander of the 32nd Infantry Division, and reinvigorate the Buna attack.[7] The expected rapid Allied triumph against the Japanese beachhead never materialized.

The defensive positions of the Japanese around Buna and Gona replicated the trench warfare of World War I, with intertwined trenches and bunkers. Unlike World War I in Europe, however, the setting was a jungle with its myriad of additional challenges to both combatants. The bloody confrontation continued into December and beyond, with Gona falling first to the Australians on December 9, but requiring another ten days

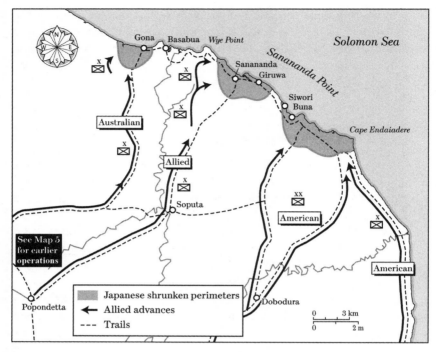

Map 7. Buna/Kokoda Trail, 1942

for the Allies to mop up remaining Japanese resistance.[8] The Americans captured Buna on the third day of 1943.[9] Many Japanese remained ensconced in the jungle at Sanananda, between Buna and Gona, an area the Allies did not clear until January 22. The Papuan campaign thus ended more than two months after MacArthur had launched his offensive, and the costs to both sides had been heavy. Between late September 1942 and the end of January 1943, the Japanese lost approximately 8,000 dead and wounded compared to Allied casualties of more than 2,300 dead and 13,000 wounded or ill from disease.[10] As along the Kokoda Trail, some Japanese troops had resorted to cannibalism during their fanatical, last-stand resistance.[11]

The End on Guadalcanal, November 1942–February 1943

The denouement of the Guadalcanal campaign began after the defeat of the Japanese in the naval Battle of Guadalcanal in mid-November.

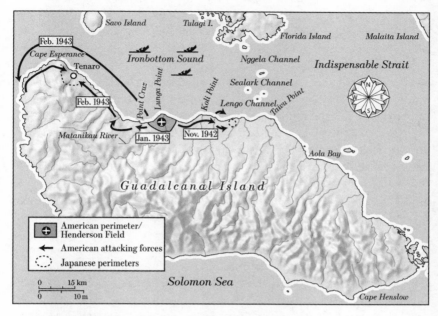

Map 8. Guadalcanal, November 1942–February 1943

Another naval tussle, the Battle of Tassafaronga, followed a fortnight later. After this series of naval engagements, the Japanese made no further attempts to capture Henderson Field. Instead, American forces on Guadalcanal, like MacArthur's in New Guinea, went over to offensive operations to eliminate the Japanese threat. (See map 8.)

The Japanese attempt to land more forces on Guadalcanal and launch another attack against Henderson Field precipitated the naval Battle of Guadalcanal on November 13–15. Unlike the regular runs of the high-speed Tokyo Express destroyer transports, in this effort the Japanese employed eleven transports in an attempt to land 7,000 soldiers, 31,000 artillery shells, and enough food to feed 30,000 men for twenty days.[12] The IJN committed capital ships to the effort to force through these much needed supplies and reinforcements, but the attrition to the Japanese carrier force and its air groups at Santa Cruz precluded the provision of any significant aircraft carrier support for the operation. Halsey, however, still had the damaged carrier *Enterprise* and its air group operating in the area.[13]

The naval Battle of Guadalcanal involved three sequential engagements. In the first, during the early hours of November 13, a force of five American cruisers and eight destroyers engaged a Japanese force of two battleships, one cruiser, and fifteen destroyers in another night surface action. In the ensuing confused action that represented something more akin to a knife fight than a naval battle, the Americans lost three cruisers and four destroyers, while the Japanese lost the battleship *Hiei* and two destroyers.[14] The Japanese broke off the action and failed to complete their primary mission of bombarding Henderson Field.[15] The next day, aircraft from Henderson Field, including air squadrons from the *Enterprise* operating off the airstrip, attacked a Japanese bombardment force that had hit Henderson Field in the early-morning darkness. The same air element also located and attacked the large Japanese transport force headed to Guadalcanal. In addition to sinking one cruiser and six transports and damaging three cruisers and two destroyers, these air attacks forced one transport to abort the run, while the remaining four later beached themselves on Guadalcanal. In the third and final encounter of the battle, during the night hours of November 14–15, American and Japanese battleships met head-to-head for the first time. This fight pitted two American battleships and four destroyers against a Japanese force of one battleship, four cruisers, and nine destroyers. Losses amounted to three American destroyers sunk and one battleship and one destroyer damaged, while the Japanese lost one battleship and one destroyer sunk.[16] This round of the battle represented an American victory in terms of fleet damage, but it enabled the remaining four Japanese transports that had survived the air attacks on the 14th to get through and beach on Guadalcanal, where they were subjected to repeated attacks by the Cactus Air Force. In overall terms, the Americans won the battle handily, allowing the Japanese to land only 2,000 troops, four days' worth of rice, and 260 boxes of artillery shells for the loss of ten valuable transports.[17]

The next naval engagement occurred at the end of November in the Battle of Tassafaronga, yet another night fight. The Japanese attempted to make another Tokyo Express run with eight destroyers to provision their forces on Guadalcanal, while the Americans sought to stop them with a force of five cruisers and six destroyers. The Americans achieved tactical surprise but, despite their superior force, got the worst of the fight. The US Navy lost one cruiser sunk plus three that sustained major damage from Japanese torpedoes, while the IJN lost only one destroyer with a second lightly damaged. The defeat was a tactical embarrassment for the Americans and another clear demonstration of Japanese skill in night fighting and torpedo technology. Again, however, the Japanese turned back without having delivered the badly needed supplies to Guadalcanal, so that success at sea did not translate into any change on land.[18]

The naval Battle of Guadalcanal demonstrated the growing air and sea control enjoyed by the Allies around that island, but much ground fighting remained ahead. Throughout November, the Americans began to expand their perimeter around the airfield, particularly to the west; but the lines soon stabilized and remained relatively static into January 1943. In early December, the 1st Marine Division departed for rest and rehabilitation, and Major General Alexander M. Patch, US Army, took command of the forces on the island. On January 2, 1943, the South Pacific Area activated the US XIV Corps, under Patch's command, consisting of the Americal (23rd) Division, the 25th Infantry Division, and the 2nd Marine Division.[19] That month XIV Corps conducted a series of offensives pushing west from the airfield to clear the Japanese. Unbeknownst to the Americans, the Japanese, realizing the increasing American control over the seas and air around the island, had decided on New Year's Eve to abandon Guadalcanal and evacuate their remaining troops. Under American pressure, but in a coordinated and largely successful evacuation, the last of the Japanese left the island on February 8, thus ending the campaign for Guadalcanal.[20] During this tumultuous campaign, the Americans had lost a total of 7,100 killed and permanently missing on land, sea, and in the air, while Japanese losses exceeded 30,300.[21]

THE ALLIES SEIZE THE STRATEGIC INITIATIVE

With the successful conclusions of the Papua New Guinea and Guadalcanal campaigns, the Allies had finally seized the strategic initiative in the Pacific War. The Japanese decision to evacuate Guadalcanal also carried with it changes in their plans for New Guinea, changes that imply the Japanese knew they had ceded the initiative to the Allies. Without giving up on potential future operations against Port Moresby, the Japanese decided to pull back from Papua while reinforcing other positions such as Lae and Salamaua on the northern coast of New Guinea. The Japanese also decided to prepare strong positions in the central and northern Solomons to shield Rabaul from the growing American presence in the area.[22] These decisions represented tacit admission that the situation in early 1943 precluded Japan from isolating Australia, meaning Japan could no longer pursue its aims in expanding the perimeter of its conquests in the Pacific. Instead, Tokyo could only react to forthcoming Allied moves, a

telling sign that the initiative had indeed passed to the Allies. Reviewing
the elements contributing to this important shift in the strategic initiative
will help us grasp its underlying dynamics.

Resources

The manpower situation during this phase changed but slightly.[23] On
New Guinea, Allied forces continued to outnumber the Japanese at the
point of contact. The weakened Australian 7th Division and the fresh but
inexperienced US 32nd Infantry Division squared off against remnants
of multiple Japanese units around Buna and Gona that totaled between
6,000 and 8,000 troops.[24] On Guadalcanal in mid-November the Japanese achieved parity for the first time in the campaign with an estimated
30,000 troops against the American presence of 29,000 troops. Despite
this brief advantage, the Japanese defeat at the naval Battle of Guadalcanal precluded any Japanese land offensive on the island. Soon the balance
shifted back to the Allies: on December 9, the Americans had 40,000
troops on the island to Japan's 25,000, and Tokyo's decision to withdraw
from Guadalcanal in late December meant that the Japanese numbers
continued to shrink while the Americans' grew.[25]

The material situation remained similar to that of the previous phase,
but superior American aircraft production did begin to show in the southern and southwestern Pacific.[26] Through November 1942, the JNAF had
carried the fight alone in the region, but this soon changed. At the end of
November the Japanese organized the 6th Air Division under the command of the 8th Area Army to direct the JAAF units that would soon arrive to support the ongoing operations and lift some of the burden from
the IJN. JAAF aircraft moved to Rabaul in December, and fifteen aircraft
operating from Buna engaged in their first combat against the Allies in the
last ten days of the year. This influx of Japanese army aircraft sustained
Japanese airpower in the southern Pacific, despite the heavy attrition of
Japanese naval aircraft. After the evacuation of Guadalcanal, the combined Japanese air strength in the combat area still exceeded 200 strike
and fighter aircraft.[27] During this period, the JAAF sent the 1st and 11th
Air Divisions, totaling 100 fighters, from the 12th Air Regiment, the 10th
Air Division of reconnaissance aircraft, and the 14th Air Division with
its 27 bombers to Rabaul.[28] On Guadalcanal, total American air strength
increased from just 29 aircraft on October 26 to 188 aircraft of all types
by the end of November.[29] Meanwhile, during this period, US Fifth Air
Force's strength in the SWPA remained nearly the same as it had been in

September and October, in part because of the priority the Allies placed on the South Pacific Area, which enabled the increased numbers of aircraft on Guadalcanal.[30]

The material balance during the naval confrontations for this period still generally favored the Japanese. American industrial might began to assert itself at home but had not yet tilted the balance at the point of engagement in the Pacific.[31] In the two surface naval engagements that opened and closed the naval Battle of Guadalcanal, the Japanese significantly outnumbered their American opponents. But in the last battle, at Tassafaronga, the Americans employed a superior force. No carrier actions took place during this period of the war, as the *Enterprise* remained the only operational, if damaged, American fleet carrier in the Pacific following Santa Cruz. The Japanese carriers had also been damaged in that battle, but the losses in their carrier aircraft had been heavier and with greater impact. As a result, the carrier actions that characterized mid- to late 1942 temporarily ceased until both sides rebuilt their carrier fleets.

Technology remained essentially a constant, with some minor changes around the edges mostly favoring the Allies. The P-38s that made their appearance earlier in the SWPA began to overcome their teething troubles and entered the fray on Guadalcanal in late November 1942.[32] P-38s fought their first real action against the Japanese on December 27 over New Guinea. While their contribution during this period of the war remained limited, they represented a portent of things to come.[33] Japanese naval and army pilots would come to respect the P-38, with Lieutenant Kunie Iwashita, IJN, rating it the best American fighter he encountered during the war.[34] The Americans also innovated with technology, modifying the A-20 and B-25 bombers to make those platforms more effective. As early as July–August 1942, Lieutenant Colonel Paul I. "Pappy" Gunn had installed multiple .50-caliber machine guns in a modified nose on the A-20, making the aircraft a devastating gun platform.[35] Kenney liked the modification and in November ordered Gunn to undertake similar efforts with the B-25 aircraft in the Fifth Air Force.[36] Like the P-38, these modifications were destined to play a more important role later in the conflict, but they demonstrated slight improvements in US aircraft technology in late 1942. The introduction of JAAF aircraft also altered the composition of Japanese airpower. Aircraft such as the light, twin-engine Kawasaki Ki-48 "Lily" and the nimble Nakajima Ki-43 "Oscar" fighter now rose to meet the Allied threat.[37] However, these aircraft did not represent large steps forward in technology. The Oscar was even more maneuverable than the Zero, but it used the same engine and had lighter armament, while its lighter airframe restricted its speed.[38] In the main, however, both sides continued to employ the same or similar aerial technology with which they had started the two campaigns.

As in the air, technology on land and sea remained very similar. The weaponry employed by both sides did not undergo any major upgrades during this period. At sea, however, the Americans were beginning to demonstrate a better understanding of the employment of radar during night surface engagements. Admiral Willis Lee, who led the Americans to victory during the battleship engagement that closed the naval Battle of Guadalcanal, attributed his success almost entirely to his possession of radar.[39] This advantage remained fleeting, however. The Battle of Tassa-faronga later that month once again demonstrated that a smaller force of Japanese destroyers could still best a larger American force that contained cruisers and enjoyed the advantage of radar. American naval command-ers were improving their employment of radar unevenly; at Tassafaronga improper coordination meant that all the American cruisers fired on the same enemy ship because of its prominent radar signature, leaving the remaining Japanese ships unmolested.[40] The battle represented a perfect example of the pitfalls of overreliance on radar technology by the US Navy.

The resource competition remained a tight contest during this phase of the war. For the most part, the Allies retained a slight advantage in manpower at the point of contact. In the air the Japanese fielded a large air force, while the American air forces on New Guinea and Guadalcanal grew and finally surpassed the Japanese. Japan retained a preponderance of air, naval, and ground strength, but that would change as 1943 pro-gressed.[41] Technologically, the Allies made minor gains but still fought with inferior torpedoes and with fighter aircraft that could not match the performance and range of the Japanese Zero. By January 1943, Allied strength had grown significantly in the Solomons and the South Pacific Area. Although the overall resource advantage remained marginally in the Japanese favor for this period, the strategic initiative passed to the Allies after the victories on Guadalcanal and in Papua New Guinea.

Intelligence

Neither side shone in the intelligence arena during this four-month period of the war. The Americans anticipated the Japanese activity around Gua-dalcanal prior to and during the naval Battle of Guadalcanal and kept track of Japanese shipping in and around the Solomon Islands.[42] Such intelligence allowed the Allies to meet and defeat the repeated Japanese assaults. Intelligence also precipitated the Battle of Tassafaronga when the Americans, probably through radio decrypts, learned of the forthcoming Japanese attempt to land supplies on Guadalcanal and maneuvered to block the attempt.[43] Still, US estimates of Japanese strength on the ground in the Buna and Gona areas left much to be desired. The intelligence summary for General Headquarters, South West Pacific Area, on November 27–28, 1942, estimated a total of 3,000 Japanese troops in that area, when in reality the Japanese had more than 6,000.[44] MacArthur's intelligence chief, General Charles A. Willoughby, also underestimated the Japanese ability to reinforce the Buna area with fresh troops. These misperceptions contributed to the unexpectedly long and bloody action required to clear the area of Japanese forces. However, the Japanese were largely reacting to Allied moves, unable to anticipate Allied operations through their murky intelligence picture. When the Allies landed forces at Oro Bay to assist in the attack against Buna, the first Japanese knowledge of the operation came just two hours before the landing when a patrol plane spotted the Allied convoy in the bay.[45]

In terms of security, the Allies generally protected their operations while the Japanese had mixed results. Japanese code encryption failures continued to reveal much to the Allies. US Navy ULTRA intercepts detected the forthcoming influx of JAAF airplanes to Rabaul in mid-December and at the same time detected the movement of enemy troops to Madang on New Guinea.[46] However, the Japanese shielded their most important operation, the evacuation of Guadalcanal, quite effectively. Until the last Japanese soldiers had departed Guadalcanal in early February 1943, the Americans believed the Japanese were *reinforcing* the island, leading Nimitz to praise Japanese skill in masking the operation, which allowed thousands of IJA soldiers to fight another day.[47] This evacuation helped the Japanese avoid an even greater debacle and represents an important security achievement; yet, given their other security failures, the Japanese still ceded the advantage to the Allies here.

Overall, from November 1942 through February 1943, the Allies bested the Japanese in intelligence proficiency. The Allies generally held a better appreciation of the situation and could and often did counter Japanese moves. Like the Germans in Europe, the Japanese in the Pacific never realized the full extent to which their communications security had failed. Although not as beneficial to the Allies as it was at Midway, communications intelligence did contribute to the more accurate Allied appreciation of the situation in the southern Pacific.

Strategic Acumen

The strategic decisions made in the wake of Midway tied both combatants to the dual campaigns in the South Pacific. During this phase of the war, however, the actual conduct of the two campaigns led to strategic reevaluations by both sides.

The Japanese had entered the period planning to retake Guadalcanal, after which they would build up strength using an influx of army units and army aircraft to settle the issue in the South Pacific. After their push on Guadalcanal in mid-November 1942 failed, the Japanese high command decided to occupy other strategic areas in the Solomons and to secure their lodgments in New Guinea. Tokyo sent orders to both the IJA and IJN elements in the region, directing them to cooperate to neutralize Allied airpower on Guadalcanal and then retake both that island and Tulagi.[48] Plans changed over the course of late November and December, resulting in the December 31, 1942, decision by the Japanese to withdraw. The Japanese estimate of the situation in January 1943 anticipated future Allied moves against Rabaul and acknowledged that air and sea superiority belonged to the Allies over Guadalcanal and eastern New Guinea. The Japanese recognized that the decision to cede Guadalcanal and eastern New Guinea represented a major shift in the war in the South Pacific.[49] Once again, the Allies had foiled Japanese plans.

American plans had not gone smoothly either. Faulty intelligence estimates led MacArthur and his command to expect rapid occupation of the Buna–Gona–Sanananda area on New Guinea, yet those operations lasted from November 1942 well into January 1943, and they cost the Allies much in men and equipment.[50] Nevertheless, the Allies eventually seized those positions and evicted the Japanese from Guadalcanal and secured that island as well.

Surprise did not shape this period of the two campaigns. Neither side conceived of, nor executed, any operations designed to achieve strategic surprise along the lines of Pearl Harbor, Midway, or the amphibious landings at Guadalcanal. Both remained committed to the bitter struggles of attrition on Guadalcanal and New Guinea, resulting in warfare over predictable terrain and in the surrounding seas and air lanes.

The Americans missed one potential opportunity to deal further significant damage to the Japanese. The Japanese expected heavy losses in the evacuation of Guadalcanal and anticipated removing approximately 5,000 soldiers but in the end were able to evacuate more than twice that number.[51] Had the Americans pressed the Japanese more closely on Guadalcanal in January and February, they probably could have inflicted greater losses. Still, as Nimitz noted, effective Japanese security for the evacuation made the Americans fear a renewed Japanese offensive and to advance cautiously in the face of a potentially growing threat. This missed opportunity did not, however, negate the victory on Guadalcanal.

During this period of the war, the Allies clearly came out ahead of the Japanese in the arena of strategic acumen. The Allies better matched plans to reality and achieved their ends. Neither side gained an advantage from surprise. The Allies missed a minor opportunity to inflict greater damage on the IJA at Guadalcanal, but this mistake did not represent a decisive element in the campaign.

Combat Effectiveness

On land, the two sides largely switched roles during this period. The Allies transitioned to the attack on both New Guinea and Guadalcanal, while the Japanese reverted to the tactical defensive and withdrawal. Allied ground effectiveness was mixed. The Allied forces around Buna struggled to defeat a well-entrenched but numerically inferior foe. The green American 32nd Infantry Division, in particular, struggled against the Japanese at Buna. The report from Colonel H. F. Handy, US Army, who observed the early stages of the Buna operation, claimed the US forces underestimated the Japanese soldiers' capabilities in defense and noted that the American division had not had any artillery support for its attack against the Japanese fortified line.[52] (The lack of artillery was due to the hasty air deployment of infantry elements of the 32nd.) Another report on Buna, from Colonel Harry Knight, cited training deficiencies, overreliance on artillery or mortar support, and leadership "from the rear" as strong inhibitors to the American performance around Buna in late 1942.[53] On Guadalcanal, the US Army troops involved in the closing battles on the island moved slowly and methodically, in part because of terrain and logistics and in part because they remained wary that another Japanese offensive lay just around the corner.[54] Nevertheless, in the end the Allied forces achieved their objectives on both New Guinea and Guadalcanal, while the Japanese forces failed.

A large part of the Japanese failure and Allied success traced back to their respective abilities to sustain their combat power at the front. Lieutenant General Shuichi Miyazaki, chief of staff of the Japanese 17th Army during the Guadalcanal campaign, described Japan's logistical struggles in his postwar report titled "Personal Experiences during the Solomons

Campaign." Miyazaki stated that as early as October only 20 percent of the supplies sent from Rabaul could make it to Guadalcanal owing to US air superiority and the vulnerability of Japanese transport vessels to air attack. In his estimate, the supply shortage caused the Japanese defeat, as approximately one-third of the Japanese forces on Guadalcanal died of starvation.[55] The situation around Buna deteriorated in similar fashion for the Japanese. The rice ration for the IJA's soldiers around Sanananda steadily dwindled between December 1942 and January 1943 from the normal 28 ounces per day, to 10 ounces, and finally to 2 ounces until the food ran out.[56] By comparison, following the naval Battle of Guadalcanal, American sea and air control enabled supplies to flow steadily to the island. The supply situation for the Allies on northeastern New Guinea remained challenging and relied predominantly on airlift, later augmented by sealift. According to Kenney, the food situation for the troops around Buna in late November balanced on a knife's edge as adverse weather hampered airlift; when the weather cleared, the situation immediately eased.[57] Whatever the supply struggles the Allies experienced on New Guinea and Guadalcanal, they paled in comparison to the levels of deprivation experienced by their Japanese counterparts.

On land, therefore, the Americans proved more combat effective than the Japanese. Although the Japanese held off superior Allied forces on New Guinea for several months and deftly covered their evacuation on Guadalcanal, their skillful defensive tactics could not overcome their sustainment deficiencies. The air and sea combat also contributed to those logistical struggles.

The Allies also edged the Japanese at sea. The US Navy clearly won the naval Battle of Guadalcanal, which paid handsome dividends: The Americans landed substantial reinforcements on Guadalcanal, while the Japanese landed only a few; the Navy traded two cruisers and seven destroyers for two Japanese battleships, one cruiser, three destroyers, and twelve transports.[58] At Tassafaronga, superior Japanese night-fighting tactics again inflicted an embarrassing defeat on a superior American force, but the Japanese failed to land supplies on Guadalcanal. Thus, the Japanese squandered their tactical success in that battle.

The first naval battle in November proved to be a tipping point with serious implications for the sustainment of forces on Guadalcanal and, therefore, for possession of the island. Following the naval Battle of Guadalcanal, the Japanese found transportation of troops and supplies to the island by destroyers and slower landing barges too difficult and costly, mostly because of Allied air superiority, which often found and attacked the barges while simultaneously whittling down Japanese air strength at Rabaul.[59] The mid-November surge had failed to give Japan sea control, and the IJN had not eliminated the Cactus Air Force through either ship bombardment or air action.

Control of the air was key to the battles on both land and sea. In the struggle for Guadalcanal, the best estimates for comparative air losses between November 16 and February 9 indicate Allied losses of 134 aircraft to all causes in this period, while Japanese losses amounted to 176–177 aircraft to all causes. Added to similar estimates for the period between August 7 and November 15, the Americans lost 615 aircraft to Japan's 682 for the entire Guadalcanal campaign.[60]

The Allies won the air war during this period, despite the relative parity in aircraft losses. Although aircraft expenditures in the Guadalcanal campaign were closely matched for both combatants, the Allies secured air superiority over the island, inflicted heavy damage on both the IJN and IJA, and, most significant, made prohibitive the costs to the Japanese of continuing to supply and reinforce Guadalcanal. By comparison, the Japanese neither isolated the Americans on Guadalcanal nor destroyed their land-based air forces. As a result, they never achieved air superiority. The same tale echoed in New Guinea, but with a twist. During this period, US Fifth Air Force repeatedly struck at the Japanese defenses in and around Buna and Gona, albeit with limited effectiveness. But, as at Guadalcanal, the key contribution the Allied air force made was the isolation of the Japanese garrison, which increased in effectiveness after November when the Allies opened the Dobodora air base adjacent to Buna.[61] The twist in New Guinea was that, while the Allied air forces isolated the Japanese from their supplies, the same air forces played a major role in sustaining the Allied ground force.

Another aspect of the air war deserves mention. The opening of Dobodura Airfield by the Allies, so close to the front and during the battle, demonstrated the Allied ability to rapidly construct forward air bases. Air bases such as Dobodura and those constructed earlier around Milne Bay laid the foundation for future Allied success in the Papuan campaign because they enabled increasingly effective employment of the Allied air forces. The Japanese understood the concept as well but did not prove as effective at air-base construction. Major General Toroshiro Kawabe, chief of the General Affairs Section of the Army Bureau of Aeronautics until April 1943, praised the American ability to build supporting air bases rapidly with good maintenance support, while lamenting Japan's inability to do either. These inabilities greatly hampered the JAAF's logistical network and increased Japanese aircraft operational losses before they even reached the combat zone.[62] The Japanese constructed a rudimentary airfield at Buna following their initial landings in August and built Buin Airfield on Bougainville in October to support the fight against Guadalcanal.[63] However, these airfields did not significantly alter the course of those campaigns.

In terms of overall combat effectiveness, the Allies came out ahead in this period. The Japanese soldiers proved very stubborn and skillful in defense, often demonstrating superior tactical skill to that of the inexperienced American troops facing them, but the IJA could not sustain its forces. The story at sea contributed to this outcome. Again, the Japanese often demonstrated better tactical skill at nighttime surface engagements, but the Japanese often did not accomplish their missions, even after tactical victories. This contributed to the Americans' ability to achieve sea superiority over the Japanese, which then allowed for the isolation of Japanese troops on Guadalcanal and the shielding of Henderson Field and the Cactus Air Force from naval bombardment. Finally, both sides fielded strong air forces, and neither side could eliminate the other's airpower; but the Allies employed their air formations more effectively. They achieved air superiority over Guadalcanal and over eastern New Guinea, which enabled them to support their own ground and sea forces, while helping to isolate the Japanese garrisons at both locations.

Chance

Chance did not affect this period of the war to the extent it had in the previous period and at Midway, though two incidents deserve mention. These examples both occurred in the first surface engagement of the naval Battle of Guadalcanal. Chance and confusion determined the very character of the engagement. The commander of the American force, Admiral Daniel Callaghan, lacked the newest radar on his flagship and entered the fray with a confused picture of the tactical situation. Callaghan hesitated during the opening moments of the engagement as he tried to make sense of the situation. This delay cost him the temporal advantage gained through early radar detection of the approaching Japanese force. As a result, instead of a standoff gunnery and torpedo engagement, the battle devolved into a melee with the two fleets intertwined with each other, which led to each ship fighting independently.[64] Such a close-range fight provided some advantages to the Americans and somewhat mitigated the Japanese advantage in gunnery ranges as well as the lethal, long-range Japanese torpedoes. The American fleet suffered greater damage, but the Japanese commander, Admiral Hiroaki Abe, decided to disengage and cancel his planned bombardment of Henderson Field, a decision that later resulted in his forced retirement from the navy.[65] Similarly, at the Battle of Tassafaronga, Rear Admiral Raizō Tanaka, despite savaging an American task force, failed to complete his mission to land supplies on Guadalcanal. Thus, Japanese tactical advantages did not translate into operational successes.

Neither of these examples gave a significant advantage to either side. At best, they amounted to a marginal advantage for the Allies. More significant for the campaign as a whole, the Japanese naval commanders demonstrated a consistent pattern that had begun at the Battle of Savo Island. Following a clash of surface forces around Guadalcanal, Japanese commanders often abandoned their primary mission regardless of the outcome of the initial engagement. This differed from the opening phase of the war in which, despite surface engagements with Allied task forces of ABDACOM, the Japanese had often, though not always, followed through with their primary mission after the clash. Reasons for the demonstrated caution are unclear, but one may speculate that the results of Coral Sea and Midway, as well as the fluid situation around Guadalcanal, may have introduced a measure of doubt in the minds of Japanese naval commanders—doubt not present when the tide of Japanese victories ran high in the opening months of the war.

CONCLUSIONS

The Allies clearly seized the strategic initiative from Japan with the victories on Papua New Guinea and Guadalcanal. Resources during this period still marginally favored the Japanese, but by early 1943 that began to change. In terms of intelligence, the Allies had again better matched their plans to realities and had more effectively balanced ends, ways, and means. Allied intelligence was not perfect, and indeed it was quite faulty around Buna, but the Allies generally formed better estimates of the situation and operated more effectively based on these more accurate appreciations. The comparison of combat effectiveness between the combatants is instructive. The Japanese fought very well on land in the tactical defense, often besting their Allied foes. The IJN also continued to display its mastery of night surface tactics. But these tactical advantages did not translate into superior combat effectiveness. The Japanese struggled to sustain their forces, a key reason for their failures on Guadalcanal and New Guinea. The IJN squandered its tactical victories and lost local command of the sea. In the air, the Allies demonstrated better combat effectiveness across the board and gained air superiority that also contributed to Japanese struggles on the land and sea. Thus, despite occasional tactical superiority, the Japanese on the whole remained less combat effective. The Allies fought adequately on land and sea, and fought well in the air, but, much more important, they sustained their forces more effectively than did the Japanese. Finally, chance at best granted the Allies a marginal advantage in the naval battles around Guadalcanal. Taken together, advantages in intelligence, strategic acumen, and overall combat effectiveness enabled the Allies to wrest the strategic initiative from Japan despite a relatively close resource balance and the latter's tactical proficiency in land defense and night surface engagements at sea.

The Pacific War would now take a different course, with the Allies in the driver's seat. The campaigns on Guadalcanal and Papua New Guinea ended within a month of each other. With these victories, the Allies gained more than just territory in the Solomon Islands and New Guinea and more than a reprieve for Australia. No longer would Japan dictate the course of the war. After February 1943, the Allies, in the main, determined the tempo and the focus of operations in the Pacific War.

Less than two weeks after the victory on Guadalcanal, the US forces occupied the Russell Islands, just northwest of Guadalcanal, their next step up the Solomon Islands chain. In early March, Allied air forces in the Battle of the Bismarck Sea destroyed a large Japanese shipping convoy carrying reinforcements and supplies for the remaining Japanese positions in northern New Guinea, an indication of the difficulties Japan would face while implementing its new strategy in the South Pacific.

At the Casablanca Conference in January 1943, the Allies struggled to come to an agreement over Pacific strategy and the associated dedication of resources. Following that conference, the American JCS crafted a directive for the conduct of the war in the Pacific: MacArthur and Halsey were to continue to establish advanced air bases, move north and west along the coast of New Guinea, and occupy the Solomons as far north as Bougainville with the objectives of inflicting losses upon the enemy, retaining the initiative, and preparing for the seizure of the entire Bismarck Archipelago.[66] The Allies successfully proceeded along those lines in the ensuing months, culminating with the invasions of Bougainville and Tarawa in November 1943. The latter assault belatedly opened the Central Pacific offensive that navy planners had envisioned before the war.

The dual campaigns in eastern New Guinea and Guadalcanal had another important effect on the later stages of the war. These battles and the follow-on actions in the central Solomons and western New Guinea throughout 1943 severely depleted the JNAF and JAAF, which noticeably hampered Japan's ability to counter the Allied offensive in the Central Pacific.[67] Beginning with the Battle of Midway, the experience of Japanese naval pilots decreased continuously, slowly declining in the rest of 1942 and then dramatically ebbing in 1943.[68] The JAAF also suffered similarly after its introduction to the southern Pacific in 1943. According to Lieutenant General Kawabe, the army lost its best pilots defending these areas, significantly reducing its ability to resist Allied efforts in later campaigns on New Guinea and in the Philippine Islands.[69]

Taken together with the losses inflicted on the Japanese land forces and on the Japanese navy, the cost of these campaigns did not bode well for Japan. The Japanese war machine of 1943 to 1945 could not match its predecessor of 1941 and 1942, much less the vastly expanded American forces—which now enjoyed the strategic initiative on the road to Tokyo.

10

Conclusions

During the eight-month period between July 1942 and February 1943, the Allies and Japanese engaged in two concurrent campaigns in the South Pacific, campaigns that resulted in attritional warfare for the possession of strategic locations in the Solomon Islands and in Papua New Guinea. More than territory was at stake, however. The outcome of these struggles determined which side would possess the strategic initiative in the conflict and, therefore, who would wield greater influence over the future course of the war. Neither side's prewar planning had envisioned warfare on this scale in the South Pacific, but the early course of the war and the rapid Japanese successes at limited cost altered the strategic calculus for both combatants. The Japanese felt they now had the ability to extend their perimeter farther to secure their gains and isolate Australia. The Americans felt they had to react to the tide of Japanese conquest and, specifically, had to protect the lines of communication between Hawaii and Australia. Thus the operations in the South Pacific, originally envisioned by both sides as limited operations preceding the decisive naval battle in the Central Pacific, instead evolved into the decisive effort in 1942 and 1943. Indeed, combat continued in and around the Solomon Islands, New Guinea, and New Britain well into 1944, while the Allies' Central Pacific drive did not commence until November 1943, opening with the Battle of Tarawa. By that point, the Allies had held the strategic initiative for nine months, an initiative they retained until the end of the war.

Strategic initiative in war represents the ability to influence the course of the conflict by waging those battles, operations, and campaigns most suited to the accomplishment of one's own political ends while avoiding those detrimental to the same. Possession of strategic initiative implies greater influence but not necessarily total control over the course of events in war. Strategic initiative is important because it grants the side possessing it greater flexibility than its adversary and thus more options for future operations. Rather than simply reacting to the impulses of the foe, the side holding the strategic initiative enjoys freedom to pursue those aims and objectives best suited to meeting its goals. One must add the caveat that such freedom should be used responsibly, which implies the need for wise strategic choice. As the Japanese ruefully discovered after the Battle of Midway, strategic initiative can be lost through miscalculation. In many ways, possession of the initiative can complicate the strategist's task by offering too wide an array of options. Hypothetically, it would seem that the side that possesses the strategic initiative toward the end of a conflict is more likely to prevail, but this hypothesis clearly requires detailed analysis. There is no doubt that the Allies, having seized the initiative in early 1943, held it throughout the remainder of the Pacific War and exploited it until achieving victory.

Possession of strategic initiative results from a myriad of factors. This analysis has identified five areas of comparison that contribute in varying degrees to the possession of strategic initiative: resources, intelligence, strategic acumen, combat effectiveness, and chance. Political will is another ingredient in that, at times, political judgment may preclude the possession of strategic initiative or, to the contrary, may demand an untimely attempt to seize it. One cannot assume that both sides are fully politically engaged in a conflict at all times. This list is not exhaustive, given all the factors that affect and contribute to strategy; but it provides a useful construct for analyzing shifts in strategic initiative during a given conflict. Understanding how these elements influenced possession of the initiative and how they interacted with one another in the Pacific War may assist in gaining a greater understanding of the causes, course, and outcomes of a conflict and the thought processes of the combatants.

Japan seized and held the strategic initiative in the opening months of World War II in the Pacific. The Japanese exploited their resource advantage, based on materiel superiority and technology, as well as their more effective intelligence collection and security. Their early strategic acumen greatly exceeded that of the Allies, as they achieved strategic surprise and matched their plans with reality to reach their goals rapidly. In terms of combat effectiveness, the Japanese demonstrated superior tactical and operational skills while also sustaining their forces; they bested the Allies on land, sea, and in the air. Chance, in the form of human capacity to deal with the unknown, favored the Allies at this point, with Nagumo's cautious decision against launching a third attack wave at Pearl Harbor and with the absence of any US aircraft carriers in the harbor during the attack.

Japan's leaders manifested strong political will by launching this war of conquest. Thus, with the political will to wage a war of conquest, the

Japanese seized and held the strategic initiative with advantages in four
of the five comparative categories; as a result, the war initially proceeded
according to their plans. The slim advantages given to the Americans by
chance could not overcome their other deficits. Nevertheless, the continued survival of the American aircraft carriers and submarines along with
the facilities at Pearl Harbor played a key role for the Allies later in the
Pacific War.

The Japanese suffered a setback at the Battle of the Coral Sea and a
disaster at the Battle of Midway. At the start of the Midway battle, the
Japanese had a significant, seemingly insurmountable, resource advantage. However, the Americans enjoyed a large advantage in intelligence
that enabled them to make superior strategic judgments. This time the
Americans reversed the tables from Pearl Harbor and negated the surprise
upon which the Japanese had based their entire plan. During the battle,
both sides demonstrated uneven operational performance. The Japanese
divided their fleet and squandered their resource superiority, but they still
coordinated strikes involving multiple aircraft carriers better than did the
Americans. Tactically, the Japanese pilots demonstrated remarkable skill
and on an individual level bested the Americans, but the Americans were
skilled fliers in their own right and performed well enough tactically to
defeat the Japanese. Meanwhile, American aircraft carriers, specifically
the *Yorktown*, demonstrated endurance and survivability in the form of
damage control that the four Japanese carriers sunk at Midway could not
match. In this battle, the Americans proved to be more combat effective.
The element of chance also favored the Americans. Admiral Nagumo
struggled to adapt effectively when his plans went awry, and Japanese
search efforts were frequently misdirected. For their part, American pilots
demonstrated individual initiative that serendipitously produced a devastating, multi-axis air attack on the Japanese carrier fleet. This battle did
not transfer the strategic initiative to the Allies, but it did even the naval
odds in the Pacific and allow the Allies to dispute the initiative.

Following Midway, the Japanese believed they still held the strategic
initiative and sought to exercise it through continued expansion in the
South Pacific. Although the Japanese canceled the occupation of Midway
and the planned invasions of Fiji–Samoa–New Caledonia, they still envisioned isolating Australia through the presumably less ambitious plans
of advancing in eastern New Guinea and the lower Solomon Islands. The
Allies continued to react to Japanese moves and hoped to take advantage
of the Midway victory with counteroffensives that would protect the vital
lifeline to Australia. By placing the initiative in dispute at Midway, the

Allies achieved the freedom of action needed to conceive of and conduct these operations. These conditions set the stage for the epic struggles on Papua New Guinea and Guadalcanal—struggles that ultimately ended with the Allies seizing the strategic initiative.

The first phase of these campaigns lasted from July 1942 to the end of October. They incorporated several dramatic, high-intensity confrontations on land, sea, and in the air. The resource gap at this stage had narrowed, but the Japanese still retained an edge. As they had at Midway, the Allies bested the Japanese in intelligence collection and security. They also demonstrated more perceptive strategic acumen by artfully matching objectives with capabilities, although the landing on Guadalcanal left no margin for error. The Japanese achieved none of their objectives during this phase of the war. The Allies also achieved strategic surprise with their landing at Guadalcanal, and, in general, they recognized and exploited opportunities more adroitly than did the Japanese. At sea and in the air the Japanese often, although not always, demonstrated superior tactical skill. On the ground, however, Allied soldiers performed more effectively. On the whole, the Allies again demonstrated superior combat effectiveness by achieving their aims even in the face of tactical setbacks and by sustaining their forces more robustly. Four out of six significant examples of chance and human capacity to operate in the unknown favored the Allies, with the most important being Admiral Mikawa's failure to attack the Allied invasion fleet after the Battle of Savo Island. Had he done so the Guadalcanal campaign—and perhaps even the course of the Pacific War—could have turned out much differently.

The influence of political will was clearly evident during this phase of the war. Throughout the summer and autumn of 1942, President Franklin Roosevelt clung doggedly to the Allies' Germany First strategy and diverted only the bare minimum of resources to the Pacific to counter the Japanese threat to Australia. If he had sent more personnel and materiel to the Pacific, perhaps at the expense of the invasion of North Africa, the precarious Allied resource situation in the South Pacific could have been significantly eased. The Guadalcanal and New Guinea campaigns may then have followed a different course, strategic initiative in the Pacific may have shifted to the Allies more quickly, and the war could have taken a different turn. Instead, Roosevelt aimed to seize the strategic initiative in the European Theater of Operations first.

In late October 1942, the strategic initiative in the Pacific was still up for grabs. Neither side had complete freedom of action in its operations and both were locked into the bloody, costly campaigns on New Guinea and in the Solomons. The Allies had exploited their advantages in intelligence, strategic acumen, combat effectiveness, and chance to overcome the Japanese advantage in resources and keep the strategic initiative in dispute. Allied political will, personified by Roosevelt, delayed a shift of the initiative to the Allies during the preceding four months. The Japanese reaction to the campaigns in the Solomons and New Guinea, with the heavy commitment of the IJN and the growing involvement of the IJA, demonstrated that the Japanese political will remained strong.

Nevertheless, between November 1942 and February 1943, the Allies defeated the Japanese in eastern New Guinea and evicted them from Guadalcanal. In so doing, they gained the strategic initiative for the first time in the Pacific War. This period did not have as many named naval battles as did the previous period, but the fighting remained constant and grueling. On land, the Allies went over to the tactical offensive, while the Japanese troops reverted to the defensive and withdrawal. The resource gap continued to close. The Allies developed superior, though not perfect, intelligence and enhanced security. Neither side achieved any strategic surprises, but the Allies demonstrated better judgment in the matching of ends, ways, and means. Combat effectiveness followed a similar pattern. At sea during night engagements and on land in defense, the Japanese possessed excellent tactical skills, but the Allies did better in accomplishing their objectives and sustaining their combat power. Allied control of the air above and around Guadalcanal helped gain control of the seas as well, effectively isolating the Japanese garrison on the island. Around Buna, Allied air superiority accomplished the same goal, isolating that Japanese bastion. The Japanese fought remarkably well despite starvation and unimaginable deprivations, but their effectiveness inexorably waned. Chance was not a major factor in this phase. With advantages in intelligence, strategic acumen, and combat effectiveness, the Allies finally seized the strategic initiative. They exploited that initiative in 1943 by continuing operations in the Solomons and on New Guinea, establishing the conditions that eventually isolated the strong Japanese bastion at Rabaul. By the end of 1943, the Allies had sufficient resources to open a second offensive with a drive across the Central Pacific while General Douglas MacArthur continued his push across the Southwest Pacific. The Japanese, meanwhile, did their best to counter Allied moves, but after February 1943 they could no longer determine the course of the war.

How, then, did the elements examined in this study interact with one another to bring about this significant shift in strategic initiative? Resources represent a critical component of war-making capacity. Generally speaking, having more resources eases the strategist's task by allowing for more options and greater flexibility in the implementation of those options. Yet, having more resources than one's opponent does not guarantee the possession of strategic initiative. The Japanese had resource superiority for much of the period examined here. Nevertheless, by February 1943, they had lost the strategic initiative to the Allies. At Midway, the IJN's proclivity for division of forces undercut its resource advantage and contributed to its defeat. The Japanese can be similarly faulted in August 1942, when they divided their land forces between Kokoda, Milne Bay, and Guadalcanal, leaving them at a tactical disadvantage in each location. A more concentrated effort in one direction may well have yielded better results. Thus, poor strategic decisions can all too easily negate resource advantages.

The quality of intelligence was a key ingredient in determining who held the initiative and why the initiative shifted. From December 1941 until about April/May 1942, the Japanese held an intelligence advantage that contributed significantly to their holding the initiative. In the weeks leading up to Midway, however, the Americans evened the odds. The Allies held an intelligence advantage in the last two periods of this study. From July to October 1942, the initiative was in dispute. Between November 1942 and February 1943, the Allies seized the initiative, and gradually improving intelligence was a major factor underlying these shifts.

The intelligence competition was a product of the intelligence organizations employed by both sides. During the first phase of the war, the Japanese intelligence system worked quite well. The Japanese had more time to develop their intelligence for their opening moves than they would once the fighting commenced and the situation became more fluid. With the exception of Hawaii, the opening Japanese moves took place in areas closer and more familiar to Japan than did the campaigns of Buna and Guadalcanal. Thus, it was easier to gather a more accurate picture in these areas than would be the case after the perimeter had expanded farther from the Japanese home islands. As the Japanese operated farther from home in the less-familiar reaches of the Solomon Islands and New Guinea, they had to collect and gather information under the pressures of war, resulting in a deterioration of the Japanese intelligence system. Human intelligence dropped off, and the Japanese struggled with radio intelligence and codebreaking. Furthermore, the IJA and IJN never created a joint intelligence center, and the army commanders on Guadalcanal could not get accurate information about their American foes from their higher echelon based in Rabaul. As a result, Japanese intelligence achieved much less fidelity than that of their Allied opponents. This, in turn, hampered strategic decisions and the conduct of operations.

The Allies improved their intelligence capabilities as the war progressed. The US Army and US Navy shared intelligence more productively than did their Japanese counterparts. The Allies also did a better job sharing intelligence among nations. MacArthur set up several agencies that integrated intelligence from various services and Allied nations. The South Pacific Area and the South West Pacific Area also coordinated well with regard to intelligence. On the whole, the Allies practiced their intelligence activities in a more integrated manner than did the Japanese. In addition, the Allies in the Pacific, particularly the US Navy, often performed brilliantly with respect to radio intelligence, which conferred significant advantages at Coral Sea and Midway. When the Japanese changed their codes after Midway, much of the information from this source dried up temporarily, but the Allies continued to exploit radio-traffic analysis to garner important information on the whereabouts and possible activities of the Imperial Japanese Navy. While waging campaigns in the Solomon Islands and on New Guinea, the Allies also benefited significantly from human intelligence provided by the Coastwatcher network. They also developed a rudimentary but effective photo-intelligence capability. With a more integrated and comprehensive intelligence effort, the Allies produced far better intelligence products and operated with a clearer picture than did their Japanese foe.

Yet, combatants must properly use intelligence for it to be effective and contribute to the war effort. In every period here examined, the side with the intelligence advantage made better strategic decisions. The Japanese excelled in the beginning, but the Allies did much better at Midway, New Guinea, and Guadalcanal. A little knowledge went a long way and enabled commanders to calculate their moves more effectively. Proper security also assisted with the achievement of strategic surprise on several occasions, such as at Pearl Harbor, Midway, and Guadalcanal. The Japanese exhibited superb strategic acumen during their opening moves, but following that phase the Allies consistently made better strategic judgments, typically supported with better intelligence.

Intelligence, however, is not the sole explanation for the Allies' seizure of the strategic initiative. The decision-making organizations employed by each side shaped their strategies. The Japanese operated by making army-navy agreements that stipulated the responsibilities of each service with regard to agreed-upon strategy. The divergent foci of the two Japanese services also hampered effective strategy in the South Pacific. The IJA continued to focus on and prepare for possible war with its traditional enemies: the Soviet Union, China, and Manchuria. When the conquest of the "southern resource area" ended successfully, the IJA remained content to return its focus to the Asian mainland and let the IJN fight against its traditional foe: the United States. The IJA grudgingly agreed to expand the defensive perimeter. In so doing it made its own demands, which included occupying the Aleutians, thus stretching Japan's resources even further. The IJA, having already rejected an invasion of Australia, also demonstrated little interest in the operations north of that continent, which were favored by the IJN.

These divergent priorities were symptomatic of the Japanese system. Because the emperor rarely intervened in interservice disputes, there was no single authority above the two service chiefs to forge a common strategy. Neither did the Japanese develop a true joint staff that worked together to blend service concerns and develop joint plans. Integration occurred only at the highest levels of the Imperial General Headquarters, if at all. This resulted in mid-1942 in a compromise to expand beyond the originally planned defensive perimeter in three divergent directions: the northern, the central, and the southern Pacific. The Japanese secured success only in the North Pacific, occupying Attu and Kiska in the Aleutians, but for little gain. Exacerbating the Japanese problems, when things began to heat up in the South Pacific, the IJA was late to the fight. Few JAAF aircraft arrived until late 1942. The IJA eventually diverted a number of army divisions to the area, but it fed troops into the battle in small increments, while its main strength remained in Manchuria and China. While the IJA reacted slowly, the JNAF and the Japanese fleet suffered steady attrition in the air and waters around New Guinea and Guadalcanal. The Japanese also maintained separate field commands for the IJA and the IJN, expecting commanders to make local agreements that supported the direction given in the central agreements. Thus, while the Americans were at times discomfited by their own problems of divided command in the Pacific, the Japanese could not replicate the unity of effort that was achieved under the South Pacific and Southwest Pacific commands of Bull Halsey and MacArthur.

American and Allied commanders clearly benefited from a more integrated command system than the Japanese possessed. The creation of the Joint Chiefs of Staff, modeled on the British system, facilitated just enough interservice cooperation to develop an American strategy that eventually succeeded. As the pointed post-Midway exchanges between George Marshall and Ernest King demonstrated, American interservice relations were not all sweetness and light. Nevertheless, the JCS system generally kept the Allied war machine in the Pacific focused on the same objectives. Additionally, when necessary, President Roosevelt could and did override his military leaders to ensure that the military strategy matched his grand strategy. General MacArthur and Admirals Robert Ghormley and Halsey also enjoyed relatively unfettered command over nearly all military personnel in their designated areas of responsibility. They could employ their resources as they saw fit without having to reach an army-navy compromise in the field. Allied commanders integrated aircraft, ships, intelligence, and ground troops from different services and nations into a single force directed toward common objectives. Unlike the Japanese arrangements, under which the IJN focused on the Solomons and the IJA centered its efforts on New Guinea, the Allies operated joint commands in both areas. With the JCS guiding the overall effort from the top, the Allies operated more cooperatively and implemented a more effective strategy.

Sooner or later, even the most efficacious strategy must be accompanied by battlefield success, making combat effectiveness an important ingredient of strategic initiative. Here, the findings are quite interesting. In several cases, the Japanese remained tactically superior yet were less effective than the Allies. The Allies learned quickly how to counter the Japanese night infantry tactics that had succeeded earlier in the war and also how to use teamwork in the air to counter the capable and nimble Japanese aircraft and their experienced, skillful pilots. The Japanese infantry, naval personnel, and aircrews remained skilled warriors throughout these campaigns, but the Allies performed well enough at the tactical level to counter their highly trained adversaries. After the opening phase of the war, the Allies sustained their forces much more effectively than did the Japanese, which proved a key component of Allied victories. Tactical prowess does not feed and arm the soldier, and as the Japanese sustainment effort deteriorated, so too did the combat capabilities of their fielded forces. This assessment reveals that the Allies achieved their objectives with slightly fewer resource expenditures than the Japanese, who failed to meet their objectives despite heavy losses.

Finally, chance played an important role in a number of ways, the most important of which favored the Allies. One of the most important conclusions with respect to chance in the Pacific between 1942 and February 1943 is the difference between the willingness of the Allied and Japanese commanders to accept risk. Although not always the case—Frank Fletcher at Guadalcanal is an important exception—the Allied commanders dealt better with calculated risks and the unknown. Chester Nimitz's boldness at Midway is one example, as is the tactical conduct of Admirals Fletcher and Raymond Spruance during that battle. The JCS's determination to launch the Guadalcanal operation over the objections of MacArthur and Ghormley is another. In contrast, the Japanese often hesitated or hedged, even after winning a battle. Chuichi Nagumo flailed at Midway when the Japanese plan went awry. Gunichi Mikawa missed his golden opportunity to destroy the American invasion fleet at Guadalcanal following his victory at Savo Island. Despite their tactical victory at Tassafaronga, the Japanese turned back and did not land their supplies on Guadalcanal. During the naval Battle of Guadalcanal, the Japanese bombardment force abandoned its objectives on the first night after a short, sharp fight with an inferior American cruiser force. In sum, the IJN frequently failed to accomplish its missions, despite having won an engagement.[1] Often satisfied with a tactical victory, the IJN abandoned its primary missions without taking the further risks necessary to complete them. Such hesitancy greatly reduced Japanese combat effectiveness during this period of the Pacific War.

The division of Japanese forces between Kokoda, Milne Bay, and Guadalcanal in August 1942 reinforces the close interrelationships between the New Guinea and Solomons campaigns. The brief window from mid- to late August 1942 presented a significant opportunity for the Japanese to avert having to fight two long, attritional struggles. Following Mikawa's naval victory at Savo Island, had the Japanese diverted the forces destined for Milne Bay and Kokoda to Guadalcanal, they might have been able to retake the airfield at a time when the Americans might not have been able to mount a credible defense. Had they secured Guadalcanal, they might have then been able to refocus on New Guinea with a similar concentration of effort. Instead, they employed inferior resources at all three locations and failed at each. The dual campaigns also influenced the air war, with New Guinea taking a backseat to Guadalcanal for the Japanese. The Japanese essentially yielded air superiority to the Allies on New Guinea while simultaneously failing to win it over Guadalcanal. This analysis demonstrates the importance of examining the New Guinea and Solomon Islands campaigns as part of a whole, in which the Southwest and South Pacific theaters were intimately connected.

In sum, during the period from August 1942 to the winter of 1942–1943, the Allies wrested the strategic initiative from the Japanese. They did so without a preponderance of resources, without superior aircraft or ships, and with a mixed assortment of experienced and inexperienced ground troops. They challenged the Imperial Japanese war machine at the zenith of its power and came out on top after two long, grueling campaigns on New Guinea and Guadalcanal. Superior strategic acumen, supported by good intelligence and enacted with combat-effective forces that could be sustained over time, enabled the Allies to bring about a fundamental shift in the dynamics of the Pacific War. A different outcome on New Guinea or Guadalcanal would certainly have altered the course of the war. Yet, fortune often favored the Allies, who took calculated risks and punished the hesitant Japanese who did not. While seizing the initiative, the Allies inflicted damaging losses on the IJA, the IJN, and the air forces of both services. These losses frequently came from the elite of the Japanese forces and made the Japanese task of resistance much more difficult in the later stages of the war. In contrast, after they had seized the initiative, the Allies could count on steadily increasing resources and combat power. Although they did not have those resources in the South Pacific at the time, Allied commanders knew they were on the way. This knowledge undoubtedly figured into the strategic calculations of both sides, even during this period of relative Japanese advantage. Yet, the fact remains that the Allies seized the strategic initiative and were winning the war well before they had the overwhelming resource advantages needed to defeat the Japanese empire in the Pacific.

NOTES

CHAPTER 1. INTRODUCTION

1. See John T. Kuehn, *Agents of Innovation: The General Board and the Design of the Fleet That Defeated the Japanese Navy* (Annapolis, MD: Naval Institute Press, 2008), 26, 125–143.
2. Samuel Eliot Morison, *The Two-Ocean War: A Short History of the United States Navy in the Second World War* (Boston: Little, Brown, 1963), 285.
3. John L. Zimmerman, *The Guadalcanal Campaign* (Washington, DC: Historical Division, Headquarters, US Marine Corps, 1949), 165.
4. John Miller, *Guadalcanal: The First Offensive*, United States Army in World War II: The War in the Pacific (Washington, DC: Center of Military History, 1989), 350.
5. Maurice Matloff and Edwin Marion Snell, *Strategic Planning for Coalition Warfare, 1941–1942*, United States Army in World War II: The War Department (Washington, DC: Office of the Chief of Military History, 1953), 167, 296, 350, 366.
6. Wesley Frank Craven and James Lea Cate, *The Pacific: Guadalcanal to Saipan, August 1942 to July 1944*, vol. 4, *The Army Air Forces in World War II* (Washington, DC: Office of Air Force History, 1983), 670.
7. See, for example, John Keegan, *The Second World War* (New York: Penguin Books, 1990), 278, and R. J. Overy, *Why the Allies Won*, 1st American ed. (New York: W. W. Norton, 1996), 15.
8. Williamson Murray and Allan R. Millett, *A War to Be Won: Fighting the Second World War* (Cambridge: Belknap Press of Harvard University Press, 2000), 195.
9. Dan van der Vat, *The Pacific Campaign: World War II, the U.S.-Japanese Naval War, 1941–1945* (New York: Simon & Schuster, 1991), 121, 177.
10. Ronald H. Spector, *Eagle against the Sun: The American War with Japan* (New York: The Free Press, 1985), 178.
11. Ibid., 217–218.
12. James B. Wood, *Japanese Military Strategy in the Pacific War: Was Defeat Inevitable?* (New York: Rowman & Littlefield, 2007), 7, 19.
13. H. P. Willmott, *The War with Japan: The Period of Balance, May 1942–October 1943* (Wilmington, DE: Scholarly Resources, 2002), 90.
14. United States Strategic Bombing Survey, ed., "U.S. Strategic Bombing Survey (Pacific): Interrogations of Japanese Leaders and Responses to Questionnaires, 1945–1946" (Washington, DC: National Archives Microfilm

Publications, 1991) (hereafter cited as USSBS Interrogations): No. 497: Lieutenant General Shuichi MIYAZAKI, IJA; Subject: Effect of Allied Air Activity on Japanese Planning of the SOLOMONS, RABAUL, and NEW GUINEA Operations and on Japan's Ability to Carry out Those Plans; Planning and Objectives of the Burma Campaign; Date: 3 December 1945, Tokyo; Microfilm Publication M1654, Reel #9, 497-5. Lieutenant General Miyazaki represented many Japanese attitudes when he stated "there is no longer any secrecy about anything as far as we are concerned, so I will be glad to write everything I can remember on the matter" during his postwar USSBS interrogation.

15. The *Australian War Memorial Project* and its associated *Australia-Japan Research Project* have provided online access to some such materials: ajrp .awm.gov.au/AJRP/AJRP2.nsf/Web-Pages/HomePage?OpenDocument. This book has incorporated portions of these materials.

CHAPTER 2. STRATEGIC INITIATIVE

1. B. H. Liddell Hart, *Strategy*, 2nd rev. ed. (New York: Meridian Books, 1991), 322.

2. Paul M. Kennedy, *Grand Strategies in War and Peace* (New Haven, CT: Yale University Press, 1991), 4–5.

3. Joint Publication 1-02: 12 April 2001 (as Amended through 30 September 2010): *Department of Defense Dictionary of Military and Associated Terms* (Washington, DC: US Department of Defense, 2010), 317.

4. Outlining three "levels" of war including the tactical, operational, and strategic levels represents an artificial construct and one open to serious debate and discussion. The three often overlap significantly. Capabilities in each of these aspects of war may also influence policy choices and development of a grand strategy. Nevertheless, the construct helps clarify much about each aspect, even if its presumed isolation appears overstated.

5. Joint Publication 1-02, 457.

6. Ibid., 340.

7. See, for example, Liddell Hart, *Strategy*, 321; Edward Luttwak, *Strategy: The Logic of War and Peace*, rev. and enlarged ed. (Cambridge, MA: Belknap Press of Harvard University Press, 2001), 269; Colin S. Gray, *Modern Strategy* (New York: Oxford University Press, 1999), 17–18; and Williamson Murray, MacGregor Knox, and Alvin H. Bernstein, *The Making of Strategy: Rulers, States, and War* (New York: Cambridge University Press, 1994), 1.

8. Carl von Clausewitz, *On War,* trans. Michael Howard and Peter Paret (Princeton: Princeton University Press, 1976), 178; Luttwak, *Strategy*, 2.

9. John R. Boyd, "SAASS Course 600 Reader: A Discourse on Winning and Losing by John R. Boyd, August 1987" [unpublished], Air University School

of Advanced Air and Space Studies (SAASS) (Maxwell Air Force Base, AL: Air University Press, Academic Year 2007–2008), Abstract, 1, and "Patterns of Conflict" Section, Slide 5.

10. Dima Adamsky, *The Culture of Military Innovation: The Impact of Cultural Factors on the Revolution in Military Affairs in Russia, the US, and Israel* (Stanford: Stanford University Press, 2010), 131.

11. Allan R. Millett and Williamson Murray, "Lessons of War," *National Interest* (Winter 1988/89), 83–95.

12. David J. Lonsdale, *The Nature of War in the Information Age: Clausewitzian Future,* Cass Series—Strategy and History 9 (London and New York: Frank Cass, 2004), 80.

13. Joint Publication 5-0, 26 December 2006: *Joint Operation Planning* (Washington, DC: US Department of Defense, 2006), IV-32.

14. Air Force Doctrine Document 2-1, 22 January 2000: *Air Warfare* (Washington, DC: US Air Force, 2000), 6.

15. Field Manual 1–02, September 2004: *Operational Terms and Graphics* (Washington, DC: US Department of the Army, 2004), 1–100.

16. Edward J. Drea, *Japan's Imperial Army: Its Rise and Fall, 1853–1945* (Lawrence: University Press of Kansas, 2009), 239–240.

17. Murray, Knox, and Bernstein, *The Making of Strategy*, 236–237.

18. James M. McPherson, *Battle Cry of Freedom: The Civil War Era* (New York: Oxford University Press, 1988), 534.

19. Ibid., 647.

20. Murray, Knox, and Bernstein, *The Making of Strategy*, 238–239.

21. David M. Glantz and Jonathan M. House, *The Battle of Kursk* (Lawrence: University Press of Kansas, 1999), 21.

22. David M. Glantz, *The Role of Intelligence in Soviet Military Strategy in World War II* (Novato, CA: Presidio Press, 1990), 9. See also Robert M. Citino, *Death of the Wehrmacht: The German Campaigns of 1942* (Lawrence: University Press of Kansas, 2007), 91–92.

23. David M. Glantz, *Zhukov's Greatest Defeat: The Red Army's Epic Disaster in Operation Mars, 1942* (Lawrence: University Press of Kansas, 1999), 2. Glantz writes of Soviet operations in 1942: "Taken together, the twin strategic operations [Mars: an attack near Moscow, and Uranus: an attack around Stalingrad] . . . represented the Red Army's effort to regain the strategic initiative on the Eastern Front."

24. Mao Tse-tung, *On the Protracted War*, 2nd ed. (Peking: Foreign Languages Press, 1960). Though derived independently of Mao, the first four categories loosely correspond to those mentioned in his dissection of initiative and superiority: Resources (p. 88), Intelligence (pp. 88–89), Strategic Acumen (p. 89), and Operational and Tactical flexibility (p. 97).

25. Dr. Harold Winton identified this thematic connection and brought it to the author's attention.

26. Clausewitz, *On War*, 177.
27. Eric Larrabee, *Commander in Chief: Franklin Delano Roosevelt, His Lieu-tenants, and Their War*, 1st ed. (New York: Harper & Row, 1987), 133–139.
28. Bryan I. Fugate and L. S. Dvoretskii, *Thunder on the Dnepr: Zhukov-Stalin and the Defeat of Hitler's Blitzkrieg* (Novato, CA: Presidio, 1997), 20.
29. Peter R. Mansoor, *The GI Offensive in Europe: The Triumph of American Infantry Divisions, 1941–1945* (Lawrence: University Press of Kansas, 1999), 3.
30. Clausewitz, *On War*, 85.
31. Personal electronic mail correspondence concerning the topic of chance in war between John F. Guilmartin and the author on 23 March 2010.

CHAPTER 3. THE NATIONAL COMMAND STRUCTURES

1. Graham T. Allison and Philip Zelikow, *Essence of Decision: Explaining the Cuban Missile Crisis*, 2nd ed. (New York: Longman, 1999), 143–160.
2. John Toland, *The Rising Sun: The Decline and Fall of the Japanese Empire, 1936–1945* (New York: Random House, 2003 [1970]), 35.
3. USSBS Interrogations: No. 426: Prince HIGASHI-KUNI; Subject: Japanese War Economy; Date: 14 November 1945, Tokyo; Microfilm Publication M1654, Reel #9, 426-7.
4. Masuo Kato, *The Lost War: A Japanese Reporter's Inside Story* (New York: A. A. Knopf, 1946), 40.
5. Harry A. Gailey, *The War in the Pacific: From Pearl Harbor to Tokyo Bay* (Novato, CA: Presidio, 1995), 57.
6. Edward J. Drea, *Japan's Imperial Army: Its Rise and Fall, 1853–1945* (Lawrence: University Press of Kansas, 2009), 191–192.
7. Toland, *The Rising Sun*, 23.
8. Military History Section, Far East Command, Japanese Research Division, "Japanese Monograph No. 45: Imperial General Headquarters Army High Command Record, Mid 41- Aug 45," in *Japanese Monographs*, 2.
9. Dan van der Vat, *The Pacific Campaign: World War II, the U.S.-Japanese Naval War, 1941–1945* (New York: Simon & Schuster, 1991), 42–43.
10. United States War Department, *Handbook on Japanese Military Forces* (reproduced Baton Rouge: Louisiana State University Press, 1995), 10.
11. David C. Evans and Mark R. Peattie, *Kaigun: Strategy, Tactics, and Technology in the Imperial Japanese Navy, 1887–1941* (Annapolis, MD: Naval Institute Press, 1997), 29–31.
12. United States Strategic Bombing Survey, *The Campaigns of the Pacific War* (Washington, DC: US Strategic Bombing Survey [Pacific], Naval Analysis Division, 1946), 2. Evans and Peattie, *Kaigun*, 31; USSBS Interrogations: No. 426: Prince HIGASHI-KUNI, 426-5 to 426-6.

13. USSBS, *Campaigns of the Pacific War*, 1.
14. USSBS Interrogations: No. 373: Prince Fumimaro KONOYE; Subject: Interrogation of Prince Konoye; Date: 9 November 1945, Tokyo; Microfilm Publication M1654, Reel #9, 373-4; see also Kato, *The Lost War*, 51–52.
15. War Department, *Handbook on Japanese Military Forces*, 10, 53, 11.
16. Evans and Peattie, *Kaigun*, 25–27.
17. Drea, *Japan's Imperial Army*, 192–193.
18. Ibid., 193.
19. War Department, *Handbook on Japanese Military Forces,* 10; Far East Command, "Japanese Monograph No. 45: Imperial General Headquarters Army High Command Record, Mid 41–Aug 45," 2.
20. Evans and Peattie, *Kaigun*, 458.
21. Far East Command, "Japanese Monograph No. 45: Imperial General Headquarters Army High Command Record, Mid 41–Aug 45," 3.
22. Ibid., 7.
23. Drea, *Japan's Imperial Army*, 193.
24. Evans and Peattie, *Kaigun*, 460.
25. USSBS Interrogations: No. 392: Fleet Admiral Osami NAGANO, IJN; Subject: Japanese Naval Plans; Date: 20 November 1945, Tokyo; Microfilm Publication M1654, Reel #9, 392-2. Admiral Nagano was the chief of the Naval General Staff from April 1941 to February 1944. He stated that, when the Japanese decided to increase their defensive perimeter to the east and south in 1942, it was as a result of "complete agreement" between the army and navy. Had the army objected to the expansion, it is unlikely that Emperor Hirohito would have overridden the decision. Because the emperor did not decide situations but merely granted his approval, the Japanese structure needed agreement before the plan reached Hirohito. Without consensus and compromise between the services, the operations in New Guinea and the Solomon Islands would likely not have transpired.
26. Walter J. Boyne, *Clash of Titans: World War II at Sea* (New York: Simon & Schuster, 1995), 128.
27. Jonathan B. Parshall and Anthony P. Tully, *Shattered Sword: The Untold Story of the Battle of Midway* (Washington, DC: Potomac Books, 2005), 24–25. See also Matome Ugaki et al., *Fading Victory: The Diary of Admiral Matome Ugaki, 1941–1945*, trans. Masataka Chihaya (Pittsburgh: University of Pittsburgh Press, 1991), 13.
28. *Japanese Army Operations in the South Pacific Area: New Britain and Papuan Campaigns, 1942–43*, trans. Steven Bullard, translated extracts of: Bōeichō Bōei Kenshūjo Senshishitsu, ed., Senshi Sōsho: Minami Taiheiyō Rikugun Sakusen. Pōto Moresubi–Gashima Shoko Sakusen [War History Series: South Pacific Area Army Operations (Volume 1), Port Moresby–Guadalcanal First Campaigns] (Tokyo: Asagumo Shinbunsha, 1968): 1–230, 335–384, 514–532; and Bōeichō Bōei Kenshūjo Senshishitsu, ed.,

Senshi Sōsho: Minami Taiheiyō Rikugun Sakusen. Gadarukanaru–Buna Sakusen [War History Series: South Pacific Area Army Operations (Volume 2), Guadalcanal–Buna Campaigns] (Tokyo: Asagumo Shinbunsha, 1969): 196–218, 324–362, 577–601 (Canberra: Australian War Memorial, 2007), 1, iii (hereafter Senshi Sōsho, *Japanese Army Operations*), ajrp.awm.gov.au /ajrp/ajrp2.nsf/WebI/JpnOperations/$file/JpnOpsText.pdf?OpenElement.

29. Ibid., 1.

30. Ibid., 93.

31. Ibid., 182.

32. Edward J. Drea, *MacArthur's ULTRA: Codebreaking and the War against Japan, 1942–1945* (Lawrence: University Press of Kansas, 1992), 55.

33. National Archives and Records Administration: Record Group 550: Records of the U.S. Army, Pacific, 1945–1985 (hereafter NARA 550): Series: Organizational History Files, compiled 1959–1973, documenting the period 1931–1973: Box 10: Japanese Monographs Nos. 31–35. NARA 550: Supreme Commander Allied Powers G-2 Section, Allied Translator and Interpreter Section, "Monograph #32 (Army): Southeast Pacific Area Aerial Open Record," in *Japanese Monographs*, 2.

34. Senshi Sōsho, *Japanese Army Operations*, 113–116.

35. Kato, *The Lost War*, 107. Kato writes, "There is no doubt that a major portion of the responsibility for Japan's failure at Guadalcanal, Bougainville, the Gilbert Islands, and later at all-important Saipan may be traced to the failure of the Army and Navy to set aside their differences when the future of the nation was at stake."

36. USSBS Interrogations: No. 392: Fleet Admiral Osami NAGANO, IJN, 392-2.

37. Grace P. Hayes, *The History of the Joint Chiefs of Staff in World War II: The War against Japan* (Annapolis, MD: Naval Institute Press, 1982), 8–9. Note that Admiral Stark occupied the position of CNO at the time, while Admiral King, who was to hold the dual positions of CNO and Commander-in-Chief, US Fleet, rose to those positions after the Germany First option became agreed Allied strategy.

38. Mark A. Stoler, *Allies and Adversaries: The Joint Chiefs of Staff, the Grand Alliance, and U.S. Strategy in World War II* (Chapel Hill: University of North Carolina Press, 2000), 46. Louis Morton, *Strategy and Command: The First Two Years*, United States Army in World War II: The War in the Pacific (Washington, DC: Office of the Chief of Military History, 1962), 226.

39. Morton, *Strategy and Command*, 227.

40. Joint History Office, "World War II Inter-Allied Conferences—Declassified," (Washington, DC: Joint History Office, 2003). This is an electronic resource in the form of CDs/DVDs containing digitized copies of the Allies' conferences' records and minutes.

41. Morton, *Strategy and Command*, 168–169, 179–180.
42. Eric Larrabee, *Commander in Chief: Franklin Delano Roosevelt, His Lieutenants, and Their War*, 1st ed. (New York: Harper & Row, 1987), 2–3.
43. Ibid., 142.
44. Russell F. Weigley, *The American Way of War: A History of United States Military Strategy and Policy* (Bloomington: Indiana University Press, 1973), 200, 245.
45. Stoler, *Allies and Adversaries*, 64; Morton, *Strategy and Command*, 166.
46. Stoler, *Allies and Adversaries*, 65; see also Morton, *Strategy and Command*, 226.
47. Morton, *Strategy and Command*, 227–230.
48. Ibid., 245–250.
49. Ibid., 249.
50. Richard B. Frank, *MacArthur*, 1st ed. (New York: Palgrave Macmillan, 2007), 56–58.
51. Morton, *Strategy and Command*, 256–261.

CHAPTER 4. JAPANESE INTELLIGENCE ORGANIZATION IN WORLD WAR II

1. Joint Publication 1-02: 12 April 2001 (as Amended through 17 October 2007), *Department of Defense Dictionary of Military and Associated Terms* (Washington, DC: US Department of Defense, 2007), 249, 109.
2. Joint Publication 1-02: 12 April 2001 (as Amended through 30 September 2010), *Department of Defense Dictionary of Military and Associated Terms*, 425–26.
3. Joint Publication 1-02: 12 April 2001 (as Amended through 17 October 2007), 269.
4. Ken Kotani, *Japanese Intelligence in World War II*, trans. Chiharu Kotani (New York: Osprey Publishing, 2009), 1.
5. USSBS Interrogations: No. 236: Commander Nobohiko IMAI, IJN; Subject: Japanese Naval and Operational Intelligence; Date: 3 November 1945, Tokyo; Microfilm Publication M1654, Reel #8, 236-3.
6. Kotani, *Japanese Intelligence in World War II*, 163.
7. David MacIsaac, *Strategic Bombing in World War Two: The Story of the United States Strategic Bombing Survey* (New York: Garland Publishing, 1976), 118. MacIsaac relates how the exceptional Japanese candor surprised and engendered suspicion in the Americans conducting the survey.
8. Kotani, *Japanese Intelligence in World War II*, 6, 8.
9. Ibid., 8.
10. USSBS Interrogations: No. 222: Rear Admiral Kaoru TAKEUCHI, IJN; Subject: Japanese Naval Intelligence Organization; Date: 5 November 1945, Tokyo; Microfilm Publication M1654, Reel #8, 222-1 to 222-9.

11. USSBS Interrogations: No. 238: Lieutenant General Seizo ARISUE, IJA; Subject: Organization and Operation of Japanese Army Intelligence Activities; Date: 1 November 1945, Tokyo; Microfilm Publication M1654, Reel #2, 238-6 to 238-7.

12. Ibid., 238-2 to 238-4.

13. Kotani, *Japanese Intelligence in World War II*, 14, 16–17.

14. Martin Gilbert, *The Second World War: A Complete History*, rev. ed. (New York: H. Holt, 1991), 429.

15. USSBS Interrogations: No. 402: Colonel Kazuji SUGITA, IJA; Subject: Intelligence Organization and Procedure, Japanese Army; Date: 21 November 1945, Tokyo; Microfilm Publication M1654, Reel #9, 402-1 to 402-3; United States War Department, *Handbook on Japanese Military Forces* (reproduced Baton Rouge: Louisiana State University Press, 1995), 16.

16. USSBS Interrogations: No. 364, 364-2. See also Interrogation No. 398: Lieutenant Colonel J. YAMAZAKI, IJA; Subject: Intelligence Duties of TOKUMU KIKAN (Special Service Organization); Date: 15 November 1945, Tokyo; Microfilm Publication M1654, Reel #7, 298-1 to 398-4.

17. Ibid., Interrogation No. 402, 402-6; Edward J. Drea, *MacArthur's ULTRA: Codebreaking and the War against Japan, 1942–1945* (Lawrence: University Press of Kansas, 1992), 82.

18. USSBS Interrogations: No. 402, 402-3; see also War Department, *Handbook on Japanese Military Forces*, 16.

19. USSBS Interrogations: No. 402, 402-4, and No. 238, 238-5.

20. Kotani, *Japanese Intelligence in World War II*, 12–14.

21. David Kahn, *The Reader of Gentlemen's Mail: Herbert O. Yardley and the Birth of American Codebreaking* (New Haven, CT: Yale University Press, 2004), 130–131.

22. Kotani, *Japanese Intelligence in World War II*, 14–20.

23. Drea, *MacArthur's ULTRA*, xii–xiii.

24. Ibid., 7.

25. Kotani, *Japanese Intelligence in World War II*, 56; USSBS Interrogations: No. 364, 364-2.

26. Kotani, *Japanese Intelligence in World War II*, 26, 56.

27. USSBS Interrogations: No. 238, 238-4, 238-10, and No. 402, 402-6. Reasons for the Japanese neglect of information from prisoners of war remain unclear and require further investigation. One speculative cause may be military cultural differences with the Western Allies. The Japanese looked upon surrender and capture as a disgrace, and members of the Japanese military, particularly their officers, did not expect to fall into enemy hands. If they mirror-imaged their foes, they likely expected to capture few prisoners, and certainly fewer still of any rank with potentially valuable information.

28. USSBS Interrogations: No. 238, 238-5.

29. Ibid., 238-11.

30. Ibid., 238-10.
31. Ibid., 238-11.
32. USSBS Interrogations: No. 238, 238-11, and No. 364, 364-3.
33. USSBS Interrogations: No. 402, 402-5.
34. USSBS Interrogations: No. 412: Major Akito SAEKI, IJA; Subject: Squadron (Army) Intelligence Procedure; Date: 16 November 1945, Tokyo; Microfilm Publication M1654, Reel #3, 412-2.
35. USSBS Interrogations: No. 270: Colonel Minoru MIYASHI, JAAF; Subject: Japanese Army Air Intelligence Organization and Operations; Date: 6 and 7 November 1945, Tokyo; Microfilm Publication M1654, Reel #8, 270-6; see also War Department, *Handbook on Japanese Military Forces*, 54.
36. USSBS Interrogations: No. 343: General Masakazu KAWABE, IJA; Subject: Intelligence Operations at Air General Headquarters (KOKU SOGUN SHIRIEBU); Date: 13 November 1945, Tokyo; Microfilm Publication M1654, Reel #8, 343-3.
37. USSBS Interrogations: No. 238, 238-7.
38. USSBS Interrogations: No. 449: Major Hideo ANNO, IJA; Subject: Intelligence Instruction in the Army War College; Date: 26 November 1945, Tokyo; Microfilm Publication M1654, Reel #9, 449-2; No. 604: Colonel Takeo SHIMIZU, IJA; Subject: Instruction Relating to Intelligence at the War College; Date: 27 November 1945, Tokyo; Microfilm Publication M1654, Reel #6, 604-2 to 604-3.
39. War Department, *Handbook on Japanese Military Forces*, 10; Kotani, *Japanese Intelligence in World War II*, 58.
40. Kotani, *Japanese Intelligence in World War II*, 65, 67.
41. United States Strategic Bombing Survey, ed., "Japanese Military and Naval Intelligence," Japanese Military and G-2 Naval Intelligence Division, Japanese Intelligence Section (Washington, DC: US Government Printing Office, 1946), 43.
42. Kotani, *Japanese Intelligence in World War II*, 60.
43. USSBS Interrogations: No. 607: Lieutenant Colonel YAMAMURA and 2nd Lieutenant OGATA, IJA; Subject: KEMPEI TAI; Date: 17 November 1945, Tokyo; Microfilm Publication M1654, Reel #9, 607-3 to 607-4.
44. "Japanese Military and Naval Intelligence," 43.
45. USSBS Interrogations: No. 402, 402-5.
46. USSBS Interrogations: No. 452: Lieutenant Colonel Tatsuo NOZAKI, IJA; Subject: Intelligence Instruction at the Kempeitai School at NAKANO KU, TOKYO; Date: 26 November 1945, Tokyo; Microfilm Publication M1654, Reel #3, 452-2.
47. Ibid.
48. United States Strategic Bombing Survey, *Japanese Military and Naval Intelligence Division, Japanese Intelligence Section, G-2. Dates of Survey: 1 November 1945 through 1 February 1946* [Reports. Pacific War, 97] (Wash-

ington, DC: US Government Printing Office, 1946), 15; War Department, *Handbook on Japanese Military Forces*, 53.

49. USSBS Interrogations: No. 270, 270-6.

50. USSBS Interrogations: No. 362: Lieutenant Colonel T. ASHIHARA, IJA; Subject: Organization and Operation of Japanese Army Air Force; Date: November 1945, Tokyo; Microfilm Publication M1654, Reel #3, 362-2.

51. Ibid.; Interrogation No. 284: Major Hiroshi TOGA, IJA; Subject: Intelligence Organization and Procedure in Japanese Army Air Division (HIKO-SHIDAN); Date: 7 November 1945, Tokyo; Microfilm Publication M1654, Reel #8, 284-2.

52. War Department, *Handbook on Japanese Military Forces*, 53–54; "Japanese Military and Naval Intelligence," 16.

53. War Department, *Handbook on Japanese Military Forces*, 54; "Japanese Military and Naval Intelligence," 16.

54. USSBS Interrogations: No. 270, 270-3.

55. War Department, *Handbook on Japanese Military Forces*, 54.

56. USSBS Interrogations: No. 307: Lieutenant Colonel Shizuma MATSU-MURA, IJA; Subject: Japanese Army Air Intelligence at HIKOSENTAI, HIKODAN, and HIKOSHIDAN Level; Date: 8 November 1945, Tokyo; Microfilm Publication M1654, Reel #8, 307-4 to 307-5.

57. War Department, *Handbook on Japanese Military Forces*, 54; "Japanese Military and Naval Intelligence," 17.

58. "Japanese Military and Naval Intelligence," 119, Exhibit D: Special Report—Japanese Photographic Intelligence.

59. Ibid.

60. Ibid.; see also USSBS Interrogations: No. 284, 284-2.

61. USSBS Interrogations: No. 307, 307-3.

62. "Japanese Military and Naval Intelligence," 120, Exhibit D: Special Report—Japanese Photographic Intelligence. USSBS Interrogations: No. 219: Captain Y. ARITA, IJN; Subject: Japanese Naval Intelligence Organization; Date: 2 November 1945, Tokyo; Microfilm Publication M1654, Reel #8, 219-2.

63. Kotani, *Japanese Intelligence in World War II*, 69.

64. USSBS Interrogations: No. 219: Captain Y. ARITA, IJN; Subject: Japanese Naval Intelligence Organization; Date: 2 November 1945, Tokyo; Microfilm Publication M1654, Reel #8, 219-2.

65. USSBS Interrogations: No. 222, 222-2.

66. USSBS Interrogations: No. 246: Rear Admiral Takeji ONO, IJN; Subject: Japanese Naval Intelligence; Date: 5 November 1945, Tokyo; Microfilm Publication M1654, Reel #8, 246-4; and No. 222, 222-2.

67. USSBS Interrogations: No. 309: Commander Chikataka NAKAJIMA, IJN; Subject: Fleet Intelligence Organization and Procedure; Date: 10 November 1945, Tokyo; Microfilm Publication M1654, Reel #8, 309-2.

68. USSBS Interrogations: No. 219, 219-2; "Japanese Military and Naval Intelligence," 18.
69. USSBS Interrogations: No. 246, 246-6.
70. USSBS Interrogations No. 437: Commander Tonosuke OTANI, IJN; Subject: Operational Intelligence in the Second Fleet; Date: 24 November 1945, Tokyo; Microfilm Publication M1654, Reel #9, 437-3.
71. "Japanese Military and Naval Intelligence," 18.
72. USSBS Interrogations: No. 437, 437-4; USSBS Interrogations No. 433: Commander Nikichi HANDA, IJN; Subject: Intelligence Duties of a Communications Officer on Staff of Destroyer and Cruiser Squadrons; Date: 24 November 1945, Tokyo; Microfilm Publication M1654, Reel #9, 433-1 to 433-2.
73. Kotani, *Japanese Intelligence in World War II*, 69–72.
74. Ibid., 72.
75. USSBS Interrogations: No. 208: Commander Hideo OZAWA, IJN; Subject: Japanese Communications Intelligence; Date: 2 November 1945, Tokyo; Microfilm Publication M1654, Reel #8, 208-2.
76. Kotani, *Japanese Intelligence in World War II*, 72.
77. Ibid., 90.
78. Drea, *MacArthur's ULTRA*, 13, 37.
79. Edwin P. Hoyt, *Carrier Wars: Naval Aviation from World War II to the Persian Gulf* (New York: McGraw-Hill, 1989), 118.
80. Matome Ugaki et al., *Fading Victory: The Diary of Admiral Matome Ugaki, 1941–1945*, trans. Masataka Chihaya (Pittsburgh: University of Pittsburgh Press, 1991), 359–360. Drea, *MacArthur's ULTRA*, 73.
81. Winston Groom, *1942: The Year That Tried Men's Souls*, 1st ed. (New York: Atlantic Monthly Press, 2005), 197–198.
82. David Kahn, *The Codebreakers: The Story of Secret Writing* (New York: Macmillan, 1967), 590.
83. USSBS Interrogations: No. 421: Captain Y. SANEMATSU, IJN; Subject: Intelligence Activities of "D" Department, 5th Section, Naval General Staff; Date: 22 November 1945, Tokyo; Microfilm Publication M1654, Reel #9, 421-2.
84. USSBS Interrogations: No. 236, 236-5.
85. USSBS Interrogations: No. 246, 246-7.
86. Kahn, *The Codebreakers*, 603–604.
87. USSBS Interrogations: No. 455: Rear Admiral Ichiro YOKOYAMA, IJN; Subject: Activities of Naval Attaché Staff, Washington, DC, Before PEARL HARBOR Attack; Date: 27 November 1945, Tokyo; Microfilm Publication M1654, Reel #7, 455-3.
88. Quotation from USSBS Interrogations: No. 222, 222-5; see also No. 236, 236-5; "Japanese Military and Naval Intelligence," 22.
89. "Japanese Military and Naval Intelligence," 21–22. See also USSBS Interro-

gations: No. 246, 246-9. Interrogation No. 222, 222-8, and, on executions, Jonathan B. Parshall and Anthony P. Tully, *Shattered Sword: The Untold Story of the Battle of Midway* (Washington, DC: Potomac Books, 2005), 288, 319–320.

90. USSBS Interrogations: No. 350: Captain Toshikazu OHMAE, IJN; Subject: The Contribution of Naval Intelligence to War Planning; Date: 11 November 1945, Tokyo; Microfilm Publication M1654, Reel #8, 350-2.

91. USSBS Interrogations: No. 236, 236-5.

92. "Japanese Military and Naval Intelligence," 22.

93. USSBS Interrogations: No. 222, 222-5.

94. USSBS Interrogations: No. 219, 219-3; No. 222, 222-2; No. 246, 246-4.

95. "Japanese Military and Naval Intelligence," 21.

96. "Japanese Military and Naval Intelligence," 21; USSBS Interrogations: No. 246, 246-10.

97. USSBS Interrogations: No. 222, 222-8.

98. USSBS Interrogations: No. 350, 350-4.

99. USSBS Interrogations: No. 246, 246-4.

100. USSBS Interrogations: No. 432: Captain Taisuke ITO, IJN; Subject: Selection and Assignment of Intelligence Personnel; Date: 24 November 1945, Tokyo; Microfilm Publication M1654, Reel #9, 432-1.

101. "Japanese Military and Naval Intelligence," 18–20.

102. USSBS Interrogations: No. 219, 219-3; No. 222, 222-2; No. 246, 246-4; No. 432, 432-3.

103. "Japanese Military and Naval Intelligence," 23, as depicted in Chart X of this USSBS report.

104. USSBS Interrogations: No. 246, 246-5.

105. USSBS Interrogations: No. 250: Commander Sashizo YOKURA, IJN; Subject: Japanese Naval Intelligence; Date: 5 November 1945, Tokyo; Microfilm Publication M1654, Reel #8, 250-2 to 250-3.

106. USSBS Interrogations: No. 374: Commander N. TAKITA, IJN; Subject: Procedure and Functions of Aviation Unit of Section Five, Naval General Staff, 3d Department; Date: 17 November 1945, Tokyo; Microfilm Publication M1654, Reel #9, 374-2 to 374-3.

107. USSBS Interrogations: No. 384: Lieutenant Takogo TOYODA, IJN; Subject: Organization and Operation of First Naval Air Technical Arsenal; Date: 19 November 1945, Tokyo; Microfilm Publication M1654, Reel #9, 384-1.

108. USSBS Interrogations: No. 291, 291-2.

109. USSBS Interrogations No. 329: Commander Masatake OKUMIYA, IJN; Subject: Combat Intelligence for Air Operations—Briefing and Interrogation Procedure; Date: 12 November 1945, Tokyo; Microfilm Publication M1654, Reel #8, 329-1.

110. USSBS Interrogations: No. 605: Lieutenant Commander Masuo YANAG-

ITA, IJN; Subject: Training and Duties of YOMUSHI; Date: 28 November 1945, Tokyo; Microfilm Publication M1654, Reel #7, 605-1.

111. USSBS Interrogations: No. 250, 250-3.
112. USSBS Interrogations: No. 365: Commander Moriyoshi YAMAGUCHI, IJN; Subject: Briefing and Interrogation of Navy Pilots and Photographic Reconnaissance; Date: 16 November 1945, Tokyo; Microfilm Publication M1654, Reel #9, 365-5 to 365-6.
113. "Japanese Military and Naval Intelligence," 119–120.
114. USSBS Interrogations: No. 365, 365-6.
115. USSBS Interrogations: No. 350, 350-4.
116. Kotani, *Japanese Intelligence in World War II*, 108.
117. "Japanese Military and Naval Intelligence," 3.

CHAPTER 5. AMERICAN INTELLIGENCE ORGANIZATION IN THE PACIFIC DURING WORLD WAR II

1. FM 7-25 Infantry Field Manual: *Headquarters Company, Intelligence and Signal Communication, Rifle Regiment*, 7 October 1942 (Washington, DC: War Department, 1942), 9.
2. John D. Millett, "The War Department in World War II," *American Political Science Review* 40, no. 5 (1946): 867, 875.
3. James L. Gilbert and John P. Finnegan, eds., *U.S. Army Signals Intelligence in World War II: A Documentary History* (Washington, DC: Center of Military History, 1993), 3–4.
4. FM 7-25, 16, and FM 100-5 *Field Service Regulations: Operations*, 22 May 1941 (Fort Leavenworth, KS: US Army Command and General Staff College Press, 1992 reprint [1941]), 46.
5. FM 7-25, 16, 18.
6. Ibid., 18–19.
7. Edward J. Drea, *MacArthur's ULTRA: Codebreaking and the War against Japan, 1942–1945* (Lawrence: University Press of Kansas, 1992), 8; David Kahn, *The Codebreakers: The Story of Secret Writing* (New York: Macmillan, 1967), 360.
8. Drea, *MacArthur's ULTRA*, 8–9.
9. Ibid., 10.
10. FM 7-25, 19.
11. Ibid., 50–51.
12. Kahn, *The Codebreakers*, 584–585.
13. Ken Kotani, *Japanese Intelligence in World War II*, trans. Chiharu Kotani (New York: Osprey Publishing, 2009), 18.
14. National Archives and Records Administration: Record Group 496: Records of General Headquarters, South West Pacific Area and United States Army Forces Pacific (World War II), 1941–1947 (hereafter NARA 496):

Series: General Correspondence, 1942–45, Box 321. Colonel C. G. Roberts, "Basis for Training," (Allied Intelligence Bureau, 26 August 1943), 1. See also FM 7-25, 15.

15. NARA 496: Series: HQ Allied AF Intelligence Summaries: Box 279: HQ Allied Air Forces Intelligence Summaries, 1942–1943. "Headquarters Allied Air Forces South West Pacific Area Directorate of Intelligence: Intelligence Summary Serial No. 8 (on information up to 12th June—1942.)," Sections 53–54; and NARA 496: "Headquarters Allied Air Forces South West Pacific Area Directorate of Intelligence: Intelligence Summary Serial No. 39 (on information up to 2nd October—1942.)," Section 77.

16. FM 7-25, 15; and NARA 496: Series: General Correspondence, 1942–45, Box 321. Colonel C. G. Roberts, "Basis for Training," (Allied Intelligence Bureau, 26 August 1943), 1.

17. National Archives and Records Administration: Record Group 127: Records of the U.S. Marine Corps, 1775–9999 (hereafter NARA 127): Series: Records of Amphibious Corps, compiled 1940–1946: Box 22, Folder 1 #2265. Lieutenant Colonel Warren J. Clear, "Problems of Taking Jap Prisoners" (Military Intelligence Division, 10 May 1943), 1–3.

18. John W. Dower, *War without Mercy: Race and Power in the Pacific War* (New York: Pantheon, 1986), 60–71.

19. NARA 127: Clear, "Problems of Taking Jap Prisoners," 2–3.

20. Ibid., 4. Having been disgraced, Japanese prisoners had nothing more to lose.

21. National Archives and Records Administration: Record Group 337: Records of Headquarters Army Ground Forces, 1916–1956 (hereafter NARA 337): Series: Intelligence Reports, compiled 1943–1946: Box 51, Folder 10. Colonel Gordon B. Rogers, "Memorandum for Ground General and Special Staff Sections, Headquarters, Army Ground Forces; Subject: Observations in Southwest and South Pacific Theaters during the Period 5 April, 1943 to 14 July, 1943" (Headquarters, Army Ground Forces, 25 August 1943), 4.

22. Ibid., Folder 5. Colonel H. F. Handy, "Subject: Report of Military Observer Southwest Pacific Theater of Operations, Col. H. F. Handy, September 26 to December 23, 1942," 1–19.

23. Ibid., Folder 6. Colonel Harry Knight, "Report of Colonel Harry Knight, Cavalry, covering observations in the Southwest Pacific Theatre, during the Period October 16 to December 30, 1942," 1–11.

24. John Winton, *Ultra in the Pacific: How Breaking Japanese Codes & Cyphers Affected Naval Operations against Japan, 1941–45* (Annapolis, MD: Naval Institute Press, 1993), 68.

25. Drea, *MacArthur's ULTRA*, 73.

26. National Archives and Records Administration: Record Group 338: Records of the U.S. Army Operational, Tactical, and Support Organizations

(World War II and Thereafter) (hereafter NARA 338): Series: Unit Histories 1940–1967, Infantry Division Section, 1940–1967, Box 2934: Americal Division (Intelligence Bulletins) Thru Americal Division (Memorandums), Folder: Americal Division—Memos 1942–43. Colonel C. M. McQuarrie, "Training in Jap Weapons" (Headquarters, Americal Division, 27 July 1943), 1–2.

27. Roy M. Stanley, *World War II Photo Intelligence* (New York: Scribner, 1981), 60.

28. FM 21-26 Basic Field Manual: *Advanced Map and Aerial Photograph Reading*, 17 September 1941 (Washington, DC: US Government Printing Office, 1941), 6, 87–92, 148–192.

29. Ronald H. Spector, *Listening to the Enemy: Key Documents on the Role of Communications Intelligence in the War with Japan* (Wilmington, DE: Scholarly Resources, 1988), 175–176. This information is taken from portions of "History of the Special Branch, MIS, War Department, 1942–44," reproduced in Spector's edited volume.

30. Kahn, *The Codebreakers*, 574.

31. FM 100-5: Field Service Regulations: *Operations*, 22 May 1941, 57.

32. TM 30-215: Technical Manual: *Counter Intelligence Corps*, 22 September 1943 (Washington, DC: War Department, 1943), 1.

33. John Patrick Finnegan and Romana Danysh, *Military Intelligence*, Army Lineage Series (Washington, DC: Center of Military History, 1998), 72–73.

34. Judith A. Bennett, "Fears and Aspirations: US Military Intelligence Operations in the South Pacific, 1941–1945," *Journal of Pacific History* 39, no. 3 (2004): 284–287.

35. John F. Kreis, *Piercing the Fog: Intelligence and Army Air Forces Operations in World War II* (Bolling AFB, Washington, DC: Air Force History and Museums Program, 1996), 116–117, 46.

36. This paragraph is based primarily on ibid., 126–127, 130.

37. FM 1-40: Air Corps Field Manual: *Intelligence Procedures in Aviation Units,* (Washington, DC: Chief of the Air Corps, US Government Printing Office, 1940), 33.

38. Air Force Historical Research Agency (hereafter AFHRA): Call # 223.606: "Army Air Forces Gulf Coast Flying Training Center Summaries: A-2 Summaries Nos. 14 (18 May 1942) through 62 (18 November 1942)."

39. Stanley, *World War II Photo Intelligence*, 65–66.

40. Ibid., 83, 89–90.

41. AFHRA: Call # 730.308–1: "0005 Air Force: Scale of Effort," Fifth Air Force: Hours Flown per Assigned Combat Crew, 1. The action in the Bismarck Sea may explain why the bomber crews exceeded the reconnaissance crews in flight time for the month of March 1943. See also AFHRA: Call # 749.607: "Solomon Islands Air Command: Weekly Intelligence Summaries,

7 February 1943–28 April 1944," and NARA 496: Series: HQ Allied AF Intelligence Summaries: Box 279: HQ Allied Air Forces Intelligence Summaries, 1942–1943.

42. This paragraph is based primarily on Julius Augustus Furer, *Administration of the Navy Department in World War II* (Washington, DC: US Government Printing Office, 1959), 113, 116, 119–120.

43. Ibid., 139, 156–157.

44. This paragraph is based on Jeffrey M. Moore, *Spies for Nimitz: Joint Military Intelligence in the Pacific War* (Annapolis, MD: Naval Institute Press, 2004), 3–8.

45. Furer, *Administration of the Navy Department,* 553–554.

46. Frank Cain, "Signals Intelligence in Australia during the Pacific War," chapter 3 in *Allied and Axis Signals Intelligence in World War II*, ed. David J. Alvarez, Cass Series—Studies in Intelligence (London: Frank Cass, 1999), 48–49. See also Drea, *MacArthur's ULTRA,* 13.

47. Winton, *Ultra in the Pacific,* 7. ULTRA originated as the British code name for intelligence derived from cryptanalysis. The United States at first applied the name to information the British shared with America, and its use then spread to encompass all intelligence garnered from cryptanalysis.

48. Kahn, *The Codebreakers,* 574.

49. This excerpt is taken from portions of the report "Narrative, Combat Intelligence Center, Joint Intelligence Center, Pacific Ocean Area," reproduced in Spector, *Listening to the Enemy,* 157.

50. Winton, *Ultra in the Pacific,* 8.

51. NARA 127: Series: Records of Amphibious Corps, compiled 1940–1946, Box 10, Folder 1520: Education—College—School: K. E. Rockey, MARCORPS (Headquarters, U.S. Marine Corps, Washington, MAILBRIEF Serial No. AO-341-gmn [06A35242], 18 December 1942), 1; Box 10, Folder 1520: Education—College—School: Memo: B.B. Wilson Jr., Commanding Officer (United States Pacific Fleet Amphibious Force Communication School, Camp Pendleton, 5 February 1943).

52. NARA 127: Series: Records of Amphibious Corps, compiled 1940–1946, Box 21, Folder 5–1900: Notes on Japanese: Daily Summaries, Division Intelligence Section, Headquarters, 1st Marine Division, Fleet Marine Force (22–26 November 1942).

53. Ibid. Memo: R. K. Turner, Amphibious Force, South Pacific Force, Office of the Commander, File No. FE25/A8 Serial 087 (19 November 1942).

54. NARA 127: Box 22, Folder 6 2430: Operations 1 Nov 42–13 Dec 43: Memo A. F. Howard, "Combat Observations, South Pacific," (Headquarters, First Marine Amphibious Corps, 6 April 1943), 1–8.

55. NARA 127: Box 23, Folder 4 2550: Plans (10 Nov 42–24 Mar 43): Memo: Lieutenant Colonel Evan F. Carlson, "Discussion of and suggestion for improvement in the combat efficiency in Raider battalions, based on experience

gained in operations against the enemy," (Headquarters, Second Marine Raider Battalion, First Marine Amphibious Corps, 27 January 1943), 1–6.

56. NARA 127: Series: Records of Amphibious Corps, compiled 1940–1946, Box 10, Folder 1580-65: Pacific Fleet Memos and Letters: Memo by R. A. Spruance, "Pacific Fleet Confidential Letter 4CL-43" (Chief of Staff, United States Pacific Fleet, Flagship of the Commander in Chief, 27 February 1943).

57. Ibid., Box 21, Folder 5 1900: Notes on Japanese: Memo by P.V. Mercer, "Captured Enemy Documents—Translation Of" (United States Pacific Fleet, Flagship of the Commander in Chief, 30 November 1942).

58. Spector, *Listening to the Enemy*, 80.

59. John Prados, *Combined Fleet Decoded: The Secret History of American Intelligence and the Japanese Navy in World War II*, 1st ed. (New York: Random House, 1995), 399–402.

60. Ibid., 412.

61. Stanley, *World War II Photo Intelligence*, 66. See also Prados, *Combined Fleet Decoded*, 358.

62. Stanley, *World War II Photo Intelligence*, 66.

63. Prados, *Combined Fleet Decoded*, 413.

64. National Archives and Records Administration: Record Group 38: Records of the Office of the Chief of Naval Operations, 1875–2006 (hereafter NARA 38): Series: World War II Oral Histories, Interviews and Statements, compiled ca. 04/1942–ca. 12/1946, documenting the period ca. 12/07/1941–ca. 09/02/1945, Box 3: World War II Oral Histories and Interviews, 1942–1946: Borley, CA to Buracker, WH: Chief Photographer Fred W. Bottomer, (Lieutenant Porter, 10 September 1945), 1–5.

65. NARA 38: Series: Former Security Classified Chronological File ("Adm King Pinks"), 1942–45, Box 1: 9/13/1942–3/31/43: Memo from E. J. King to Joint Chiefs of Staff, Serial #001284 (United States Fleet, Headquarters of the Commander in Chief, Navy Department, Washington, DC, 26 October 1942).

66. Report reproduced in Spector, *Listening to the Enemy*, 156–157.

67. Prados, *Combined Fleet Decoded*, 413.

68. Ibid., 352.

69. Wyman H. Packard, *A Century of U.S. Naval Intelligence* (Washington, DC: Office of Naval Intelligence: Naval Historical Center, 1996), 210, 254.

70. Jeffery M. Dorwart, *Conflict of Duty: The U.S. Navy's Intelligence Dilemma, 1919–1945* (Annapolis, MD: Naval Institute Press, 1983), 117–118, 190.

71. Packard, *A Century of U.S. Naval Intelligence*, 278.

72. Dorwart, *Conflict of Duty*, 191.

73. Packard, *A Century of U.S. Naval Intelligence*, 255.

74. Furer, *Administration of the Navy Department*, 8, 370.

75. NARA 127: Series: Records of Amphibious Corps, compiled 1940–1946, Box 21, Folder 4 1900: Notes on Japanese. Enclosure (B) Memo Forrest

Sherman, "Notes on the duties of Air Intelligence Officers" (Commander, USS *Wasp*), 1, 6–7.

76. Kreis, *Piercing the Fog*, 256.

77. Stanley, *World War II Photo Intelligence*, 66.

78. Ibid.

79. Furer, *Administration of the Navy Department*, 654.

80. Louis Morton, *Strategy and Command: The First Two Years*, United States Army in World War II: The War in the Pacific (Washington, DC: Office of the Chief of Military History, 1962), 232.

81. Moore, *Spies for Nimitz*, xiii.

82. D. Clayton James, *The Years of MacArthur*, vol. 2, *1941–1945* (Boston: Houghton Mifflin, 1975), 178.

83. NARA 496: Series: Histories 1942–45, Box 326 "MIS Histories 1942–1945," Folder "History of ATIS (Draft Copy)" (Colonel Harold Doud), Foreword, 1, 78–83.

84. James, *The Years of MacArthur*, vol. 2, 178–179. Fourteen thousand prisoners may seem a significant number that undermines claims of the capture of only limited numbers of Japanese prisoners, but this covered the period between 1942 and 1945. By means of comparison, in May 1942 the Japanese captured more than 76,000 American and Filipino soldiers on Bataan alone. See John Toland, *But Not in Shame: The Six Months after Pearl Harbor* (New York: Random House, 1961), 335.

85. Drea, *MacArthur's ULTRA*, 20, 23, 27; Cain, "Signals Intelligence in Australia," chapter 3 in Alvarez, ed., *Allied and Axis Signals Intelligence in World War II*, 44.

86. James, *The Years of MacArthur*, vol. 2, 179; Allison Ind, *Allied Intelligence Bureau* (New York: McKay, 1958), 11–12, 25; Drea, *MacArthur's ULTRA*, 54.

87. "National Archives and Records Administration: Record Group 457: Records of the National Security Agency/Central Security Service [NCA/CCS]: SRH-268 Redman Correspondence," Department of the Navy, Naval Historical Center, www.history.navy.mil/research/library/online-reading-room /title-list-alphabetically/a/advanced-intelligence-centers-in-the-us-navy.html. Memorandum from J. R. Redmon to Admiral F. J. Horne, paragraph 6.

88. Cain, "Signals Intelligence in Australia," 50. ; Moore, *Spies for Nimitz*, 17.

89. Kreis, *Piercing the Fog*, 256.

90. NARA 127: Series: Records of Amphibious Corps, compiled 1940–1946, Box 20, Folder 31060-2: Aviation S+C Combined: Memo from Commander, South Pacific, "Directive for Establishing a Photographic Wing (Composite), South Pacific" (COMSOPAC, 21 June 1943), 1.

91. AFHRA: Call # 749.01: "Commander Aircraft Solomons (COMAIRSOLS)," extracts from diary of Major Victor Dykes, 1.

92. "Narrative, Combat Intelligence Center, Joint Intelligence Center, Pacific Ocean Area," reproduced in Spector, *Listening to the Enemy*, 164. The

report also states that the Radio Intelligence Section of JICPOA, which had
been the CIU inherited from ICPOA, transformed into FRUPAC.

CHAPTER 6. "EAST WIND, RAIN": THE JAPANESE SEIZE
THE INITIATIVE

1. "East Wind, Rain" was the diplomatic code phrase Japan sent to its foreign
   missions indicating imminent war with the United States. See Dan van der
   Vat, *The Pacific Campaign: World War II, the U.S.-Japanese Naval War,
   1941–1945* (New York: Simon & Schuster, 1991), 96.
2. John Keegan, *The Second World War* (New York: Penguin Books, 1990),
   249.
3. Gerhard L. Weinberg, *Visions of Victory: The Hopes of Eight World War II
   Leaders* (Cambridge, UK: Cambridge University Press, 2005), 252–257.
4. van der Vat, *The Pacific Campaign*, 120, 59–65.
5. Weinberg, *Visions of Victory*, 66–67.
6. Saburō Ienaga, *The Pacific War: World War II and the Japanese, 1931–
   1945*, 1st American ed. (New York: Pantheon Books, 1978), 139.
7. Weinberg, *Visions of Victory*, 179, 196–197, 203–205.
8. Ibid., 185–186.
9. John W. Dower, *War without Mercy: Race and Power in the Pacific War*
   (New York: Pantheon, 1986), x.
10. Keegan, *The Second World War*, 252.
11. van der Vat, *The Pacific Campaign*, 121.
12. Hiroyuki Agawa, *The Reluctant Admiral: Yamamoto and the Imperial
    Navy*, trans. John Bester, 1st paperback ed. (Tokyo and New York: Kodan-
    sha International, 1982), 219–220.
13. Richard J. Overy, *Why the Allies Won*, 1st American ed. (New York: W. W.
    Norton, 1996), 33; Ienaga, *The Pacific War*, 141.
14. James B. Wood, *Japanese Military Strategy in the Pacific War: Was Defeat
    Inevitable?* (New York: Rowman & Littlefield, 2007), 9.
15. Masuo Kato, *The Lost War: A Japanese Reporter's Inside Story* (New York:
    A. A. Knopf, 1946), 40.
16. Louis Morton, *Strategy and Command: The First Two Years*, United States
    Army in World War II: The War in the Pacific (Washington, DC: Office of
    the Chief of Military History, 1962), 88. Admiral Harold Stark, CNO prior
    to the war, had drafted his own memorandum, known as the "Plan Dog"
    memorandum, in November 1940. This memo stressed that, given the cur-
    rent military situation in Europe, only a US-led invasion of the European
    continent could defeat the stronger enemy, Hitler, and the Allied strategy
    should therefore focus on such an effort. The Allies, according to Stark,
    should accept the temporary loss of the western Pacific to the Japanese in
    the event of war in order to defeat Germany first. See Edward S. Miller, *War*

Plan Orange: The U.S. Strategy to Defeat Japan, 1897–1945 (Annapolis, MD: Naval Institute Press, 1991), 269–271.

17. Miller, *War Plan Orange*, 24.

18. This paragraph is based on ibid., 61–62; John Costello, *Days of Infamy: MacArthur, Roosevelt, Churchill, the Shocking Truth Revealed: How Their Secret Deals and Strategic Blunders Caused Disasters at Pearl Harbor and the Philippines* (New York: Pocket Books, 1994), 9; and Harry A. Gailey, *The War in the Pacific: From Pearl Harbor to Tokyo Bay* (Novato, CA: Presidio, 1995), 47.

19. Lewis H. Brereton, *The Brereton Diaries: The War in the Air in the Pacific, Middle East and Europe, 3 October 1941–8 May 1945* (New York: W. Morrow and Company, 1946), 12.

20. John T. Kuehn, "The War in the Pacific, 1941–1945," *The Cambridge History of the Second World War*, ed. John Ferris and Evan Mawdsley, vol. 1 (Cambridge, UK: Cambridge University Press, 2015), 423.

21. USSBS Interrogations: No. 479: Captain Minoru GENDA; Subject: Japanese Naval Air Force; Date: 28–29 November 1945, Tokyo; Microfilm Publication M1654, Reel #9, 479-2 to 479-3.

22. Agawa, *The Reluctant Admiral*, 251–252.

23. Ibid., 250, 278–279; Keegan, *The Second World War*, 254.

24. Mitsuo Fuchida et al., *Midway: The Battle That Doomed Japan* (Annapolis, MD: Naval Institute Press, 1992), 38–39.

25. van der Vat, *The Pacific Campaign*, 21.

26. Fuchida et al., *Midway*, 43; Costello, *Days of Infamy*, 4.

27. Jonathan Parshall, "Reflections on Fushida, or 'A Tale of Three Woppers,'" *Naval War College Review* 63, no. 2 (Spring 2010): 128–130. Parshall attributes the fuel-tank issue and other legends to the misleading recollections of Mitsui Fushida, the airborne commander of the Pearl Harbor strike force.

28. Matome Ugaki et al., *Fading Victory: The Diary of Admiral Matome Ugaki, 1941–1945*, trans. Masataka Chihaya (Pittsburgh: University of Pittsburgh Press, 1991), 47.

29. D. Clayton James, *The Years of MacArthur*, vol. 2, *1941–1945* (Boston: Houghton Mifflin, 1975), 3; Williamson Murray and Allan R. Millett, *A War to Be Won: Fighting the Second World War* (Cambridge: Belknap Press of Harvard University Press, 2000), 182. Much debate continues about MacArthur's and Brereton's failure to act proactively and launch their own airstrike against the Japanese airfields on Formosa. Brereton felt he did not have MacArthur's authorization to strike and therefore withheld his long-range bombers until it was too late.

30. Brereton, *The Brereton Diaries*, 44.

31. Saburō Sakai, Martin Caidin, and Fred Saito, *Samurai!*, 1st ed. (New York: Dutton, 1957), 46.

32. Brereton, *The Brereton Diaries*, 51, 20, 22.

33. Sakai, Caidin, and Saito, *Samurai!*, 41.

34. Brereton, *The Brereton Diaries*, 35, 51.

35. James, *The Years of MacArthur*, vol. 2, 23.

36. Gailey, *The War in the Pacific*, 51, 109–110.

37. Weinberg, *A World at Arms*, 313–315.

38. Saburō Hayashi, *Kogun: The Japanese Army in the Pacific War* (Quantico, VA: Marine Corps Association, 1989 [1959]), 37–38.

39. Costello, *Days of Infamy*, 3.

40. Hayashi, *Kogun*, 36.

41. United States Strategic Bombing Survey, *The Campaigns of the Pacific War* (Washington, DC: US Strategic Bombing Survey [Pacific] Naval Analysis Division, 1946), 28.

42. Murray and Millett, *A War to Be Won*, 179–181.

43. NARA 127: Series: Records of Amphibious Corps, compiled 1940–1946, Box 21, Folder 1900 Notes on Japanese. Memo from the Commander, South Pacific Area and South Pacific Force, "Lessons from Malaya" (Assistant Chief of Staff J. W. Smith, 15 November 1942), 3–4, 5, 7, 10–12.

44. Hayashi, *Kogun*, 38; United States Strategic Bombing Survey, *Campaigns of the Pacific War*, 29.

45. USSBS Interrogations: No. 601: Commander Ryosuke NOMURA, IJN; Subject: Japanese Land Based Air Operations in the CELEBES and RABAUL Area; Date: 28 November 1945, Tokyo; Microfilm Publication M1654, Reel #9, 2; Hayashi, *Kogun*, 39.

46. Ugaki et al., *Fading Victory*, 95.

47. United States Strategic Bombing Survey, *Campaigns of the Pacific War*, 31.

48. Paul S. Dull, *A Battle History of the Imperial Japanese Navy, 1941–1945* (Annapolis, MD: Naval Institute Press, 1978), 53, 55–60.

49. Agawa, *The Reluctant Admiral*, 288–289.

50. Dull, *A Battle History*, 22, 25–26.

51. Fuchida et al., *Midway*, 45–46.

52. Dull, *A Battle History*, 104–111.

53. Murray and Millett, *A War to Be Won*, 190–191.

54. Ugaki et al., *Fading Victory*, 114.

55. Fuchida et al., *Midway*, 72.

56. USSBS Interrogations: No. 503: Vice Admiral Shigeru FUKUDOME, IJN; Subject: The Naval War in the PACIFIC; Date: 9 December 1945, Tokyo; Microfilm Publication M1654, Reel #9, 39.

57. Winston Groom, *1942: The Year That Tried Men's Souls*, 1st ed. (New York: Atlantic Monthly Press, 2005), 197.

58. Dull, *A Battle History*, 120; Keegan, *The Second World War*, 271–272.

59. Ugaki et al., *Fading Victory*, 119; Dull, *A Battle History*, 121.

60. Dull, *A Battle History*, 128–129. Gailey, *War in the Pacific*, 151–152.

61. USSBS Interrogations: No. 524: Admiral Shigeru FUKUDOME, IJN; Sub-

ject: War in the PACIFIC; Date: 12 December 1945, Tokyo; Microfilm Publication M1654, Reel #9, 10–11.

62. Senshi Sōsho, *Japanese Army Operations,* 1.

63. Far East Command, "Japanese Monograph No. 45: Imperial General Headquarters Army High Command Record, Mid 41- Aug 45," 48, 50.

64. NARA 550: Series: Organizational History Files, compiled 1959–1973, documenting the period 1931–1973: "Imperial General Headquarters Army Directives, Volume II, Directives No. 901- No. 1600 (19 Jul 41–26 Aug 43)" (General Headquarters, Far East Command, Military Intelligence Section, General Staff Military Historical Section), 61–63.

65. Far East Command, "Japanese Monograph No. 45: Imperial General Headquarters Army High Command Record, Mid 41- Aug 45," 51.

66. Ibid., 12.

67. Gailey, *War in the Pacific,* 63–64.

68. Wood, *Japanese Military Strategy,* 92.

69. Gailey, *War in the Pacific,* 64.

70. Fuchida et al., *Midway,* 28–29.

71. Military Supplies Division, United States Strategic Bombing Survey, *Japanese Naval Shipbuilding* (Washington, DC: US Government Printing Office, 1946), 6; James F. Dunnigan and Albert A. Nofi, *Victory at Sea: World War II in the Pacific,* 1st ed. (New York: William Morrow, 1995), 4.

72. William Frederick Halsey and J. Bryan, *Admiral Halsey's Story* (New York: Whittlesey House, 1947), 70.

73. Dunnigan and Nofi, *Victory at Sea,* 245; Overy, *Why the Allies Won,* 331.

74. B. H. Liddell Hart, *History of the Second World War* (New York: G. P. Putnam's Sons, 1970), 209.

75. USSBS Interrogations: No. 414 (Annex A): Commander FUKANIZU, IJN; Subject: Production, Wastage and Strength, Japanese Naval Air Force; Date: November 1945, Tokyo; Microfilm Publication M1654, Reel #9, Plate 86-1.

76. Fuchida et al., *Midway,* 62.

77. Ugaki et al., *Fading Victory,* 116.

78. Overy, *Why the Allies Won,* 331.

79. This discussion of Japanese aircraft characteristics is based on Sakai, Caidin, and Saito, *Samurai!,* 129, 42, 63–66; Wood, *Japanese Military Strategy,* 90–91; Eric M. Bergerud, *Fire in the Sky: The Air War in the South Pacific* (Boulder: Westview Press, 2000), 9; Gailey, *War in the Pacific,* 60–61, and van der Vat, *The Pacific Campaign,* 124.

80. Gailey, *War in the Pacific,* 60; Liddell Hart, *History of the Second World War,* 224.

81. Fuchida et al., *Midway,* 27; David C. Evans and Mark R. Peattie, *Kaigun: Strategy, Tactics, and Technology in the Imperial Japanese Navy, 1887–1941* (Annapolis, MD: Naval Institute Press, 1997), 206–207.

82. Fuchida et al., *Midway*, 209 (for reference to the optics). Dull, *A Battle History*, 60 (for comparative torpedo ranges).

83. Halsey and Bryan, *Admiral Halsey's Story*, 72.

84. Wood, *Japanese Military Strategy*, 48.

85. Ienaga, *The Pacific War*, 141.

86. Keegan, *The Second World War*, 268.

87. Agawa, *The Reluctant Admiral*, 251–252.

88. USSBS Interrogations: No. 222, 222-3.

89. USSBS Interrogations: No. 495: Captain Toshikazu OHMAE, IJN, and Commander Meriyoshi YAMAGUCHI, IJN; Subject: Japanese Navy Air Force; Date: 6 December 1945, Tokyo; Microfilm Publication M1654, Reel #9, 495-2.

90. NARA 550: Series: Organizational History Files, compiled 1959–1973, documenting the period 1931–1973, Box 22: Japanese Monographs: Nos. 143–152. Army Force Far East Headquarters, Military History Section, "Japanese Monograph No. 152: Political Strategy Prior to the Outbreak of War, Part V," in *Japanese Monographs*, 16–17.

91. John Costello, *The Pacific War, 1941–1945: The First Comprehensive One-Volume Account of the Causes and Conduct of World War II in the Pacific* (New York: Quill, 1981), 118.

92. Brereton, *The Brereton Diaries*, 37.

93. Roberta Wohlstetter, *Pearl Harbor: Warning and Decision* (Stanford: Stanford University Press, 1962), 382.

94. Dower, *War without Mercy*, 5, 11, 259.

95. Fuchida et al., *Midway*, 54.

96. Ugaki et al., *Fading Victory*, 74.

97. Wood, *Japanese Military Strategy*, 15.

98. Overy, *Why the Allies Won*, 34.

99. Wood, *Japanese Military Strategy*, 63; van der Vat, *The Pacific Campaign*, 140; Joel Ira Holwitt, *"Execute against Japan": The U.S. Decision to Conduct Unrestricted Submarine Warfare* (College Station: Texas A&M University Press, 2013), 141–142.

100. van der Vat, *The Pacific Campaign*, 140.

101. This paragraph is based on NARA 550: Series: Organizational History Files, compiled 1959–1973, documenting the period 1931–1973, Box 3: Japanese Night Combat parts 1 & 2: "Japanese Night Combat: Part 1 of 3 Parts, Principles of Night Combat" (Headquarters, United States Army Forces Far East, and Eighth United States Army, Military History Section, Japanese Research Division, 1955), 5, 13–15, 51, 165.

102. Agawa, *The Reluctant Admiral*, 174.

103. Fuchida et al., *Midway*, 34; Wood, *Japanese Military Strategy*, 75.

104. Jonathan B. Parshall and Anthony P. Tully, *Shattered Sword: The Untold Story of the Battle of Midway* (Washington, DC: Potomac Books, 2005),

65; Edwin P. Hoyt, *Blue Skies and Blood: The Battle of the Coral Sea* (New York: Paul S. Eriksson, 1975), 54; USSBS Interrogations: No. 46: Commander H. SEKINO, IJN; Subject: CORAL SEA Battle, 7–8 May 1942; Date: 17 October 1945, Tokyo; Microfilm Publication M1654, Reel #6, 46-3. Interrogation No. 53: Captain M. YAMAOKA, IJN; Subject: SOLOMON ISLAND Operation and Battle of CORAL SEA; Date: 19 October 1945, Tokyo; Microfilm Publication M1654, Reel #8, 53-4.

105. Ugaki et al., *Fading Victory*, 122.
106. Sakai, Caidin, and Saito, *Samurai!*, 10, 17; AFHRA: Call # 168.1703-62: United States Strategic Bombing Survey, *Japanese Air Power* (Washington, DC: US Strategic Bombing Survey [Pacific], Military Analysis Division, 1946), 5.
107. Dunnigan and Nofi, *Victory at Sea*, 256.
108. Sakai, Caidin, and Saito, *Samurai!*, 88.
109. van der Vat, *The Pacific Campaign*, 135–136.
110. USSBS Interrogations: No. 479, 479-5; For the 21st Air Flotilla see: Interrogation No. 424: Captain Bunzo SHIBATA, IJN; Subject: 21st Air Flotilla; Date: 18 November 1945, Tokyo; Microfilm Publication M1654, Reel #9, 424-6. For the 23rd Air Flotilla see: Interrogation No. 601: Commander Ryosuke NOMURA, IJN; Subject: Japanese Land Based Air Operations in the CELEBES and RABAUL Area; Date: 28 November 1945, Tokyo; Microfilm Publication M1654, Reel #6, 601-2.
111. Mark R. Peattie, *Sunburst: The Rise of Japanese Naval Air Power, 1909–1941* (Annapolis, MD: Naval Institute Press, 2001), 309–312.
112. USSBS Interrogations: No. 424, 424-5–424-6; No. 601, 601-2, 601-3.

CHAPTER 7. MIDWAY: THE INITIATIVE IN DISPUTE

1. Matome Ugaki et al., *Fading Victory: The Diary of Admiral Matome Ugaki, 1941–1945*, trans. Masataka Chihaya (Pittsburgh: University of Pittsburgh Press, 1991), 75; Gordon W. Prange, Donald M. Goldstein, and Katherine V. Dillon, *Miracle at Midway* (New York: McGraw-Hill, 1982), 22–23.
2. Saburō Hayashi, *Kogun: The Japanese Army in the Pacific War* (Quantico, VA: Marine Corps Association, 1989 [1959]), 51.
3. Jonathan B. Parshall and Anthony P. Tully, *Shattered Sword: The Untold Story of the Battle of Midway* (Washington, DC: Potomac Books, 2005), 431.
4. Ibid., 37.
5. Ibid., 65.
6. Ugaki et al., *Fading Victory*, 123.
7. United States Strategic Bombing Survey, *The Campaigns of the Pacific War* (Washington, DC: US Strategic Bombing Survey [Pacific], Naval Analysis Division, 1946), 58.

8. John Prados, *Combined Fleet Decoded: The Secret History of American Intelligence and the Japanese Navy in World War II*, 1st ed. (New York: Random House, 1995), 315–317.

9. Ibid., 317–321.

10. E. B. Potter, *Nimitz* (Annapolis, MD: Naval Institute Press, 1976), 79–81, 87.

11. United States Strategic Bombing Survey, *Campaigns of the Pacific War*, 74–76, 99–101.

12. Mitsuo Fuchida et al., *Midway: The Battle That Doomed Japan* (Annapolis, MD: Naval Institute Press, 1992), 216–222.

13. Parshall and Tully, *Shattered Sword*, 95–96.

14. Ibid., 433–434, 90.

15. Ibid., 93; Ugaki et al., *Fading Victory*, 126.

16. Fuchida et al., *Midway*, 86; Potter, *Nimitz*, 88.

17. Fuchida et al., *Midway*, 117.

18. Ibid., 123, 125, 130–135.

19. Ibid., 130–135, 138–139; Parshall and Tully, *Shattered Sword*, 134–135.

20. Parshall and Tully, *Shattered Sword*, 154–155.

21. USSBS Interrogations: No. 165: Captain H. OHARA, IJN; Subject: Battle of MIDWAY, 4–6 June 1942. Damage to Aircraft Carrier, SORYU; Date: 25 October 1945, Tokyo; Microfilm Publication M1654, Reel #2, 165-2. See also Interrogation No. 11: Captain Susumu KAWAGUCHI, IJN; Subject: HIRYU (CV) at the Battle of MIDWAY; Date: 10 October 1945, Tokyo; Microfilm Publication M1654, Reel #5, 11-4. Interrogation No. 138: Lieutenant Commander Hiroshi TOXUNO, IJN; Subject: Battle of GUADALCANAL, 12–14 November 1942, Battle of MIDWAY, 4–5 June 1942, Battle of VILLA STANMORE, 6 March 1943; Date: 25 October 1945, Tokyo; Microfilm Publication M1654, Reel #8, 138-4.

22. Parshall and Tully, *Shattered Sword*, 154–155. It is worth noting that, given Japanese estimates of the outcome at Coral Sea, the presence of a single American carrier closely matched their estimate of American strength.

23. Ibid.

24. USSBS Interrogations: No. 165, 165-2 to 165-3.

25. Parshall and Tully, *Shattered Sword*, 154–155, 209, 219.

26. Fuchida et al., *Midway*, 156–157.

27. Ibid., 168; Parshall and Tully, *Shattered Sword*, 297, 311–318; 324–328.

28. United States Strategic Bombing Survey, *Campaigns of the Pacific War*, 77; Parshall and Tully, *Shattered Sword*, 417.

29. Samuel Eliot Morison, *The Two-Ocean War: A Short History of the United States Navy in the Second World War* (Boston: Little, Brown, 1963), 161–162; United States Strategic Bombing Survey, *Campaigns of the Pacific War*, 77.

30. USSBS Interrogations: No. 65: Captain Y. WATANABE, IJN; Subject:

PEARL HARBOR—MIDWAY—SOLOMONS; Date: 15 October 1945, Tokyo; Microfilm Publication M1654, Reel #8, 65-4.

31. Fuchida et al., *Midway*, 131.

32. Parshall and Tully, *Shattered Sword*, 108–110, 132, 159–164.

33. USSBS Interrogations: No. 11: Captain Susumu KAWAGUCHI, IJN; Subject: *HIRYU* (CV) at the Battle of MIDWAY; Date: 10 October 1945, Tokyo; Microfilm Publication M1654, Reel #8, 11-7.

34. Alvin B. Kernan, *The Unknown Battle of Midway: The Destruction of the American Torpedo Squadrons*, Yale Library of Military History (New Haven: Yale University Press, 2005), 30–32.

35. John B. Lundstrom, *The First Team: Pacific Naval Air Combat from Pearl Harbor to Midway*, 1st Naval Institute Press (Annapolis, MD: Naval Institute Press, 2005), 343–363.

36. Parshall and Tully, *Shattered Sword*, 481.

37. Lundstrom, *The First Team*, 441, 445.

38. Parshall and Tully, *Shattered Sword*, 482–483.

39. Kernan, *Unknown Battle of Midway*, 26.

40. Lundstrom, *The First Team*, 300.

41. Parshall and Tully, *Shattered Sword*, 164–171.

42. This paragraph is based on ibid., 129, 216–217, 274.

43. Potter, *Nimitz*, 85–86.

44. Parshall and Tully, *Shattered Sword*, 65, 276–278. Japanese air groups operated organically with their carriers and did not rotate to other vessels in the same manner as US Navy flying squadrons.

45. Samuel Eliot Morison, *Coral Sea, Midway and Submarine Actions, May 1942–August 1942*, vol. 4, *History of United States Naval Operations in World War II* (Annapolis, MD: Naval Institute Press, 2010 [1949]), 33–37.

46. Parshall and Tully, *Shattered Sword*, 174–175, 217.

47. USSBS Interrogation No. 252: Captain Yasumi TOYAMA, IJN; Subject: (1) Transports at MIDWAY; (2) Transports at the Battle of EASTERN SOLOMONS 25 August 1942; (3) Battle of TASSAFARONGA 30 November 1942; Date: 1 November 1945, Tokyo; Microfilm Publication M1654, Reel #2, 252-4.

48. Parshall and Tully, *Shattered Sword*, 418–419.

49. Morison, *Coral Sea*, 257.

50. Parshall and Tully, *Shattered Sword*, 385–387.

51. NARA 550: Series: Organizational History Files, compiled 1959–1973, documenting the period 1931–1973: "Imperial General Headquarters Army Directives, Volume II, Directives No. 901–No. 1600, (19 Jul 41–26 Aug 43)," Imperial General Headquarters Army Department Directive #1,179 (General Headquarters, Far East Command, Military Intelligence Section, General Staff Military Historical Section), 81; Imperial General Headquarters Army Department Directive #1, 180, 81–82, 218, 123.

52. *Naval History and Heritage Command, Operational Archives Branch, Washington Navy Yard: Collection 505: Papers of FADM Chester W. Nimitz, USN 1902–1976* (hereafter NHHC 505): Box 1: Command Summary Fleet Admiral C. W. Nimitz, US Navy, Book 1: 7 December 1941–31 August 1942, Volumes 1, 2, and 3, pages 1–861, 570.

53. Ibid., 571.

54. National Archives and Records Administration: Record Group 165: Records of the War Department General and Special Staff, 1903–1947 (hereafter NARA 165): Series: Classified General Correspondence 1942–47, Box 118: 1942–43: Projects—Area Central Pacific—South Pacific, Folder: SW Pacific Area: 24 May 1942 Memo Subject: Situation in the Pacific, 1–4.

55. Ibid., 31 May 1942 Naval Message #010100, From: COMINCH, For Action: CINCPAC, Information: COMSOPACFOR, COMSWPACFOR, 1.

56. Ibid., AG 913, June 8,1942, From: GHQ SWPA, To: Chief of Staff, Signed MacArthur, 1; Louis Morton, *Strategy and Command: The First Two Years*, United States Army in World War II: The War in the Pacific (Washington, DC: Office of the Chief of Military History, 1962), 99.

57. NARA 165: Series: Security Classified General Correspondence 1942–47, Box 118: 1942–43: Projects—Area Central Pacific—South Pacific, Folder: SW Pacific Area: COMINCH FILE: FF1/A16-3(1) Serial #00482, Memorandum dated June 11,1942, 1–2. See also Morton, *Strategy and Command*, 296. King and his chief naval planner, Rear Admiral Charles M. Cooke, felt that the threat of Japanese land-based aircraft in the area precluded safe operation of carrier task forces in the New Guinea–Rabaul area. King and Cooke felt a more methodical step-by-step advance, beginning in the southern Solomon Islands, afforded the best opportunity for success in the coming offensive while limiting the risk to the remaining American carriers.

58. Ibid.: June 26, 1942, Memorandum for Admiral King: Subject: Offensive Operations in the South and South West Pacific Areas. Signed: GCM Chief of Staff, 1–2; June 29,1942, Memorandum for Admiral King, Signed: GCM Chief of Staff, 1; Joint Directive for Offensive Operations in the Southwest Pacific Area: Agreed upon by the United States Chiefs of Staff, 2 July 1942, Signed by E. J. King and G. C. Marshall, 1–2.

59. Ibid.: Joint Directive for Offensive Operations in the Southwest Pacific Area: Agreed upon by the United States Chiefs of Staff, 2 July 1942, Signed by E. J. King and G. C. Marshall, 1–2.

60. *Genea Archives—BACM Research: World War II Historical Document Archive Dvd-Rom Disc 1 of 4.* FDR Presidential Papers 1: FDR06I.pdf: 6 May 1942, Memorandum for General George Marshall, Chief of Staff, Signed: FDR, 1.

61. Morton, *Strategy and Command*, 308–309.

62. NARA 165: Series: Top-Secret Card Index to Correspondence in Series 15:

Box 1: 000.1—311.2: Telegram, 7/14/42, from Pres. Roosevelt 7/14/42 to C/S (Chief of Staff), 1.

63. *Genea Archives—BACM Research: World War II Historical Document Archive Dvd-Rom Disc 1 of 4.* FDR Presidential Papers 1: FDR06H.pdf: July 15, 1942, Memorandum for General Marshall, Admiral King, Hon. Harry L. Hopkins, 1–3.

64. Richard B. Frank, *Guadalcanal: The Definitive Account of the Landmark Battle*, 1st ed. (New York: Random House, 1990), 43–44.

65. Grace P. Hayes, *The History of the Joint Chiefs of Staff in World War II: The War against Japan* (Annapolis, MD: Naval Institute Press, 1982), 157.

66. James B. Wood, *Japanese Military Strategy in the Pacific War: Was Defeat Inevitable?* (New York: Rowman & Littlefield, 2007), 15.

CHAPTER 8. NEW GUINEA AND GUADALCANAL, JULY–OCTOBER 1942: THE INITIATIVE REMAINS IN DISPUTE

1. Senshi Sōsho, *Japanese Army Operations*, 67.
2. Ibid., 98–101.
3. Ibid., 91–92.
4. Richard B. Frank, *Guadalcanal: The Definitive Account of the Landmark Battle*, 1st ed. (New York: Random House, 1990), 31.
5. Eric M. Bergerud, *Fire in the Sky: The Air War in the South Pacific* (Boulder: Westview Press, 2000), 659.
6. NARA 38: Series: Records Relating to Naval Activity During World War II: World War II War Diaries, Box 1: SCAPJAP, NSCO: 7 Dec 1941–Dec 1943 to COMINCH: 7 Dec 1941–Dec 1943. Memo dated 6/5/42 From: The Commander in Chief, United States Fleet, To: All Bureaus and Offices of the Navy Department. Subject: Instructions Relative to duties as Commander, South Pacific Area and South Pacific Force. Reference: (a) Cincpac Serial 090W, 1.
7. NHHC 505: Box 1: Command Summary Fleet Admiral C. W. Nimitz U.S. Navy, Book One: 7 December 1941–31 August 1942, Volumes 1, 2, 3, pages 1–861. War Plans CincPac Files: Subject: Captain Steele's "Running Estimates and Summary" covering the period 7 December 1941–31 August 1942, 615.
8. John Miller, *Guadalcanal: The First Offensive*, United States Army in World War II: The War in the Pacific (Washington, DC: Center of Military History, 1989), 19–20.
9. NHHC 505: Box 1, Captain Steele's "Running Estimates and Summary" covering the period 7 December 1941–31 August 1942, 615.
10. Samuel B. Griffith, *The Battle for Guadalcanal* (New York: Lippincott, 1963), 29.
11. Senshi Sōsho, *Japanese Army Operations*, 106.

12. Edward J. Drea, *MacArthur's ULTRA: Codebreaking and the War against Japan, 1942–1945* (Lawrence: University Press of Kansas, 1992), 40.
13. NARA 496: Series: Combined Operations Intelligence Center Situation Reports 1942–1943, Box 164: Folder: Situation Reports from the C.O.I.C. to G2 USAF: 26 June 1942–31 August 1942. General Headquarters, South West Pacific Area, Situation Report No. 313, 3–7. NARA 550: Series: Organizational History Files, compiled 1959–1973, documenting the period 1931–1973, Box 16: Japanese Monographs: Nos. 86 to 97, Folder: Japanese Monograph: No. 96: Eastern New Guinea Invasion Operations, 7–8.
14. Senshi Sōsho, *Japanese Army Operations*, 107.
15. NARA 550: Folder: Japanese Monograph: No. 96: Eastern New Guinea Invasion Operations, 9.
16. Dudley McCarthy, *South-West Pacific Area—First Year: Kokoda to Wau*, Australia in the War of 1939–1945, Series 1, Army V. 5 (Canberra: Australian War Memorial, 1959), www.awm.gov.au/collection/C1417310.
17. USSBS Interrogations: No. 503, 503-39.
18. Bergerud, *Touched with Fire: The Land War in the South Pacific* (New York: Penguin Books, 1996), 136–141; John Costello, *The Pacific War, 1941–1945: The First Comprehensive One-Volume Account of the Causes and Conduct of World War II in the Pacific* (New York: Quill, 1981), 317.
19. Senshi Sōsho, *Japanese Army Operations*, 133–135.
20. Bergerud, *Touched with Fire*, 142.
21. McCarthy, *South-West Pacific Area*, 234.
22. Saburō Hayashi, *Kogun: The Japanese Army in the Pacific War* (Quantico, VA: Marine Corps Association, 1989 [1959]), 55.
23. McCarthy, *South-West Pacific Area*, 246.
24. Bergerud, *Touched with Fire*, 142; Samuel Milner, *Victory in Papua*, United States Army in World War II: The War in the Pacific (Washington, DC: Center of Military History, 2003), 104.
25. NARA 550: Series: Organizational History Files, compiled 1959–1973, documenting the period 1931–1973, Box 16: Japanese Monographs: Nos. 86 to 97, Folder: Japanese Monograph: No. 96: Eastern New Guinea Invasion Operations, 11. Japan's Special Naval Landing Forces (SNLF) did not quite equate to US Marines. The SNLF units did make amphibious landings and often engaged in fighting. They were, however, not as proficient in infantry tactics as their army counterparts. Against light resistance or in unopposed landings they performed quite well. During an attack against a determined foe they were far less effective, although they could be very stubborn in defense. See United States War Department, *Handbook on Japanese Military Forces* (reproduced Baton Rouge: Louisiana State University Press, 1995), 76.
26. NARA 550: Series: Organizational History Files, compiled 1959–1973, documenting the period 1931–1973, Box 16: Japanese Monographs: Nos.

86 to 97, Folder: Japanese Monograph: No. 96: Eastern New Guinea Invasion Operations, 11–12.

27. NARA 496: Series: Combined Operations Intelligence Center Situation Reports 1942–1943, Box 164: Folder: Situation Reports from the COIC [Combined Operations Intelligence Center] to G2 USAAF: June 26, 1942–August 31, 1942: General Headquarters, South West Pacific Area Situation Report No. 347, dated 25 August 1942, 6–8.

28. Drea, *MacArthur's ULTRA*, 44.

29. McCarthy, *South-West Pacific Area*, 159.

30. Milner, *Victory in Papua*, 79, 83–87.

31. NARA 496: Series: Combined Operations Intelligence Center Situation Reports 1942–1943, Box 163: April 1, 1942–June 26, 1942, Folder 2: Situation Reports from COIC to G2 USAF: Situation Report No. 249, dated 20/5/42, 3, and Situation Report No. 282, dated 21/6/42, 3.

32. Griffith, *Battle for Guadalcanal*, 20–21.

33. Senshi Sōsho, *Japanese Army Operations*, 122.

34. Matome Ugaki et al., *Fading Victory: The Diary of Admiral Matome Ugaki, 1941–1945*, trans. Masataka Chihaya (Pittsburgh: University of Pittsburgh Press, 1991), 77.

35. Frank, *Guadalcanal*, 64–69, 86–87.

36. Dan van der Vat, *The Pacific Campaign: World War II, the U.S.-Japanese Naval War, 1941–1945* (New York: Simon & Schuster, 1991), 213.

37. William Frederick Halsey and J. Bryan, *Admiral Halsey's Story* (New York: Whittlesey House, 1947), 113.

38. van der Vat, *The Pacific Campaign*, 228; Costello, *The Pacific War*, 350–351.

39. United States Strategic Bombing Survey, *The Campaigns of the Pacific War*, (Washington, DC: US Strategic Bombing Survey [Pacific], Naval Analysis Division, 1946), 110–113, 119.

40. Ibid., 119–120, 123.

41. NARA 127: Series: Reports, Studies, and Plans re World War II Military Operations, 1941–1956, Box 13: Quantico Newsletter, 1941 to Intell. Section, Tsingtao, Trial of Russians, Folder: Intelligence Center Pacific Ocean Areas Office of the Marine Liaison Officer "Japanese Land Forces (No. 2) Tactics," 20 October 1942. Translation of the captured documents detailing the "IKKI [Ichiki] Detachment Orders" for the landing on Guadalcanal included in "Intelligence Center, Pacific Ocean Areas: Japanese Land Forces No. 2 Tactics, Oct. 20, 1942," Enclosure A, 5–7.

42. Griffith, *Battle for Guadalcanal*, 86–87.

43. Winston Groom, *1942: The Year That Tried Men's Souls*, 1st ed. (New York: Atlantic Monthly Press, 2005), 301, 303–307.

44. Hayashi, *Kogun*, 59–60.

45. NARA 550: Series: Organizational History Files, compiled 1959–1973,

documenting the period 1931–1973, Box 3: Japanese Night Combat Parts 1 and 2: "Japanese Night Combat: Part 3 of 3 Parts, Supplement: Night Combat Examples (Headquarters United States Army Forces, Far East and Eighth United States Army Military History Section," Japanese Research Division, 1955), 583.

46. Frank, *Guadalcanal*, 364–365. Frank admits that casualty calculations for the battle are problematic, but his extensive research leads him to the conclusion that the US Marines lost no more than 90 killed, while the Japanese actually sustained more than the 2,200 dead estimated by the 1st Marine Division.

47. John B. Lundstrom, *The First Team and the Guadalcanal Campaign: Naval Fighter Combat from August to November 1942* (Annapolis, MD: Naval Institute Press, 1994), 96. The first American aircraft, totaling nineteen F4F-4 Wildcat fighters and twelve SBD-3 Dauntless dive-bombers, landed at Henderson Field on Guadalcanal on 20 August.

48. AFHRA: Call # 168.1703-62: *Japanese Air Power*, 13; Call # 168.1703-65: United States Strategic Bombing Survey, Military Analysis Division, *Employment of the Forces Under the Southwest Pacific Command* (Washington, DC: US Strategic Bombing Survey, Military Analysis Division, 1947), 12.

49. AFHRA: Call # 168.1703-65: United States Strategic Bombing Survey, Military Analysis Division, *Employment of the Forces Under the Southwest Pacific Command* (Washington, DC: US Strategic Bombing Survey, Military Analysis Division, 1947), 12.

50. Frank, *Guadalcanal*, 609–610.

51. NARA 550: Series: Organizational History Files, compiled 1959–1973, documenting the period 1931–1973, Box 19: Japanese Monographs: Nos. 118–125, Folder: Japanese Monograph: No. 121: Outline of Southeast Area Naval Air Operations, Part 2: "Monograph No. 121 (Navy) Outline of Southeast Area Naval Air Operations Part II, Aug 42–Oct 42, Prepared by Second Demobilization Bureau," 44–45.

52. Richard M. Leighton and Robert W. Coakley, *Global Logistics and Strategy: 1940–1943*, vol. 1, *United States Army in World War II: The War Department* (Washington, DC: Office of the Chief of Military History, 1955), 716–717.

53. Dull, *A Battle History*, 238. Force ratios on Guadalcanal from 7 August through the end of October 1942: on 7 August 2,200 Japanese to 10,000 Americans; on 20 August 3,600 Japanese to 10,000 Americans; on 12 September 6,000 Japanese to 11,000 Americans; and on 23 October 22,000 Japanese to 23,000 Americans.

54. USSBS Interrogations: No. 424, 424-6.

55. Mark R. Peattie, *Sunburst: The Rise of Japanese Naval Air Power, 1909–1941* (Annapolis, MD: Naval Institute Press, 2001), 176; USSBS Interro-

gations: No. 446-Supp.: Captain Takashi MIYAZAKI, IJN; Subject: Air
Operations of Japanese Naval Air Forces based at RABAUL, including
NEW GUINEA and SOLOMONS; Date: January 1946, Washington, D.C.;
Microfilm Publication M1654, Reel #9, 446-Supplement, Plate 97-1.

56. Intelligence Assistant Chief of Air Staff, Historical Division, "Army Air
Forces Historical Studies: No. 17: Air Action in the Papuan Campaign, 21
July 1942 to 23 January 1943," (August 1944), 8–9.

57. Lundstrom, *The First Team*, 238.

58. United States Strategic Bombing Survey, *The Campaigns of the Pacific War*,
108, 110–113.

59. Frank, *Guadalcanal*, 167–173.

60. United States Strategic Bombing Survey, *The Campaigns of the Pacific War*,
115–117, 119–123.

61. Frank, *Guadalcanal*, 374–378.

62. AFHRA: Call # 168.7103-71 V2: "General George C. Kenney Diaries Volume II, 1 September 1942–31 October 1942" (see 8 September and 17 September entries for P-38 fuel-tank problems). For the A-20 information see:
George C. Kenney, *The Saga of Pappy Gun* (New York: Duell, Sloan and
Pearce, 1959), 48.

63. Bergerud, *Fire in the Sky: The Air War in the South Pacific*, 463–464.

64. Frank, *Guadalcanal*, 122–123.

65. Richard J. Overy, *Why the Allies Won*, 1st American ed. (New York: W. W.
Norton, 1996), 222.

66. NARA 337: Series: Intelligence Reports, compiled 1943–1946, Box 51:
Folder 8: Walsh Obs Report: Memo Headquarters Army Ground Forces,
Army War College, Washington, D.C.; Subject: Observer Report, dated 13
March 1943, Appendix IV, 1.

67. Ibid., Section III, 9–10.

68. Ore J. Marion, Thomas Cuddihy, and Edward Cuddihy, *On the Canal: The
Marines of L-3-5 on Guadalcanal, 1942*, 1st ed., Stackpole Military History
series (Mechanicsburg, PA: Stackpole Books, 2004), 225.

69. NHHC Collection 505: Papers of FADM Chester W. Nimitz, USN 1902–
1976, Box 1: Command Summary Fleet Admiral C.W. Nimitz, US Navy, Book
1: 7 December 1941–31 August 1942, Volumes 1, 2, 3, pages 1–861, 791.

70. Ibid., 832.

71. NHHC 505: "Nimitz Diary" (Reference Library), only 1 Box, 23 October
1942 entry.

72. Frank, *Guadalcanal*, 206–207.

73. USSBS Interrogations: No. 402, 402-4 to 402-5.

74. Senshi Sōsho, *Japanese Army Operations*, 1.

75. Griffith, *The Battle for Guadalcanal*, 44.

76. NHHC 505: Papers of FADM Chester W. Nimitz, USN 1902–1976, Box

1: Command Summary Fleet Admiral C. W. Nimitz, U.S. Navy, Book 1: 7 December 1941–31 August 1942, Volumes 1, 2, 3, pages 1–861, 649.

77. NHHC 505: "Nimitz Diary" (Reference Library), only 1 box, entries for 17 and 14 October 42.

78. Halsey and Bryan, *Admiral Halsey's Story*, 117.

79. Frank, *Guadalcanal*, 335–336.

80. Ugaki et al., *Fading Victory*, 177.

81. Frank, *Guadalcanal*, 121.

82. Ibid., 79.

83. NARA 550: Series: Organizational History Files, compiled 1959–1973, documenting the period 1931–1973, Box 3: Japanese Night Combat parts 1 & 2: "Japanese Night Combat: Part 1 of 3 Parts, Principles of Night Combat" (Headquarters, United States Army Forces, Far East, and Eighth United States Army Military History Section, Japanese Research Division, 1955), 166–167.

84. NARA 127: Series: Reports, Studies, and Plans re World War II Military Operations, 1941–1956, Box 1: Amphib Corps Pac Flt to 1st Corps, Tank Bn., Folder: 1st Parachute Battalion; Operations Report September 13–14, 1942, "Operations Report First Parachute Battalion," Document 23689, 1–2; and NARA 127: Series: Reports, Studies, and Plans re World War II Military Operations, 1941–1956, Box 13: Quantico Newsletter, 1941 to Intell. Section, Tsingtao, Trial of Russians, Folder: Correspondence Between Gen Vandegrift & Gen Holcomb Concerning Fighting on Pacific Islands 1942: 15 September 1942 letter from General Vandegrift to US Marine Corps Commandant, General Holcomb, 1–5.

85. NARA 550: Series: Organizational History Files, compiled 1959–1973, documenting the period 1931–1973, Box 3: Japanese Night Combat parts 1 & 2: "Japanese Night Combat: Part 1 of 3 Parts, Principles of Night Combat" (Headquarters, United States Army Forces, Far East, and Eighth United States Army Military History Section, Japanese Research Division, 1955), 167.

86. Frank, *Guadalcanal*, 261–263.

87. USSBS Interrogations: No. 495, 495-3. The Japanese tried to air-drop supplies to the Japanese soldiers retreating along the Kokoda Trail using the G4M "Betty" bombers at night with untrained crews. Ohmae estimates a recovery rate of the supplies as 25 percent. To this author, having extensive training and experience in nighttime tactical airdrops, even 25 percent seems rather high given the nature of the terrain with both jungle and mountains and a lack of trained aircrews. Regardless, the Japanese clearly could not sustain their efforts despite the airdrops.

88. Senshi Sōsho, *Japanese Army Operations*, 133.

89. NARA 550: Series: Organizational History Files, compiled 1959–1973,

documenting the period 1931–1973, Box 3: Japanese Night Combat parts 1 & 2: "Japanese Night Combat: Part 1 of 3 Parts, Principles of Night Combat" (Headquarters, United States Army Forces, Far East, and Eighth United States Army Military History Section, Japanese Research Division, 1955), 166.

90. NARA 496: Series: Reports of the Commander, Fleet Marine Force Guadalcanal 1943, Box 731: G-3 Admin: Reports of the Commander, Fleet Marine Force, Relating to Operations on Guadalcanal 1943, Folder: Division Commander's Final Report Guadalcanal Phase III: "DIVISION COMMANDER'S FINAL REPORT ON GUADALCANAL OPERATION PHASE III," 11.

91. AFHRA: Call # 168.7103-71 V2: "General George C. Kenney Diaries Volume II, 1 September 1942–31 October 1942," entries for 18 and 24 September 1942.

92. AFHRA: Call # 168.1703-71: United States Strategic Bombing Survey (Pacific), Military Analysis Division, *The Fifth Air Force in the War against Japan* (Washington, DC: US Strategic Bombing Survey, June 1947), 27.

93. Jeff Reardon, "Breaking the U.S. Navy's 'Gun Club' Mentality in the South Pacific," *Journal of Military History* 75, no. 2 (April 2011): 533–534, 538, 541.

94. Bergerud, *Fire in the Sky*, 424.

95. Peter Young, *The World Almanac Book of World War II: The Complete and Comprehensive Documentary of World War II* (Englewood Cliffs, NJ: World Almanac Publications and Prentice-Hall, 1981), 168.

96. Saburō Sakai, Martin Caidin, and Fred Saito, *Samurai!*, 1st ed. (New York: Dutton, 1957), 163.

97. Frank, *Guadalcanal*, 320.

98. Ibid., 60.

99. Costello, *The Pacific War*, 324–325.

100. John B. Lundstrom, *Black Shoe Carrier Admiral: Frank Jack Fletcher at Coral Sea, Midway, and Guadalcanal* (Annapolis, MD: Naval Institute Press, 2006), 368–383. Historians have widely criticized Fletcher for this decision, but Lundstrom makes a cogent argument in the admiral's defense. Regardless, the invasion remained exposed at a critical juncture, which provided a fleeting opportunity for the Japanese.

101. Samuel Eliot Morison, *The Two-Ocean War: A Short History of the United States Navy in the Second World War* (Boston: Little, Brown, 1963), 175–176.

102. Frank, *Guadalcanal*, 165, 370–371.

103. Reardon, "Breaking," 541.

104. Ugaki et al., *Fading Victory*, 193, 221, 251, 255–256.

105. Edwin Palmer Hoyt, *Yamamoto: The Man Who Planned Pearl Harbor*, 1st Lyons Press ed. (Guilford, CT: Lyons Press, 2001), 219.

106. NHHC 505: "Nimitz Diary" (Reference Library), only 1 Box, entry for 30 October 42.
107. Grace P. Hayes, *The History of the Joint Chiefs of Staff in World War II: The War against Japan* (Annapolis, MD: Naval Institute Press, 1982), 191, 191–193. Roosevelt ordered his military leaders to make sure that every weapon needed to hold in the Pacific made its way there, but he phrased his memo in such a manner to ensure that transfers came at the expense of the buildup in England and not through diversion from Operation Torch in North Africa.
108. van der Vat, *The Pacific Campaign*, 232.

CHAPTER 9. NEW GUINEA AND GUADALCANAL, NOVEMBER 1942–
FEBRUARY 1943: THE ALLIES SEIZE THE INITIATIVE

1. NARA 550: Series: Organizational History Files, compiled 1959–1973, documenting the period 1931–1973, Box 11: Japanese Monographs Nos. 41 and 45, Folder: Japanese Monograph No. 45: Imperial General Head-quarters Army High Command Record, 67–68. Much of this Japanese view-point approximated MacArthur's own vision for future operations in the region.
2. NHHC Collection 505: Papers of FADM Chester W. Nimitz, USN 1902–1976, Box 2: Command Summary Fleet Admiral C. W. Nimitz U.S. Navy, Book Two: 1 September 1942–31 December 1942, Volumes 1, 2, pages 862–1262. War Plans CincPac Files: Subject: Captain Steele's "Running Es-timates and Summary" covering the period 1 September 1942–31 December 1942, 1150–1151.
3. Samuel Milner, *Victory in Papua*, United States Army in World War II: The War in the Pacific (Washington, DC: Center of Military History, 2003), 116–119.
4. Robert L. Eichelberger and Milton Mackaye, *Jungle Road to Tokyo* (Lon-don: Odhams Press Limited, 1951), 41.
5. Milner, *Victory in Papua*, 119–123.
6. Ibid., 126–127, 130–131, 147–150.
7. Eichelberger and Mackaye, *Jungle Road to Tokyo*, 41–42.
8. John Costello, *The Pacific War, 1941–1945: The First Comprehensive One-Volume Account of the Causes and Conduct of World War II in the Pacific* (New York: Quill, 1981), 380.
9. Milner, *Victory in Papua*, 321.
10. Eichelberger and Mackaye, *Jungle Road to Tokyo*, 80–81.
11. Winston Groom, *1942: The Year That Tried Men's Souls*, 1st ed. (New York: Atlantic Monthly Press, 2005), 343.
12. Richard B. Frank, *Guadalcanal: The Definitive Account of the Landmark Battle*, 1st ed. (New York: Random House, 1990), 428.

13. United States Strategic Bombing Survey, *The Campaigns of the Pacific War,* (Washington, DC: US Strategic Bombing Survey, [Pacific] Naval Analysis Division, 1946), 125–126.

14. Ibid., 127.

15. Frank, *Guadalcanal: The Definitive Account of the Landmark Battle,* 451.

16. United States Strategic Bombing Survey, *The Campaigns of the Pacific War,* 126, 128–129.

17. Frank, *Guadalcanal: The Definitive Account of the Landmark Battle,* 487–490.

18. United States Strategic Bombing Survey, *The Campaigns of the Pacific War* 139–140.

19. John Miller, *Guadalcanal: The First Offensive*, United States Army in World War II: The War in the Pacific (Washington, DC: Center of Military History, 1989), 209, 213, 218.

20. Saburō Hayashi, *Kogun: The Japanese Army in the Pacific War* (Quantico, VA: Marine Corps Association, 1989 [1959]), 62–65.

21. Frank, *Guadalcanal,* 614.

22. Hayashi, *Kogun,* 62–64.

23. John Keegan, *The Second World War* (New York: Penguin Books, 1990), 297. One should also note that the balance of US troops in the Pacific and the European theaters began to shift. In January 1943, the United States had 460,000 troops in the Pacific, but the build-up in England and operations in the Mediterranean now drew 380,000 American troops. Since September, 60,000 American soldiers had headed to the Pacific against 180,000 that had departed for Europe, despite the precarious situation in the South Pacific. This division of effort amply demonstrates Roosevelt's commitment to Europe.

24. D. Clayton James, *The Years of MacArthur*, vol. 2, *1941–1945* (Boston: Houghton Mifflin, 1975), 240.

25. E. B. Potter and Chester W. Nimitz, eds., *Triumph in the Pacific: The Navy's Struggle against Japan*, A Spectrum Book (Englewood Cliffs, NJ: Prentice-Hall, 1963), 28.

26. Richard J. Overy, *Why the Allies Won*, 1st American ed. (New York: W. W. Norton, 1996), 331. According to Overy, the United States produced 47,826 aircraft in 1942 while Japan produced a total of 8,861.

27. NARA 550: Series: Organizational History Files, compiled 1959–1973, documenting the period 1931–1973, Box 10: Japanese Monographs Nos. 31–35, Folder: Japanese Monograph No. 32: Southeast Area Air Operations Record: "Monograph #32 (Army): Southeast Pacific Area Aerial Opn Record," 2, 4, 5.

28. USSBS Interrogations: No. 485, 485-1.

29. Miller, *Guadalcanal,* 173–174.

30. AFHRA: Call # 168.1703-71, *The Fifth Air Force in War Against Japan,* 13.

31. Admiral Ernest J. King, *Our Navy at War: A Report to the Secretary of the Navy, Covering Our Peacetime Navy and Our Wartime Navy and Including Combat Operations up to March 1, 1944* (Washington, DC: United States News, 1944), 9–11. American naval construction times decreased markedly once hostilities commenced. Battleship construction time reduced by 18 percent to thirty-two months, carrier construction time by over 50 percent to just over 15 months, submarines by 50 percent to seven months, and destroyers by 64 percent to just over five months. Indeed, the average construction of US destroyers in 1942 amounted to 6.75 ships per month. These numbers presaged the American materiel dominance that characterized the last two years of the Pacific War as, in 1943, the US Navy stood on the cusp of a commissioning boom whose roots could be traced back to prewar planning. The Imperial Japanese Navy received one battleship, six carriers, two cruisers, nine destroyers, and twenty-two submarines from its shipyards in 1942 (United States Strategic Bombing Survey, *Japanese Naval Shipbuilding*, 2.) As time passed, however, the Japanese could not hope to match American construction.

32. Miller, *Guadalcanal*, 173–174.

33. AFHRA: Call # 168.7103-71 V3: "General George C. Kenney Diaries, Volume III, 1 November 1942–31 December 1942," entry for 27 December 1942.

34. USSBS Interrogations: No. 496: Lieutenant Kunie IWASHITA, IJN; Subject: Japanese Naval Air Combat & Tactics; Date: 3 December 1945, Tokyo; Microfilm Publication M1654, Reel #9, 496-2. Interrogation No. 386: Senior Private Guy TOKO, IJA; Subject: Combat Techniques of the JAAF; Date: 20 November 1945, Tokyo; Microfilm Publication M1654, Reel #9, 496-3.

35. George C. Kenney, *The Saga of Pappy Gun* (New York: Duell, Sloan and Pearce, 1959), 48–49.

36. AFHRA: Call # 168.7103-71 V3: "General George C. Kenney Diaries, Volume III, 1 November 1942–31 December 1942," entry for 19 November 1942.

37. Frank, *Guadalcanal*, 574.

38. Eric M. Bergerud, *Fire in the Sky: The Air War in the South Pacific* (Boulder: Westview Press, 2000), 219–221.

39. Frank, *Guadalcanal*, 486.

40. Jeff Reardon, "Breaking the U.S. Navy's 'Gun Club' Mentality in the South Pacific," *Journal of Military History* 75, no. 2 (April 2011): 547.

41. Edward J. Drea, *MacArthur's ULTRA: Codebreaking and the War against Japan, 1942–1945* (Lawrence: University Press of Kansas, 1992), 63.

42. NHHC Collection 505: Papers of FADM Chester W. Nimitz, USN 1902–1976, Box 2: Command Summary Fleet Admiral C. W. Nimitz U.S. Navy, Book Two: 1 September 1942–31 December 1942, Volumes 1, 2, pages 862–1262. War Plans CincPac Files: Subject: Captain Steele's "Running Es-

timates and Summary" covering the period 1 September 1942–31 December 1942, 1163–1168.

43. Frank, *Guadalcanal*, 504.

44. NARA 496: Series: Organization of the Allied Intelligence Bureau 1942–45, Box 469: G-2 Admin: Records Relating to the Organization of the Allied Intelligence Bureau 1942–1945, Folder: Notes on New Guinea Operations Jan 43: "Advanced Echelon General Headquarters, Southwest Pacific Area, Military Intelligence Section, General Staff: I–III: Daily Summary of Enemy Intelligence, IV: G-2 Estimate of the Enemy Situation, V: Special Intelligence—Secret, No. 250x, Date Nove. 27/28/42," 3.

45. Drea, *MacArthur's ULTRA*, 51–52, 49.

46. Ibid., 55–56.

47. Frank, *Guadalcanal*, 597.

48. NARA 550: Series: Organizational History Files, compiled 1959–1973, documenting the period 1931–1973, Box 11: Japanese Monographs Nos. 41 and 45, Folder: Japanese Monograph No. 45: Imperial General Headquarters Army High Command Record, 69. See also NARA 550: Series: Organizational History Files, compiled 1959–1973, documenting the period 1931–1973, Box 5: Imperial General Headquarters Navy Directives, Folder: Imperial General Headquarters Navy Directives: Numbers 1 to 182 (11/05/1941–12/29/1942), 138–145: "Imperial General Headquarters, Navy General Staff Directive No. 159, Appendix: Army-Navy Central Agreement Concerning South Pacific Area Operations, 18 Nov 42."

49. NARA 550: Series: Organizational History Files, compiled 1959–1973, documenting the period 1931–1973, Box 11: Japanese Monographs Nos. 41 and 45, Folder: Japanese Monograph No. 45: Imperial General Headquarters Army High Command Record, 75–77.

50. Eichelberger and Mackaye, *Jungle Road to Tokyo*, 41.

51. Frank, *Guadalcanal*, 595.

52. NARA 337: Series: Intelligence Reports, compiled 1943–1946, Box 51, Folder 5: Handy Obs Report: "Memo To: The Commanding General, Army Ground Forces, Washington, D.C.; Subject: Report of Military Observer Southwest Pacific Theater of Operations, Col. H. F. Handy, September 26 to December 23, 1942," 4, 11.

53. NARA 337: Series: Intelligence Reports, compiled 1943–1946, Box 51, Folder 6: Knight Obs Report: "Memo To: The Commanding General, Army Ground Forces, Washington, D.C.; Subject: Report of Colonel Harry Knight, Cavalry, covering observations in the Southwest Pacific Theatre, during the Period October 16 to December 30, 1942," Appendix B, 15.

54. Frank, *Guadalcanal*, 597.

55. USSBS Interrogations: Lieutenant General Shuichi MIYAZAKI, Chief of Staff of the 17th Army, "Personal Experiences During the SOLOMONS Campaign," Microfilm Publication M1654, Reel #5, 4–10, 8–11. Attempts

to sustain the force with destroyer transports, barges, and even submarines failed to meet Japanese needs.

56. Milner, *Victory in Papua*, 346.

57. AFHRA: Call # 168.7103-71 V3: "General George C. Kenney Diaries, Volume III, 1 November 1942–31 December 1942," entries for 20 and 21 November 1942.

58. Dan van der Vat, *The Pacific Campaign: World War II, the U.S.-Japanese Naval War, 1941–1945* (New York: Simon & Schuster, 1991), 237.

59. USSBS Interrogations: No. 467: Commander Tadashi YAMAMOTO, IJN, and Captain Toshikazu OHMAE, IJN; Subject: SOLOMON ISLANDS Actions 1942–1943; Date: 20 November 1945, Tokyo; Microfilm Publication M1654, Reel #9, 467-6.

60. Frank, *Guadalcanal*, 610–611.

61. Bergerud, *Fire in the Sky*, 589–590.

62. USSBS Interrogations: No. 447: Lieutenant General KAWABE, IJA; Subject: Overall Planning and Policies; Date: 26 November 1945, Tokyo; Microfilm Publication M1654, Reel #9, 447-3.

63. Frank, *Guadalcanal*, 295.

64. United States Strategic Bombing Survey, *The Campaigns of the Pacific War*, 125.

65. Frank, *Guadalcanal*, 461.

66. John Miller, *Cartwheel: The Reduction of Rabaul*, United States Army in World War II: The War in the Pacific (Washington, DC: Office of the Chief of Military History, 1959), 19.

67. USSBS Interrogations: No. 139: Commander Chika Taka NAKAJIMA, IJN; Subject: GILBERT-MARSHALLS Operations. Naval Strategic Planning; Date: 21 October 1945, Tokyo; Microfilm Publication M1654, Reel #5, 139-3.

68. USSBS Interrogations: No. 444: Capt Takeshi MIENO, IJN; Subject: Japanese Naval Air Personnel and Training; Date: 26 November 1945, Tokyo; Microfilm Publication M1654, Reel #9, 444-1.

69. USSBS Interrogations: No. 447, 447-4.

CHAPTER 10. CONCLUSIONS

1. It is worth noting that the Imperial Japanese Navy continued to demonstrate this deficiency throughout the war, perhaps reflecting the enduring Japanese preoccupation with defeating warships rather than attacking transports or support facilities. As late as October 1944, Admiral Kurita missed the opportunity to smash the US transports supporting the invasion of Leyte in the Philippines. The Japanese employed effective tactical deception to lure Admiral Halsey's powerful covering force away from the landings so that Kurita's own powerful force might stop the invasion. The plan, in part, worked

and Kurita sailed into the midst of a force of escort carriers and destroyers that were no match for his force of battleships, cruisers, and destroyers. Kurita engaged the American force, inflicted significant damage, and then turned his force around without pressing on to hit the exposed transports. In so doing, Kurita missed a real opportunity to defeat the invasion.

BIBLIOGRAPHY

ARCHIVAL SOURCES

Air Force Historical Research Agency, Maxwell Air Force Base,
Montgomery, AL

Call # 223.606: "Army Air Forces Gulf Coast Flying Training Center Summaries: A-2 Summaries Nos. 14 (18 May 1942) through 62 (18 November 1942)."

Call # 168.1703–62: United States Strategic Bombing Survey, Military Analysis Division. *Japanese Air Power.* Washington, DC: United States Strategic Bombing Survey (Pacific), Military Analysis Division, 1946.

Call # 168.1703-63: United States Strategic Bombing Survey, Military Analysis Division. *Japanese Air Weapons and Tactics.* Washington, DC: United States Strategic Bombing Survey (Pacific), Military Analysis Division, 1947.

Call # 168.1703-65: United States Strategic Bombing Survey, Military Analysis Division. *Employment of the Forces under the Southwest Pacific Command.* Washington, DC: United States Strategic Bombing Survey, Military Analysis Division, 1947.

Call # 168.1703-71: United States Strategic Bombing Survey (Pacific), Military Analysis Division. *The Fifth Air Force in the War against Japan.* Washington, DC: United States Strategic Bombing Survey (Pacific), Military Analysis Division, June 1947.

Call # 168.7103-71 V2: "General George C. Kenney Diaries Volume II, 1 September 1942–31 October 1942."

Call # 168.7103-71 V3: "General George C. Kenney Diaries, Volume III, 1 November 1942–31 December 1942."

Call # 730.308-1: "0005 Air Force: Scale of Effort," FIFTH AIR FORCE: Hours Flown per Assigned Combat Crew.

Call # 749.01: "Commander Aircraft Solomons (COMAIRSOLS)," extracts from diary of Major Victor Dykes.

Call # 749.607: "Solomon Islands Air Command: Weekly Intelligence Summaries," 7 February 1943–28 April 1944.

National Archives and Records Administration, College Park, MD

National Archives and Records Administration: Record Group 38: Records of the Office of the Chief of Naval Operations, 1875–2006.

National Archives and Records Administration: Record Group 127: Records of the US Marine Corps, 1775–9999.

National Archives and Records Administration: Record Group 165: Records of the War Department General and Special Staff, 1903–1947.

National Archives and Records Administration: Record Group 337: Records of Headquarters Army Ground Forces, 1916–1956.

National Archives and Records Administration: Record Group 338: Records of the US Army Operational, Tactical, and Support Organizations (World War II and Thereafter).

National Archives and Records Administration: Record Group 496: Records of General Headquarters, South West Pacific Area and United States Army Forces Pacific (World War II), 1941–1947.

National Archives and Records Administration: Record Group 550: Records of the U.S. Army, Pacific, 1945–1985.

Naval History and Heritage Command, Operational Archives Branch, Washington Navy Yard, Washington, DC

Collection 505: Papers of FADM Chester W. Nimitz, USN 1902–1976.

United States Strategic Bombing Survey, ed. US Strategic Bombing Survey (Pacific): Interrogations of Japanese Leaders and Responses to Questionnaires, 1945–1946. Washington, DC: National Archives Microfilm Publications, 1991.

Lieutenant General Shuichi MIYAZAKI, Chief of Staff of the 17th Army; "Personal Experiences during the SOLOMONS Campaign"; Microfilm Publication M1654.

No. 11: Captain Susumu KAWAGUCHI, IJN; Subject: *HIRYU* (CV) at the Battle of MIDWAY; Date: 10 October 1945, Tokyo; Microfilm Publication M1654.

No. 46: Commander H. SEKINO, IJN; Subject: CORAL SEA Battle, 7–8 May 1942; Date: 17 October 1945, Tokyo; Microfilm Publication M1654.

No. 53: Captain M. YAMAOKA, IJN; Subject: SOLOMON ISLAND Operation and Battle of CORAL SEA; Date: 19 October 1945, Tokyo; Microfilm Publication M1654.

No. 65: Captain Y. WATANABE, IJN; Subject: PEARL HARBOR—MIDWAY—SOLOMONS; Date: 15 October 1945, Tokyo; Microfilm Publication M1654.

No. 138: Lieutenant Commander Hiroshi TOXUNO, IJN; Subject: Battle of GUADALCANAL, 12–14 November 1942; Battle of MIDWAY, 4–5 June 1942; Battle of VILLA STANMORE, 6 March 1943; Date: 25 October 1945, Tokyo; Microfilm Publication M1654.

No. 139: Commander Chika Taka NAKAJIMA, IJN; Subject: GILBERT-MARSHALLS Operations, Naval Strategic Planning; Date: 21 October 1945, Tokyo; Microfilm Publication M1654.

No. 165: Captain H. OHARA, IJN; Subject: Battle of MIDWAY, 4–6 June 1942, Damage to Aircraft Carrier, SORYU; Date: 25 October 1945, Tokyo; Microfilm Publication M1654.

No. 208: Commander Hideo OZAWA, IJN; Subject: Japanese Communications Intelligence; Date: 2 November 1945, Tokyo; Microfilm Publication M1654.

No. 219: Captain Y. ARITA, IJN; Subject: Japanese Naval Intelligence Organization; Date: 2 November 1945, Tokyo; Microfilm Publication M1654.

No. 222: Rear Admiral Kaoru TAKEUCHI, IJN; Subject: Japanese Naval Intelligence Organization; Date: 5 November 1945, Tokyo; Microfilm Publication M1654.

No. 236: Commander Nobohiko IMAI, IJN; Subject: Japanese Naval and Operational Intelligence; Date: 3 November 1945, Tokyo; Microfilm Publication M1654.

No. 238: Lieutenant General Seizo ARISUE, IJA; Subject: Organization and Operation of Japanese Army Intelligence Activities; Date: 1 November 1945, Tokyo; Microfilm Publication M1654.

No. 246: Rear Admiral Takeji ONO, IJN; Subject: Japanese Naval Intelligence; Date: 5 November 1945, Tokyo; Microfilm Publication M1654.

No. 250: Commander Sashizo YOKURA, IJN; Subject: Japanese Naval Intelligence; Date: 5 November 1945, Tokyo; Microfilm Publication M1654.

No. 252: Captain Yasumi TOYAMA, IJN; Subject: (1) Transports at MIDWAY; (2) Transports at the Battle of EASTERN SOLOMONS, 25 August 1942; (3) Battle of TASSAFARONGA 30 November 1942; Date: 1 November 1945, Tokyo; Microfilm Publication M1654.

No. 270: Colonel Minoru MIYASHI, JAAF; Subject: Japanese Army Air Intelligence Organization and Operations; Date: 6 and 7 November 1945, Tokyo; Microfilm Publication M1654.

No. 284: Major Hiroshi TOGA, IJA; Subject: Intelligence Organization and Procedure in Japanese Army Air Division (HIKOSHIDAN); Date: 7 November 1945, Tokyo; Microfilm Publication M1654.

No. 291: Commander Y. TERAI, IJN; Subject: Japanese Intelligence, Its Organization and Use in War Plans; Date: 10 November 1945, Tokyo; Microfilm Publication M1654.

No. 307: Lieutenant Colonel Shizuma MATSUMURA, IJA; Subject: Japanese Army Air Intelligence at HIKOSENTAI, HIKODAN, and HIKOSHIDAN Level; Date: 8 November 1945, Tokyo; Microfilm Publication M1654.

No. 309: Commander Chikataka NAKAJIMA, IJN; Subject: Fleet Intelligence Organization and Procedure; Date: 10 November 1945, Tokyo; Microfilm Publication M1654.

No. 329: Commander Masatake OKUMIYA, IJN; Subject: Combat Intelligence for Air Operations—Briefing and Interrogation Procedure; Date: 12 November 1945, Tokyo; Microfilm Publication M1654.

No. 343: General Masakazu KAWABE, IJA; Subject: Intelligence Operations at

Air General Headquarters (KOKU SOGUN SHIRIEBU); Date: 13 November 1945, Tokyo; Microfilm Publication M1654.

No. 350: Captain Toshikazu OHMAE, IJN; Subject: The Contribution of Naval Intelligence to War Planning; Date: 11 November 1945, Tokyo; Microfilm Publication M1654.

No. 362: Lieutenant Colonel T. ASHIHARA, IJA; Subject: Organization and Operation of Japanese Army Air Force; Date: November 1945, Tokyo; Microfilm Publication M1654.

No. 364: Lieutenant Colonel Kokuzo OYA, IJA; Subject: Intelligence Organization in Imperial Headquarters; Date: 31 November 1945, Tokyo; Microfilm Publication M1654.

No. 365: Commander Moriyoshi YAMAGUCHI, IJN; Subject: Briefing and Interrogation of Navy Pilots and Photographic Reconnaissance; Date: 16 November 1945, Tokyo; Microfilm Publication M1654.

No. 372: Lieutenant Colonel Isamu ASAI, IJA; Subject: Operation and Organization of TOKUMU KIKAN in Manchuria; Date: 15 November 1945, Tokyo; Microfilm Publication M1654.

No. 373: Prince Fumimaro KONOYE; Subject: Interrogation of Prince Konoye; Date: 9 November 1945, Tokyo; Microfilm Publication M1654.

No. 374: Commander N. TAKITA, IJN; Subject: Procedure and Functions of Aviation Unit of Section Five, Naval General Staff, 3d Department; Date: 17 November 1945, Tokyo; Microfilm Publication M1654.

No. 384: Lieutenant Takogo TOYODA, IJN; Subject: Organization and Operation of First Naval Air Technical Arsenal; Date: 19 November 1945, Tokyo; Microfilm Publication M1654.

No. 386: Senior Private Guy TOKO, IJA; Subject: Combat Techniques of the JAAF; Date: 20 November 1945, Tokyo; Microfilm Publication M1654.

No. 392: Fleet Admiral Osami NAGANO, IJN; Subject: Japanese Naval Plans; Date: 20 November 1945, Tokyo; Microfilm Publication M1654.

No. 398: Lieutenant Colonel J. YAMAZAKI, IJA; Subject: Intelligence Duties of TOKUMU KIKAN (Special Service Organization); Date: 15 November 1945, Tokyo; Microfilm Publication M1654.

No. 402: Colonel Kazuji SUGITA, IJA; Subject: Intelligence Organization and Procedure, Japanese Army; Date: 21 November 1945, Tokyo; Microfilm Publication M1654.

No. 411: Captain M. SUGITA, IJN; Subject: Organization of the Naval Attaché Staff in BERLIN; Date: 21 November 1945, Tokyo; Microfilm Publication M1654.

No. 412: Major Akito SAEKI, IJA; Subject: Squadron (Army) Intelligence Procedure; Date: 16 November 1945, Tokyo; Microfilm Publication M1654.

No. 414 (Annex A): Commander FUKANIZU, IJN; Subject: Production, Wastage and Strength, Japanese Naval Air Force; Date: November 1945, Tokyo; Microfilm Publication M1654.

No. 421: Captain Y. SANEMATSU, IJN; Subject: Intelligence Activities of "D" Department, 5th Section, General Staff; Date: 22 November 1945, Tokyo; Microfilm Publication M1654.

No. 422: Captain Atsuo SHIGEHIRO, IJN; Subject: Organization of Naval Attaché Staff in Argentina; Date: 23 November 1945, Tokyo; Microfilm Publication M1654.

No. 423: Captain Isuneze WACHI, IJN; Subject: Organization and Operation of Naval Attaché Staff in Mexico; Date: 23 November 1945, Tokyo; Microfilm Publication M1654.

No. 424: Captain Bunzo SHIBATA, IJN; Subject: 21st Air Flotilla; Date: 18 November 1945, Tokyo; Microfilm Publication M1654.

No. 426: Prince HIGASHI-KUNI; Subject: Japanese War Economy; Date: 14 November 1945, Tokyo; Microfilm Publication M1654.

No. 432: Captain Taisuke ITO, IJN; Subject: Selection and Assignment of Intelligence Personnel; Date: 24 November 1945, Tokyo; Microfilm Publication M1654.

No. 433: Commander Nikichi HANDA, IJN; Subject: Intelligence Duties of a Communications Officer on Staff of Destroyer and Cruiser Squadrons; Date: 24 November 1945, Tokyo; Microfilm Publication M1654.

No. 437: Commander Tonosuke OTANI, IJN; Subject: Operational Intelligence in the Second Fleet; Date: 24 November 1945, Tokyo; Microfilm Publication M1654.

No. 442: Mr. E. SONE; Subject: Activities Information Available to the Navy; Date: 22 November 1945, Tokyo; Microfilm Publication M1654.

No. 444: Capt Takeshi MIENO, IJN; Subject: Japanese Naval Air Personnel and Training; Date: 26 November 1945, Tokyo; Microfilm Publication M1654.

No. 446-Supp.: Captain Takashi MIYAZAKI, IJN; Subject: Air Operations of Japanese Naval Air Forces based at RABAUL, including NEW GUINEA and SOLOMONS; Date: January 1946, Washington, DC; Microfilm Publication M1654.

No. 447: Lieutenant General Toroshiro KAWABE, IJA; Subject: Overall Planning and Policies; Date: 26 November 1945, Tokyo; Microfilm Publication M1654.

No. 449: Major Hideo ANNO, IJA; Subject: Intelligence Instruction in the Army War College; Date: 26 November 1945, Tokyo; Microfilm Publication M1654.

No. 452: Lieutenant Colonel Tatsuo NOZAKI, IJA; Subject: Intelligence Instruction at the Kempeitai School at NAKANO KU, TOKYO; Date: 26 November 1945, Tokyo; Microfilm Publication M1654.

No. 455: Rear Admiral Ichiro YOKOYAMA, IJN; Subject: Activities of Naval Attaché Staff, Washington, DC, before PEARL HARBOR Attack; Date: 27 November 1945, Tokyo; Microfilm Publication M1654.

No. 467: Commander Tadashi YAMAMOTO, IJN, and Captain Toshikazu OHMAE, IJN; Subject: SOLOMON ISLANDS Actions, 1942–1943; Date: 20 November 1945, Tokyo; Microfilm Publication M1654.

No. 479: Captain Minoru GENDA; Subject: Japanese Naval Air Force; Date: 28–29 November 1945, Tokyo; Microfilm Publication M1654.

No. 485: Lieutenant Colonel Roji TANAKA, IJA; Subject: Japanese Army Air Forces in SOLOMONS Campaign; Date: 28 November 1945, Tokyo; Microfilm Publication M1654.

No. 495: Captain Toshikazu OHMAE, IJN, and Commander Meriyoshi YAMA-GUCHI, IJN; Subject: Japanese Navy Air Force; Date: 6 December 1945, Tokyo; Microfilm Publication M1654.

No. 496: Lieutenant Kunie IWASHITA, IJN; Subject: Japanese Naval Air Combat & Tactics; Date: 3 December 1945, Tokyo; Microfilm Publication M1654.

No. 497: Lieutenant General Shuichi MIYAZAKI, IJA; Subject: Effect of Allied Air Activity on Japanese Planning of the SOLOMONS, RABAUL and NEW GUINEA Operations and on Japan's Ability to Carry out Those Plans; Planning and Objectives of the BURMA Campaign; Date: 3 December 1945, Tokyo; Microfilm Publication M1654.

No. 503: Vice Admiral Shigeru FUKUDOME, IJN; Subject: The Naval War in the PACIFIC; Date: 9 December 1945, Tokyo; Microfilm Publication M1654.

No. 524: Admiral Shigeru FUKUDOME, IJN; Subject: War in the PACIFIC; Date: 12 December 1945, Tokyo; Microfilm Publication M1654.

No. 601: Commander Ryosuke NOMURA, IJN; Subject: Japanese Land Based Air Operations in the CELEBES and RABAUL Area; Date: 28 November 1945, Tokyo; Microfilm Publication M1654.

No. 604: Colonel Takeo SHIMIZU, IJA; Subject: Instruction Relating to Intelligence at the War College; Date: 27 November 1945, Tokyo; Microfilm Publication M1654.

No. 605: Lieutenant Commander Masuo YANAGITA, IJN; Subject: Training and Duties of YOMUSHI; Date: 28 November 1945, Tokyo; Microfilm Publication M1654.

No. 607: Lieutenant Colonel YAMAMURA and 2nd Lieutenant OGATA, IJA; Subject: KEMPEI TAI; Date: 17 November 1945, Tokyo; Microfilm Publication M1654.

ELECTRONIC SOURCES

Australian War Memorial Project and its associated Australia–Japan Research Project. ajrp.awm.gov.au/AJRP/ajrp2.nsf.

Far East Command, Military History Section, Japanese Research Division. "Japanese Monograph No. 45: Imperial General Headquarters Army High Command Record, Mid 41–Aug 45." In *Japanese Monographs*. Revised edition, 1959. www.ibiblio.org/hyperwar/Japan/Monos/JM-45/index.html.

Genea Archives—BACM Research. *World War II Historical Document Archive.* DVD (4 discs).

Japanese Army Operations in the South Pacific Area: New Britain and Papuan

Campaigns, 1942–43. Translated by Steven Bullard. Translated extracts of: Bōeichō Bōei Kenshūjo Senshishitsu (ed.), *Senshi Sōsho: Minami Taiheiyō Rikugun Sakusen. Pōto Moresubi–Gashima Shoko Sakusen* [War History Series: South Pacific Area Army Operations (volume 1), Port Moresby–Guadalcanal First Campaigns] (Tokyo: Asagumo Shinbunsha, 1968): 1–230, 335–384, 514–532; and Bōeichō Bōei Kenshūjo Senshishitsu (ed.), *Senshi Sōsho: Minami Taiheiyō Rikugun Sakusen. Gadarukanaru–Buna Sakusen* [War History Series: South Pacific Area Army Operations (volume 2), Guadalcanal–Buna Campaigns] (Tokyo: Asagumo Shinbunsha, 1969): 196–218, 324–362, 577–601. Canberra: Australian War Memorial, 2007. ajrp.awm.gov.au/ajrp/ajrp2.nsf/WebI/JpnOperations

Joint History Office. "World War II Inter-Allied Conferences—Declassified." CD. Washington, DC: Joint History Office, 2003.

McCarthy, Dudley. *South-West Pacific Area—First Year: Kokoda to Wau.* Australia in the War of 1939–1945. Series 1, Army V. 5. Canberra: Australian War Memorial, 1959. www.awm.gov.au/collection/C1417310.

National Archives and Records Administration: Record Group 457: Records of the National Security Agency/Central Security Service [NCA/CCS]: SRH-268 Redman Correspondence. Department of the Navy, Naval Historical Center. www.history.navy.mil/research/library/online-reading-room/title-list-alphabetically/a/advanced-intelligence-centers-in-the-us-navy.html.

Shindo, Hiroyuki. "Journal of the Australian War Memorial: Japanese Air Operations over New Guinea during the Second World War." www.awm.gov.au/journal/j34/shindo.asp.

West Point Military Academy, Department of History, World War II Asia-Pacific Atlases.

www.usma.edu/history/SitePages/WWII%20Asian%20Pacific%20Theater.aspx.

OFFICIAL US GOVERNMENT PUBLICATIONS AND FIELD MANUALS

"Air Force Doctrine Document 2–1, 22 January 2000: Air Warfare." Edited by HQ AF DC/DR, 116: U.S. Air Force, 2000.

Assistant Chief of Air Staff, Intelligence, Historical Division. "Army Air Forces Historical Studies: No. 17: Air Action in the Papuan Campaign, 21 July 1942 to 23 January 1943." August 1944.

Boyd, John R. "SAASS Course 600 Reader: A Discourse on Winning and Losing by John R. Boyd August 1987." Edited by Air University, School of Advanced Air and Space Studies (SAASS), 340. Maxwell Air Force Base, AL: Air University Press, Academic Year 2007–2008.

Far East Command, Military History Section, Japanese Research Division. "Japanese Monograph No. 45: Imperial General Headquarters Army High Command Record, Mid 41–Aug 45." In *Japanese Monographs.*

"Field Manual 1-02, September 2004: Operational Terms and Graphics." US Department of the Army, 2004.

"Field Manual 3-0: Operations." Edited by Headquarters, Department of the Army. Washington, DC: Department of the Army, June 2001.

"FM 1-40: Air Corps Field Manual: Intelligence Procedures in Aviation Units." Edited by War Department. Washington, DC: Chief of the Air Corps, US Government Printing Office, 1940.

"FM 7-25 Infantry Field Manual: Headquarters Company, Intelligence and Signal Communication, Rifle Regiment, October 7, 1942." Washington, DC: US Government Printing Office, 1942.

"FM 21-26 Basic Field Manual: Advanced Map and Aerial Photograph Reading, September 17, 1941." Washington, DC: US Government Printing Office, 1941.

"FM 100-5 Field Service Regulations: Operations, May 22, 1941." Fort Leavenworth, KS: US Army Command and General Staff College Press, orig. publ. 1941 [reprint 1992].

G-2 Section, Supreme Commander Allied Powers, Allied Translator and Interpreter Section. "Monograph #32 (Army): Southeast Pacific Area Aerial Opn Record." In *Japanese Monographs*.

Headquarters, Army Force Far East, Military History Section. "Japanese Monograph No. 33 (Army): Southeast Area Operations Record Part 1, South Seas Detachment Operations Record (3 January–30 May 1942)." In *Japanese Monographs*.

———. "Japanese Monograph No. 152: Political Strategy Prior to the Outbreak of War, Part V." In *Japanese Monographs*.

"Japanese Military and Naval Intelligence." Edited by United States Strategic Bombing Survey. Japanese Military and G-2 Naval Intelligence Division, Japanese Intelligence Section. Washington, DC: US Government Printing Office, 1946.

Joint Publication 1-02: 12 April 2001 (as amended through 17 October 2007): *Department of Defense Dictionary of Military and Associated Terms*. Washington, DC: US Department of Defense, 2007.

Joint Publication 1-02: 12 April 2001 (as amended through 30 September 2010): *Department of Defense Dictionary of Military and Associated Terms*. Washington, DC: US Department of Defense, 2010.

Joint Publication 5-0, 26 December 2006: *Joint Operation Planning*. Washington, DC: US Department of Defense, 2006.

"TM 30-215: Technical Manual: Counter Intelligence Corps, 22 September 1943." Washington, DC: War Department, 22 September 1943.

United States Strategic Bombing Survey. *Japanese Military and Naval Intelligence Division. Japanese Intelligence Section, G-2. Dates of Survey: 1 November 1945 through 1 February 1946*. Washington, DC: US Government Printing Office, 1946.

United States Strategic Bombing Survey, Military Analysis Division. *Japanese Air Power*. Washington, DC: United States Strategic Bombing Survey (Pacific), Military Analysis Division, 1946.

United States Strategic Bombing Survey, Military Supplies Division. *Japanese Naval Shipbuilding*. Washington, DC: US Government Printing Office, 1946.

United States Strategic Bombing Survey, Naval Analysis Division. *The Campaigns of the Pacific War*. Washington, DC: United States Strategic Bombing Survey (Pacific), Naval Analysis Division, 1946.

United States War Department. *Handbook on Japanese Military Forces*. Baton Rouge: Louisiana State University Press, 1995.

PUBLISHED SOURCES

Adamsky, Dima. *The Culture of Military Innovation: The Impact of Cultural Factors on the Revolution in Military Affairs in Russia, the US, and Israel*. Stanford: Stanford University Press, 2010.

Agawa, Hiroyuki. *The Reluctant Admiral: Yamamoto and the Imperial Navy*. Translated by John Bester. 1st paperback ed. Tokyo and New York: Kodansha International, 1982.

Allison, Graham T., and Philip Zelikow. *Essence of Decision: Explaining the Cuban Missile Crisis*. 2nd ed. New York: Longman, 1999.

Alvarez, David J., ed. *Allied and Axis Signals Intelligence in World War II*. London: Frank Cass, 1999.

Bennett, Judith A. "Fears and Aspirations: US Military Intelligence Operations in the South Pacific, 1941–1945." *Journal of Pacific History* 39, no. 3 (2004): 283–307.

Bergerud, Eric M. *Fire in the Sky: The Air War in the South Pacific*. Boulder: Westview Press, 2000.

———. *Touched with Fire: The Land War in the South Pacific*. New York: Penguin Books, 1996.

Boyne, Walter J. *Clash of Titans: World War II at Sea*. New York: Simon & Schuster, 1995.

Brereton, Lewis H. *The Brereton Diaries: The War in the Air in the Pacific, Middle East and Europe, 3 October 1941–8 May 1945*. New York: W. Morrow and Company, 1946.

Citino, Robert M. *Death of the Wehrmacht: The German Campaigns of 1942*. Lawrence: University Press of Kansas, 2007.

Clausewitz, Carl von. *On War*. Translated by Michael Howard and Peter Paret. Princeton: Princeton University Press, 1976.

Clemens, Martin. *Alone on Guadalcanal: A Coastwatcher's Story*. Annapolis, MD: Naval Institute Press, 1998.

Cook, Haruko Taya, and Theodore Failor Cook. *Japan at War: An Oral History*. 1st ed. New York: New Press; distributed by W.W. Norton, 1992.

Costello, John. *Days of Infamy: MacArthur, Roosevelt, Churchill, the Shocking Truth Revealed: How Their Secret Deals and Strategic Blunders Caused Disasters at Pearl Harbor and the Philippines*. New York: Pocket Books, 1994.

———. *The Pacific War, 1941–1945: The First Comprehensive One-Volume Ac-*

260 Bibliography

count of the Causes and Conduct of World War II in the Pacific. New York: Quill, 1981.

Craven, Wesley Frank, and James Lea Cate. *The Pacific: Guadalcanal to Saipan, August 1942 to July 1944,* vol. 4, *The Army Air Forces in World War II.* Washington, DC: Office of Air Force History, 1983.

Dorwart, Jeffery M. *Conflict of Duty: The U.S. Navy's Intelligence Dilemma, 1919–1945.* Annapolis, MD: Naval Institute Press, 1983.

Dower, John W. *War without Mercy: Race and Power in the Pacific War.* New York: Pantheon, 1986.

Drea, Edward J. *Japan's Imperial Army: Its Rise and Fall, 1853–1945.* Lawrence: University Press of Kansas, 2009.

———. *MacArthur's ULTRA: Codebreaking and the War against Japan, 1942–1945.* Lawrence: University Press of Kansas, 1992.

Dull, Paul S. *A Battle History of the Imperial Japanese Navy, 1941–1945.* Annapolis, MD: Naval Institute Press, 1978.

Dunnigan, James F., and Albert A. Nofi. *Victory at Sea: World War II in the Pacific.* 1st ed. New York: William Morrow, 1995.

Eichelberger, Robert L., and Milton Mackaye. *Jungle Road to Tokyo.* London: Odhams Press Limited, 1951.

Evans, David C., and Mark R. Peattie. *Kaigun: Strategy, Tactics, and Technology in the Imperial Japanese Navy, 1887–1941.* Annapolis, MD: Naval Institute Press, 1997.

Finnegan, John Patrick, and Romana Danysh. *Military Intelligence.* Army Lineage Series. Washington, DC: Center of Military History, 1998.

Frank, Richard B. *Guadalcanal: The Definitive Account of the Landmark Battle.* 1st ed. New York: Random House, 1990.

———. *MacArthur.* The Great Generals Series. 1st ed. New York: Palgrave Macmillan, 2007.

Fuchida, Mitsuo, et al. *Midway: The Battle That Doomed Japan.* Annapolis, MD: Naval Institute Press, 1992.

Fugate, Bryan I., and L. S. Dvoretskii. *Thunder on the Dnepr: Zhukov-Stalin and the Defeat of Hitler's Blitzkrieg.* Novato, CA: Presidio, 1997.

Furer, Julius Augustus. *Administration of the Navy Department in World War II.* Washington, DC: US Government Printing Office, 1959.

Gailey, Harry A. *The War in the Pacific: From Pearl Harbor to Tokyo Bay.* Novato, CA: Presidio, 1995.

Gamble, Bruce. *Fortress Rabaul: The Battle for the Southwest Pacific, January 1942–April 1943.* Minneapolis: Zenith Press, 2010.

Gilbert, James L., and John P. Finnegan, eds. *U.S. Army Signals Intelligence in World War II: A Documentary History.* Washington, DC: Center of Military History, 1993.

Gilbert, Martin. *The Second World War: A Complete History.* Rev. ed. New York: H. Holt, 1991.

Glantz, David M. *The Role of Intelligence in Soviet Military Strategy in World War II*. Novato, CA: Presidio Press, 1990.

———. *Zhukov's Greatest Defeat: The Red Army's Epic Disaster in Operation Mars, 1942*. Lawrence: University Press of Kansas, 1999.

Glantz, David M., and Jonathan M. House. *The Battle of Kursk*. Lawrence: University Press of Kansas, 1999.

Gray, Colin S. *Modern Strategy*. New York: Oxford University Press, 1999.

Griffith, Samuel B. *The Battle for Guadalcanal*. New York: Lippincott, 1963.

Groom, Winston. *1942: The Year That Tried Men's Souls*. 1st ed. New York: Atlantic Monthly Press, 2005.

Halsey, William Frederick, and J. Bryan. *Admiral Halsey's Story*. New York: Whittlesey House, 1947.

Hayashi, Saburō. *Kogun: The Japanese Army in the Pacific War*. Quantico, VA: Marine Corps Association, 1989 [orig. publ. 1959].

Hayes, Grace P. *The History of the Joint Chiefs of Staff in World War II: The War against Japan*. Annapolis, MD: Naval Institute Press, 1982.

Hobart, Joel I. *"Execute against Japan": The U.S. Decision to Conduct Unrestricted Submarine Warfare*. College Station: Texas A&M University Press, 2009.

Holt, Thaddeus. *The Deceivers: Allied Military Deception in the Second World War*. New York: Scribner, 2004.

Holwitt, Joel Ira. *"Execute against Japan": The U.S. Decision to Conduct Unrestricted Submarine Warfare* (College Station: Texas A&M University Press, 2013), 141–142.

Hoyt, Edwin P. *Blue Skies and Blood: The Battle of the Coral Sea*. New York: Paul S. Eriksson, Inc., 1975.

———. *Carrier Wars: Naval Aviation from World War II to the Persian Gulf*. New York: McGraw-Hill, 1989.

———. *Yamamoto: The Man Who Planned Pearl Harbor*. 1st Lyons Press ed. Guilford, CT: Lyons Press, 2001.

Ienaga, Saburō. *The Pacific War: World War II and the Japanese, 1931–1945*. 1st American ed. New York: Pantheon Books, 1978.

Ind, Allison. *Allied Intelligence Bureau*. New York: McKay, 1958.

James, D. Clayton. *The Years of MacArthur: Volume II, 1941–1945*. Boston: Houghton Mifflin, 1975.

Judge, Sean. *"'Who Has the Puck?': Strategic Initiative in Modern, Conventional War."* Thesis for Air University, School of Advanced Air and Space Studies, completed under the advisement of Dr. Harold R. Winton, 2008.

Kahn, David. *The Codebreakers: The Story of Secret Writing*. New York: Macmillan, 1967.

———. *The Reader of Gentlemen's Mail: Herbert O. Yardley and the Birth of American Codebreaking*. New Haven: Yale University Press, 2004.

Kato, Masuo. *The Lost War: A Japanese Reporter's Inside Story*. New York: A. A. Knopf, 1946.

Keegan, John. *The Second World War.* New York: Penguin Books, 1990.

Kennedy, Paul M. *Grand Strategies in War and Peace.* New Haven: Yale University Press, 1991.

Kenney, George C. *The Saga of Pappy Gun.* New York: Duell, Sloan and Pearce, 1959.

Kernan, Alvin B. *The Unknown Battle of Midway: The Destruction of the American Torpedo Squadrons.* The Yale Library of Military History. New Haven: Yale University Press, 2005.

King, Admiral Ernest Joseph. *Our Navy at War: A Report to the Secretary of the Navy, Covering Our Peacetime Navy and Our Wartime Navy and Including Combat Operations up to March 1, 1944.* Washington, DC: United States News, 1944.

Kotani, Ken. *Japanese Intelligence in World War II.* Translated by Chiharu Kotani. New York: Osprey Publishing, 2009.

Kreis, John F. *Piercing the Fog: Intelligence and Army Air Forces Operations in World War II.* Bolling AFB, Washington, DC: Air Force History and Museums Program, 1996.

Kuehn, John T. *Agents of Innovation: The General Board and the Design of the Fleet That Defeated the Japanese Navy.* Annapolis, MD: Naval Institute Press, 2008.

———. "The War in the Pacific, 1941–1945." In John Ferris and Evan Mawdsley, eds., pp. 420–454 in *The Cambridge History of the Second World War*, vol. 1: Fighting the War. Cambridge, UK: Cambridge University Press, 2015.

Larrabee, Eric. *Commander in Chief: Franklin Delano Roosevelt, His Lieutenants, and Their War.* 1st ed. New York: Harper & Row, 1987.

Leighton, Richard M., and Robert W. Coakley. *Global Logistics and Strategy: 1940–1943*, vol. 1, *United States Army in World War II: The War Department.* Washington, DC: Office of the Chief of Military History, 1955.

Liddell Hart, Basil Henry. *History of the Second World War.* New York: G. P. Putnam's Sons, 1970.

———. *Strategy.* 2nd rev. ed. New York: Meridian Books, 1991.

Lonsdale, David J. *The Nature of War in the Information Age: Clausewitzian Future.* Cass Series—Strategy and History; 9. London and New York: Frank Cass, 2004.

Lundstrom, John B. *Black Shoe Carrier Admiral: Frank Jack Fletcher at Coral Sea, Midway, and Guadalcanal.* Annapolis, MD: Naval Institute Press, 2006.

———. *The First Team and the Guadalcanal Campaign: Naval Fighter Combat from August to November 1942.* Annapolis, MD: Naval Institute Press, 1994.

———. *The First Team: Pacific Naval Air Combat from Pearl Harbor to Midway.* 1st Naval Institute Press paperback ed. Annapolis, MD: Naval Institute Press, 2005.

Luttwak, Edward. *Strategy: The Logic of War and Peace.* Rev. and enlarged ed. Cambridge, MA: Belknap Press of Harvard University Press, 2001.

MacIsaac, David. *Strategic Bombing in World War Two: The Story of the United States Strategic Bombing Survey.* New York: Garland Publishing, 1976.

Mansoor, Peter R. *The GI Offensive in Europe: The Triumph of American Infantry Divisions, 1941–1945.* Lawrence: University Press of Kansas, 1999.

Mao Tse-tung. *On the Protracted War.* 2nd ed. Peking: Foreign Languages Press, 1960.

Marion, Ore J., Thomas Cuddihy, and Edward Cuddihy. *On the Canal: The Marines of L-3-5 on Guadalcanal, 1942.* Stackpole Military History series. 1st ed. Mechanicsburg, PA: Stackpole Books, 2004.

Matloff, Maurice, and Edwin Marion Snell. *Strategic Planning for Coalition Warfare, 1941–1942.* United States Army in World War II: The War Department. Washington, DC: Office of the Chief of Military History, 1953.

McCarthy, Dudley. *South-West Pacific Area—First Year: Kokoda to Wau.* Australia in the War of 1939–1945. Series 1, Army V. 5. Canberra: Australian War Memorial, 1959.

McPherson, James M. *Battle Cry of Freedom: The Civil War Era.* New York: Oxford University Press, 1988.

Miller, Edward S. *War Plan Orange: The U.S. Strategy to Defeat Japan, 1897–1945.* Annapolis, MD: Naval Institute Press, 1991.

Miller, John. *Cartwheel: The Reduction of Rabaul.* United States Army in World War II: The War in the Pacific. Washington, DC: Office of the Chief of Military History, 1959.

———. *Guadalcanal: The First Offensive.* United States Army in World War II: The War in the Pacific. Washington, DC: Center of Military History, 1989.

Millett, Allan R., and Williamson Murray. "Lessons of War." *National Interest* (Winter 1988/89), 83–95.

Millett, John D. "The War Department in World War II." *American Political Science Review* 40, no. 5 (1946): 863–897.

Milner, Samuel. *Victory in Papua.* United States Army in World War II: The War in the Pacific. Washington, DC: Center of Military History, 2003.

Moore, Jeffrey M. *Spies for Nimitz: Joint Military Intelligence in the Pacific War.* Annapolis, MD: Naval Institute Press, 2004.

Morison, Samuel Eliot. *Coral Sea, Midway and Submarine Actions, May 1942–August 1942,* vol. 4, *History of United States Naval Operations in World War II.* Annapolis, MD: Naval Institute Press, 2010 (1949).

———. *The Two-Ocean War: A Short History of the United States Navy in the Second World War.* Boston: Little, Brown, 1963.

Morton, Louis. *Strategy and Command: The First Two Years.* United States Army in World War II: The War in the Pacific. Washington, DC: Office of the Chief of Military History, 1962.

Murray, Williamson, MacGregor Knox, and Alvin H. Bernstein. *The Making of Strategy: Rulers, States, and War.* New York: Cambridge University Press, 1994.

Murray, Williamson, and Allan Reed Millett. *A War to Be Won: Fighting the Second World War.* Cambridge: Belknap Press of Harvard University Press, 2000.

Overy, Richard J. *Why the Allies Won.* 1st American ed. New York: W. W. Norton, 1996.

Packard, Wyman H. *A Century of U.S. Naval Intelligence.* Washington, DC: Office of Naval Intelligence, Naval Historical Center, 1996.

Parker, Geoffrey. *The Cambridge History of Warfare.* Rev. and updated ed. New York: Cambridge University Press, 2009 [orig. publ. 2005].

Parshall, Jonathan B. "Reflections on Fushida, or 'A Tale of Three Whoppers.'" *Naval War College Review* 63, no. 2 (Spring 2010): 127–138.

Parshall, Jonathan B., and Anthony P. Tully. *Shattered Sword: The Untold Story of the Battle of Midway.* Washington, DC: Potomac Books, 2005.

Peattie, Mark R. *Sunburst: The Rise of Japanese Naval Air Power, 1909–1941.* Annapolis, MD: Naval Institute Press, 2001.

Potter, E. B. *Nimitz.* Annapolis, MD: Naval Institute Press, 1976.

Potter, E. B., and Chester W. Nimitz, eds. *Triumph in the Pacific: The Navy's Struggle against Japan.* A Spectrum Book. Englewood Cliffs, NJ: Prentice-Hall, 1963.

Prados, John. *Combined Fleet Decoded: The Secret History of American Intelligence and the Japanese Navy in World War II.* 1st ed. New York: Random House, 1995.

Prange, Gordon William, Donald M. Goldstein, and Katherine V. Dillon. *Miracle at Midway.* New York: McGraw-Hill, 1982.

Reardon, Jeff. "Breaking the U.S. Navy's 'Gun Club' Mentality in the South Pacific." *Journal of Military History* 75, no. 2 (April 2011): 533–564.

Rottman, Gordon L. *Japanese Army in World War II: The South Pacific and New Guinea, 1942–43,* vol. 14: *Battle Orders.* Edited by Duncan Anderson. New York: Osprey Publishing, 2005.

Sakai, Saburō, Martin Caidin, and Fred Saito. *Samurai!* 1st ed. New York: Dutton, 1957.

Spector, Ronald H. *Eagle against the Sun: The American War with Japan.* New York: The Free Press, 1985.

———. *Listening to the Enemy: Key Documents on the Role of Communications Intelligence in the War with Japan.* Wilmington, DE: Scholarly Resources, 1988.

Stanley, Roy M. *World War II Photo Intelligence.* New York: Scribner, 1981.

Stoler, Mark A. *Allies and Adversaries: The Joint Chiefs of Staff, the Grand Alliance, and U.S. Strategy in World War II.* Chapel Hill: University of North Carolina Press, 2000.

Stolfi, R. H. S. *Hitler's Panzers East: World War II Reinterpreted.* 1st ed. Norman: University of Oklahoma Press, 1991.

Toland, John. *But Not in Shame: The Six Months after Pearl Harbor.* New York: Random House, 1961.

————. *The Rising Sun: The Decline and Fall of the Japanese Empire, 1936–1945*. New York: Random House, 2003 [orig. publ. 1970].

Ugaki, Matome, et al. *Fading Victory: The Diary of Admiral Matome Ugaki, 1941–1945*. Translated by Masataka Chihaya. Pittsburgh: University of Pittsburgh Press, 1991.

van der Vat, Dan. *The Pacific Campaign: World War II, the U.S.-Japanese Naval War, 1941–1945*. New York: Simon & Schuster, 1991.

Weigley, Russell Frank. *The American Way of War: A History of United States Military Strategy and Policy*. Bloomington: Indiana University Press, 1973.

Weinberg, Gerhard L. *Visions of Victory: The Hopes of Eight World War II Leaders*. Cambridge, UK: Cambridge University Press, 2005.

————. *A World at Arms: A Global History of World War II*. Cambridge, UK, and New York: Cambridge University Press, 1994.

Willmott, H. P. *The War with Japan: The Period of Balance, May 1942–October 1943*. Wilmington, DE: Scholarly Resources, 2002.

Winton, John. *Ultra in the Pacific: How Breaking Japanese Codes & Cyphers Affected Naval Operations against Japan, 1941–45*. Annapolis, MD: Naval Institute Press, 1993.

Wohlstetter, Roberta. *Pearl Harbor: Warning and Decision*. Stanford: Stanford University Press, 1962.

Wood, James B. *Japanese Military Strategy in the Pacific War: Was Defeat Inevitable?* New York: Rowman & Littlefield, 2007.

Young, Peter. *The World Almanac Book of World War II: The Complete and Comprehensive Documentary of World War II*. Englewood Cliffs, NJ: World Almanac Publications, Prentice-Hall, 1981.

Zimmerman, John L. *The Guadalcanal Campaign*. Washington, DC: Historical Division, Headquarters, US Marine Corps, 1949.

INDEX